"I have read every book that Shlomo Shoham has published in English and many articles besides. His incredible breadth and depth of knowledge of art and literature take one's breath away. *Art, Crime and Madness* represents the pinnacle of his life's work so far in embellishing and applying his personality theory to the elements that we humans consider important in our daily lives. His theory is arguably the most significant personality theory of the 20th century. Rich in detail and psychocultural analysis this book will take its place beside Freud's *Moses* and other classics of art interpretation. And as the title implies, it begins a new dialogue for the 21st century that has the temerity to link crime to art."

Graeme R. Newman
Distinguished Teaching Professor
School of Criminal Justice
University at Albany

"If there is something like real progress within science and humanities it is achieved by books like this. A truly interdisciplinary book by an author who takes interdisciplinary discourse seriously and conquers disciplinary boundaries successfully, without any reductionistic attitudes. The necessary preconditions for such an endeavor can be found on each page: broad intellectual range, curiosity, deep and profound knowledge and authenticity. The whole spirit of Shlomo Shoham's reasoning is both refreshing and challenging. A great book!"

Dr. Manfred Wimmer
Co-Editor of Evolution and Cognition
Konrad Lorenz Institute for Evolution and Cognition Research

"Those who have grown weary of the staleness and triteness of conventional criminology will find much that is fresh in Professor Shoham's compelling study of art, crime, and madness. In this book Professor Shoham applies his innovative personality theory to such legendary cases as Artaud, Van Gogh, and Caravaggio; in so doing, he shows with admirable detail and conviction how art, crime, and madness emerge from the existential projects of deviants and agents of social control alike. Professor Shoham has exquisitely prepared his flavor of interdisciplinary criminology in this volume. It conveys as well his wit, erudition, insightfulness, and authenticity."

Gregory J. Howard
Assistant Professor of Sociology
Western Michigan University

Art, Crime and Madness

Gesualdo • Caravaggio • Genet • Van Gogh • Artaud

Art, Crime and Madness

Shlomo Giora Shoham

SUSSEX
ACADEMIC
PRESS
Brighton • Chicago • Toronto

2 4 6 8 10 9 7 5 3

First published 2002, reprinted in paperback 2015
in Great Britain by
SUSSEX ACADEMIC PRESS
PO Box 139, Eastbourne BN24 9BP

Distributed in North America by
SUSSEX ACADEMIC PRESS
Independent Publishers Group
814 N Franklin St, Chicago, IL 60610, USA

British Library Cataloguing in Publication Data
A CIP catalogue record for this book is available from the British Library.

Library of Congress Cataloging-in-Publication Data
Shoham, S. Giora, 1929–
Art, crime, & madness : Gesualdo, Caravaggio, Genet, Van Gogh, Artaud / by Shlomo Giora Shoham.
p. cm.
Includes bibliographical references and index.
ISBN 978-1-903900-0-55 (alk. paper) — ISBN 978-1-903900-06-2 (pbk.)
1. Art and mental illness. 2. Artists—Psychology. 3. Creative ability. I. Title: Crime, madness and art. II. Title.
N71.5 .S53 2003
700′.1′9—dc21

2002066940

Typeset and designed by G&G Editorial, Brighton.
Printed and bound by CPI Group (UK) Ltd, Croydon, CR0 4YY
This book is printed on acid-free paper.

Contents

Foreword

by

Roger Hood

It is with great pleasure that I responded to the invitation of Professor Shlomo Giora Shoham's publisher to write a short Foreword to the latest book of one of criminology's most prolific authors.

Professor Shoham and I first met over forty years ago when I was a struggling research student embarking on my doctorate and he was a Visiting Scholar at the Department of Criminal Science, soon to be transformed, under the direction of Dr (later Professor Sir) Leon Radzinowicz, into the renowned Cambridge Institute of Criminology. Shlomo had already made his mark with an excellent study of the varying sentencing practices of judges in Israel and was, still in his twenties, an Assistant Attorney General. I had never met anyone who was so fired with enthusiasm for criminological theory, and on the occasions when we have met over the years I have marvelled at the continuing intensity, vitality and breadth of his scholarship. Shlomo Shoham is a criminologist *sui generis*, a criminologist who pushes the boundaries of the subject, and ways of approaching it, far beyond that ordinarily recognised within the discipline.

The writing of *Art, Crime and Madness* required a thorough study and appreciation of the history and aesthetics of art and of the biographies of the artists discussed. Like his other works, it draws upon philosophy, psychoanalysis, the interpretation of myths, and theories of personality development. Here Professor Shoham's concern is to shed light on how the criminal nature or madness of these artists affected their artistic imagination and how their depictions of human nature sheds light on the nature of criminality. I know of no other criminologist who has the intellectual range to attempt such a task or one who would have been bold enough to do so. *Art, Crime and Madness* is undoubtedly a ground-breaking and intellectually challenging work. Being a practitioner of the more pragmatic empirical criminological tradition myself, I shall have to leave it to others to make an informed judgment of Professor Shoham's thesis, but no one can doubt that this is the work of a criminological scholar whose intellectual curiosity shows no bounds.

OXFORD, OCTOBER 2002

Preface

The link between creativity, crime and madness has always fascinated me. Beginning with my first book, published in 1965, titled *Crime and Social Deviance*, I have pointed out the paradoxical nature of innovation. Namely that all great creators are almost never recognized during their lifetime; only after their death, when the cliques of artists and critics, and the power structures of galleries, theatres and publishers, no longer interfere with aesthetic judgment, can a work of art truly be appreciated. *Society and the Absurd*, published in the early 1970s, investigated the nature of artistically-oriented criminals who perceived a wide vista of creativity outside the realms of normativity; the nature of madness was viewed as a potential mechanism to a deeper and wider perception of consciousness and unconsciousness. *Salvation through the Gutters* (1980) demonstrated how sinners, heretics, and pariahs who were excommunicated out of the fold may yet be led to deeper insights and revelations.

The Buberian tract *The Violence of Silence*, together with the existentialist Theory of Personality laid out in *The Myth of Tantalus*, presented art as a mode of dialogue. Art has to be *communicated*, hence the vanity fair of post-modernism cannot be authentic art because its idée is too encompassing – everything goes; to paraphrase Nietzsche, if everything is possible nothing is true. *Rebellion, Creativity and Revelation* (1985) showed that the duality of human existence necessitates a dual process of revelation and creativity for a work of art to be authentic. Revelation structures the inspiration of the artist and extricates it from diachronic history into synchronic eternity; this is why a Mozart opera is eternal, whereas the hundreds of opera by Salieri have been buried under the dust of history.

Art, Crime and Madness is the culmination of the evolution of my perception of the link between creativity, crime, and madness. The ideas discussed herein are crystallized toward a universal thesis for the linkage between morbidity, deviance, and art. This thesis is a major element in the scaffolding of the Personality Theory, expounded in various books and journal articles over the last thirty years.

The initiation of the idea for a new Theory of Personality was triggered by an insight into the duality of human existence. The result was the volume entitled *Salvation through the Gutters*, which received wide acknowledgment and was translated to many languages. *Salvation* dealt with the functionality of evil in both sociology and religion. The Personality Theory was presented first in the *Myth of Tantalus* (1980), and its basic scaffolding, together with the developmental dynamics, allowed a wide scale of applications. The rather ambitious plan undertaken was to apply the Personality Theory to many areas of human existence. *Sex as Bait: Eve, Casanova, and Don Juan* (1983) explained how sexual behavior, as well as the social-biological aspects of reproduction, were linked to the Theory. *The Violence of Silence* (1983) applied the Theory to human interaction. *The Bridge to Nothingness: Gnosis, Kabbala and Existentialism* (1994), applied the Theory to religion. *Vallhala, Calvary and Auschwitz* (1995) based the rise of Nazism and the destruction of European Jews on the Theory as a macro-sociological dynamic. Finally, *God as the Shadow of Man* (2000) applied the Theory to mythology and neo-structuralism.

I am indebted to the Publisher for proposing to include synopses of my books (pp. 201–6), which has afforded an opportunity to present a micro-explanation of all my published works that together form the Theory of Personality (see pp. 24–49).

I would also like to take this opportunity to thank the many readers and scholars, especially those with an interest in Biology and Pschology, who have commented on, and confirmed, the observations and ideas put forward. Such feedback is immensely helpful in formulating one's ideas, and is appreciated from the heart. Criticisms have been equally heartily received, for they have allowed me to test the parameters of experiences and circumstances of others, set them against the theoretical aspects of the Theory, and to make adjustments where necessary. No scientist, and indeed no writer, can ask for more.

S. Giora Shoham
December 2002

Acknowledgments

I wish to acknowledge the very devoted work by my assistants, Varda Azulai, Adi Cohen, Miron Danan, Shosh Katz, Martin Ket, Sefi Sharoni, and Michelle Singer, without whose industrious good will and perseverance this book would not have been completed.

The author and publishers wish to thank the following for permission to use copyright material:

The Scala Group, SPA: Caravaggio (1573–1610), *David and Goliath*, Galleria Borghese, Rome; Vincent Van Gogh (1853–1890), *Portrait of Dr Gachet*, Musée d'Orsay, Paris.

Van Gogh Museum Foundation, Amsterdam/Vincent Van Gogh Foundation, for permission to reproduce the letters of Vincent Van Gogh.

The publishers apologize for any errors or omissions in the above list and would be grateful to be notified of any corrections that should be incorporated in the next edition or reprint of this book.

Introduction
Mytho-Empiricism

Speak not, lie hidden, and conceal
the way you dream, the things you feel.
Deep in your spirit let them rise
akin to stars in crystal skies
that set before the night is blurred:
delight in them and speak no word.

How can a heart expression find?
How should another know your mind?
Will he discern what quickens you?
A thought once uttered is untrue.
Dimmed is the fountainhead when stirred:
drink at the source and speak no word.

Live in your inner self alone,
within your soul a world has grown,
the magic of veiled thoughts that might
be blinded by the outer light,
drowned in the noise of day, unheard . . .
take in their song and speak no word.

Fyodor Thutchec, *Silentium*

The present volume sets out to explore the hitherto scantily investigated interrelationship between creativity, deviance and morbidity. We have come a long way, in time and the number of books published, since *The Mark of Cain* appeared in 1970.[1] That volume, which applied our stigma and labelling premises to crime and deviance, touched but tangentially upon the realm of creativity. We believe, however, that societal reaction to creative innovation is linked to the stigma-related premises of labelling deviants much more than may be gathered from first impressions. Our hypothesis stems from the observation that creative innovation and its acceptance, by society and its institutions, are related in a curvilinear manner: a medium of innovation is acceptable, but too much tends to be rejected, and its creators are liable to be labelled deviant or mad. This book examines the link between creativity and stigma, and the factors related to the acceptance or rejection of art and the possible labelling of its creators as criminals or lunatics. A first step is to try and clarify what constitutes art, and how it is related to crime and insanity. But no definitions will be forthcoming since as existentialists we hold with Kierkegaard that to refrain from defining is a sign of tact. Also, the polemics of whether art is a mimetic imitation, a representation or an "object" seem a waste.

Rather, we shall describe the function of art and how that function is carried out. A work of art is initiated by the artist structuring mythogenes of longing and/or experience, and implanting them in an artistic medium. The concepts to be clarified are: mythogene, structure and artistic medium. Mythogenes are the building units of myths, and are structured by individuals, whereas myths are produced by groups. The creative process involves both mythogenes and myths. Mythogenes are structured projections of the longings and experiences of individuals, whereas myths are the projections of group wishes and collective experiences onto the aggregate reservoir of these myths, or mythology.

The link between subject and object has been one of the most relevant psycho-philosophical problems from time immemorial. Solomon Maimon, a disciple of Kant, posited the matter metaphorically: "To find a passage from the external world to the mental world is more important than to find a way to East India, no matter what statesmen may say." Still, our concern is more pragmatic: we wish to understand how the mental revelation of an Archimedean cry of *Eureka* is structured into an objective creation. We hypothesize that this creative linkage is effected by a "mythogenic structure", the meaning of which will be presently explained.

Myths are also projections of the development of the species, as reflected in the development of the individual. It is interesting to note that this conception of myths as a projection of personal history may be inferred from the *Apocalypse of Baruch*, which states, "Every man is the Adam of his own soul",[2] which may in turn be interpreted to mean that every human being experiences original sin. Karl Abraham, as early as 1925 in his article *Character Formation on the Genital Level of Libido*

Development, expressed a basic idea, which is relevant for our present purposes, thus:

> In the two phases of development . . . we are able to recognize archaic types of character formation. They represent in the life of the individual recapitulations of primitive states, which the human race has passed through at certain stages of its development. Hence, in general, in biology, we find the rule holding good that the individual repeats in an abbreviated form the history of his ancestors. Accordingly, in normal circumstances, the individual will traverse those early stages of character formation in a relatively short space of time.[3]

Hence, the myth of the Fall of Man is the projection of a stage of development of the individual, yet also of a universal human developmental experience. However, myths become archetypal projections of human experience only when they are widespread. The more common a developmental experience, the greater are its chances of becoming a mythical projection. The inverse also holds: the more widespread the myth, the higher the chance that it is a projection of a widespread or even universal development. The universality of the myth of the Fall of Man, for example, points to a corresponding developmental phase; the separation of the individual self from the unified whole of early orality, which is indeed experienced by every human being.

Therefore, we hold that myths structure meaning for human behaviour and serve as motivation and prime movers for both individual and group behaviour. As myths are projected models of human behaviour at all levels, they may be records of past experience, as well as a structuring for future longings and goals. Myths are also expressions of both overt behaviour and covert dynamics, of the here and now as well as of transcendence. The dimensions of myths may also vary greatly, ranging from micro-myths, like names of persons and places, which represent meaningful experiences or quests, to meta-myths, such as those of Sisyphus and Tantalus, which represent the polar types of human behaviour on both the individual and group-levels. Myths vary with time and place. Every society and culture has its own indigenous mythology. Myths move in time from sacred myths recorded before history, to modern myths like master detectives, Sherlock Holmes and Hercule Poirot, or a Superman, who realizes the dreams of omnipotence among the downtrodden, henpecked inhabitants of the Metropolis.

Myths can relate to individuals. The offerings of Isaac and Iphigenia, signifying the sacrificial enmeshing of the young within the normative system of society, are two examples. Then there are group myths like the adventures of the Olympian gods and the tribal exploits of the German Æsir. The Nazi movement may indeed be studied as a collective myth, when the collective worms, to use Goebels's macabre simile, become effectively a fire-spitting dragon.[4] We follow in the giant footsteps of Claude Lévi-Strauss, who claimed that myths are a connecting structure between divergent polarities, like the raw and the cooked.[5] However, we attribute to mythology wider and deeper functions, a myth being a structure that functions, in Piaget's words, as:

> A system of transformation characterized by the laws of this system (in contradistinction to the attributes of its individual components). The system is preserved and enriched by the actions of these transformations, but they do not lead to outright components which are outside the (structured system). In short, a structure is characterized by holism, transformation, and self-regulation.[6]

Mythology is therefore "ahistorical" in the sense that a myth, as a holistic self-regulating structure, functions irrespective of its historical veracity. Thus Moses and the Exodus of the Jews from Egypt, which have no corroboration outside the Bible, have generated monotheistic Judaism, which is still viable regardless of Moses actually having existed or not. Also, we hold that myths link subject and object, the individual and society, consciousness and matter, revelation and creation-history, and transcendence. This linkage is a feedback cycle, since man projects myths onto metaphysics, which are structured into religions, which in turn feed the individual's faith. The creative myth, the "mythologic structure", is in our terminology not only a self-regulating mechanism, but also a self-recharging dynamic. Man uses myths, which remodel him, as role models, creative muses, ideologies, and religions. Hence, myths are our prime movers, which lift us by our own proverbial bootstraps *à la* Baron Münchausen, powered as a self-energizing *perpetuum mobilæ*.

The author's interest in mythology has been generated over almost three decades of interest in the theory and practice of labelling. When someone is stigmatized as a homosexual, a criminal or a madman, his other attributes and qualities seem to be eclipsed. The fact that the homosexual is also a good pianist, that the criminal has a sense of humour, or that the madman has a good heart becomes eclipsed by the over-arching effect of stereotyping as a deviant, jailbird or lunatic. Stigmatization of the deviant, the different person and the outsider is just one instance of the omnipotence of structure.

Piaget assures us that children start thinking in structures. This might account for the fact that the most basic structures are ingrained in us in our oral phase of development, along with the acquisition of our "mother tongue". Structures are, therefore, independent entities with internal transformation, which do not change, because self-regulation keeps them intact.

Once a structure has been formed, we get used to it by processes of "feedback". The earlier and longer one has had a structure, the more it is cherished through cognitive dissonance, and normalized and mythologized by mythogenic processes. The durability of mythogenic structures is subject to natural selection and functional adaptability. In this domain, as in so many other dynamics of creation and entropy, Darwinian evolution reigns supreme.

Creativity

The structured mythogene is then ingrained in the artistic medium, be it a canvas, a sculpture or a sonnet. The mythogenic structure of the artist is thence infused, embedded and contained, as a particle of his consciousness, within his medium. We look at a picture by van Gogh or read a novel by Dostoyevsky and the force of it strikes us with overwhelming potency a century after the artist's death. The consciousness of the artist is contained in the work of art and is transferred through his act of creation. Creation is a dialectic between the creator's consciousness and matter, as mediated by the mythogenic structure. For the mythogenic structures to pass over to an audience willing and ready "to open up" to the artist's creation, the execution of the work of art, with the mythogenic structures as blueprints, must be authentic in its dialogic, maieutic transmission.

Creation is the expression of a unique personality. In order to be authentic, the creation has to include the artist's inner self, which comprises the mythogenes ingrained in the work of art, and consists of dynamics which are as specific to the artist as his fingerprints. Consequently, imitation of another's creativity renders the creation inauthentic. Discipleship can also render a creation inauthentic, unless the master–teacher relationship to his pupil is of a maieutic nature. This is in line with the Buberian conception of reaching out towards the object as the baseline for a dialogical relationship. Hence, we envisage creativity as a real bridge between man and object. By imbuing the artistic medium with his visions, as structured by the mythogenes, and by moulding it as his creation, man the creator, the *homo faber*, entwines his psyche with the artistic medium, and through it, with the audience.

The creator's longing to communicate his artistic message to kindred souls, wherever and whenever they may be, effects a link between artist and audience outside of space and time. This mutual longing to communicate through a work of art makes creativity eternal. Such communicability of a creation is also the main criterion of its durable value. Some art, which we once appreciated, seems to us dated and stale today, but Mozart, Chekhov and van Gogh seem as fresh and relevant now as in the past. The communicative timelessness of a work of art makes it a dialogue in eternity. The author recently attended a retrospective exhibition of the works of Antonelo Da Messina, held in his native town. His works, especially a wooden Christ, raised the author to intense heights of aesthetic euphoria, as if he himself was engaged in painting or sculpting the exhibits. Da Messina thus gained a measure of immortality by infusing his authentic creation with an artistic message, which continues to be communicated beyond his own place and time.

The creator may also feel a dialogue-like affinity with his tools – a sculptor with his chisel, a painter with his brush – or the present author with his thick fountain pen, with which he has written all his books in longhand. With these personalized tools, the artist may feel that he has reached the core of his creation. This is not unlike Buber's claim that he reached a dialogue with a tree by means of a walking stick. For a creator to feel that he has achieved a rapport with a tool or a creative work, he must sense that he has imbued it with his personalized uniqueness, that his vision has been infused into its inner core. The mytho-empirical anchor for the dynamic of seeking communication with the object by means of creativity is the *avoda begashmiut*, work or worship in the concrete, based on the kabbalistic myth of "the breaking of the vessels", according to which a cosmic disaster caused sparks of Divinity to be scattered into spatio-temporality and become embedded in each object and life form.

An even earlier mytho-empirical anchor for communication with the object through creativity is the myth of the Gnostic messenger. His aim was to set in motion the ships of light and start the revolution of the cosmic spheres, in order to liberate the particles of divine light entrapped in nature. This, as well as the Manichean Jesus Potabilis, who "hangs from every tree", served up in every dish and dispersed in all creation, is the transcendental projection of the quest of *homo faber* to reach the divine core of the object, and link it to his own core-vectors by the dialectics of creativity.

Worshipping in the concrete has other manifestations. Henry Thoreau built his hut beside Wadden Pond, where he felt a dialogic affinity with the woods, air, water and stars. Camus' heroes find their Sisyphean *raison d'être* in being able to create, save and cure in the midst of the existential plague. Chomsky even proposes that the dialectical involvement with language is the base line of creativity. The creator thus tries to build a bridge between himself and the word as the object. The Hebrew poet Shlonsky went to the extent of claiming that he never used a word before making love to it.

If indeed creativity is spurred by a core need to communicate, how is communication through creativity effected? We hold that the creator transmits to his audience, through his creation or performance, the intensity and sincerity of longing and experience, as structured in the mythogenes ingrained in the artistic medium. The audience perceiving the work of art may be catalysed into feeling and a similar longing and experience. However, the mythogenic structures of the artist and the individuals in the audience, as determined by their unique bio-psychocultural configuration, are bound to be different; yet, the coincidence of their yearnings in time lends them a sense of communication, effected by their common elation. Thus, James Galway, playing his flute for an Israeli audience, may be elated by the visions of green pastures, smiling Irish eyes and laughter. The music may arouse different yearnings in the members of his audience, according to the specific aims of their personality core vectors. One may long for the red mountains of Eilat, another for the blue heat of Lake Tiberias in the summer, and a third for the black eyes and olive skin of Yemenite girls. Thus, a common longing and experience, mythogenically structured by the artist within the artistic medium, and transmitted maieutically to the audience by the performance or work of art, creates the sense of communication, irrespective of the wide discrepancies in the contents of their yearnings. It is necessary, however, that the artist be authentic and intensively sincere for his art to spur a communicative elation in his audience. Without this, his performance is liable not to "pass".

The authenticity of a work of art extricates it from diachronicity and the time- and place-bound judgement of art critics, the economic considerations of gallery owners and the biases of artistic cliques. The maieutic dialogue between artist and audience, mediated by the artistic medium, is effected by the structured mythogenes of the artist which, if authentic, are outside time. This happens by triggering the structuring of the corresponding mythogenes of longing and experience within the bio-psycho-social configurations of members of the audience. Hence, although the biological bases of personalities and social context of artist and audience are widely divergent, the inspiration of the artist is maieutically transmitted to trigger elation, over time and place. Art is thus a mode of dialogue, a goal in itself, and may (although needn't) be related to mimetic representation or entertainment. Since, according to the philosophers of dialogue, especially Kierkegaard and Buber, the I and the thou, the self and the object, are only inchoate entities, the primary ontological essence is the dialogical relationship between the I and the thou, the self and the object.

The dialogue of art is not only the bridge between human individuals, life forms and objects, but also the source of existential meaning. If an

I–thou encounter occurs by means of a work of art, a sense of revelation and meaning follows. Without this dialogue, the surrounding environment becomes menacing, loaded with an I–it opaqueness.

* * *

A lasting creation begins with a spark of insight, inspiration and direct apprehension. Such a revelatory spark is expressed by Archimedes' cry of *Eureka*. The revelatory moment in creation is the dawning on the artist that he or she may structure his mythogenes of longing and experience into a work of art. Creative revelation sprouts forth from the dynamics of the personality core. It interacts dialectically with the self, which aims to mould the mythogenes and embed them into an artistic medium, and present the creation to the outside world. This need for an audience is inherent in the process of creativity. Even the reclusive Nietzsche, who gorged himself on the rarefied heights of revelation, confessed the need to descend to man and share his wisdom in *Thus Spake Zarathustra*.

The extremely inauthentic artist is totally attuned to his audience. His audience is his master, his work merely a response to the latest market research, and is therefore completely imprisoned in diachronic time. The work of the extremely authentic artist, on the other hand, is the embodiment of the uncontrolled gushing of his revelatory mythogenic dreams, longings and experience. His creations are likely to be misunderstood and rejected by the public. The artist is often stigmatized, encountering the public resistance from which innovators have suffered since time immemorial. Yet the authenticity of his art raises it above the fetters of time, into the eternal now.

Art is a prime medium of communication. The paradox here is that the revelatory component of the self, which gives the artist a sense of authentic immediacy towards his creation, the component of the inner self, is the least communicable. On the other hand, the wide promotion and commercial success of a work of art depends on its attunement to the broadest common denominator of public taste. Consequently, the more authentic the work of art, the more sincerely it expresses the artist's revelatory inner self, the less communicable it is. The lamentable result is that creativity, the prime expression of man's uniqueness and inner self, is least communicable when it is most true to the artist.

The revelatory component of a work of art may be communicated maieutically, rendering the passive observer an interlocutor, and initiating him into the act of creativity. The artist's revelation, when expressed in his creation, may trigger a revelation in the viewer, generated by his own personality and societal imprints. The revelatory component of a work bestows on it a timelessness, a permanent freshness. Revelation is a non-temporal, synchronic measure of the value of a work. Revelation and creativity are dualistic, complementary components of the act of creation. As the creative potential of each individual is unique, the mode, medium and contents of each individual's creativity have their own specific optimum. If an individual has heeded the call to authenticity and embarked on a search for rebellious, creative expression, he still has to find the mode and medium of creativity optimally suited to his specific psycho-social configuration. He may accomplish this by intuition or by trial and error, or he may fail to find it even after an arduous search. Uncertainties may plague the artist even if he has found a mode of creative expression, and the optimal medium of creativity for any individual may change with time and place. He may not be aware of having found his one optimal mode of expression, letting Maeterlinck's proverbial bluebird fly away from his porch. Most people do not feel they have found the optimal modes and media of creative expression suitable to their talents and artistic potential. Others may not be satisfied with what they have found and are ever searching for new methods and areas of creativity. Again, the search for the right mode of creative expression is part of the never-ending Sisyphean dynamic of Ego's creative involvement with his objective and human surroundings. This search in itself may be one expression of man's authentic existence.

In his preface to the *Myth of Sisyphus*, Camus invites us "to live and to create in the very midst of the desert".[7] This is precisely what his protagonists, Dr. Rieux and Grand, endeavour within the abyss of the plague. Rieux tries to cure the sick, Grand begins to write a novel and plants a rose bush in the middle of the swamp. Not knowing the ultimate purpose of their activities, not having any decisive influence on the course of events, Rieux and Grand cling to the life raft of creativity as the only safeguard against the slump of inauthenticity in the anaesthetizing bosom of the generalized other. Grand starts his novel all over again while hoping to complete it "when all this [the plague] is over". He immerses himself in writing and rewriting its opening sentences while feeling within himself that the plague will not end and that his chances of surviving are nil. Seeking creativity within the plague is transcendental, because it generates an internal force field, which is projected onto the creator's surroundings and gives his involvement with them a measure of meaning. Indeed, without creativity, man's rat-race in a cut-throat society of achievers is like weasels biting each other in a hole or worms slithering over each other in a heap of excrement. This premise could lend a novel hue to Nietzsche's dictum that art has been given to man so that he does not die of the truth, i.e., of the numbing reality of the Camusean plague.

We project our core personality cravings, quests and longings onto our creation, which extricates us from the plague while we are still afflicted with it. Such projections imbue the creative process with a halo of fulfilment. Without them a violin sonata would be the scratching of horsetail hair on dried catgut. We therefore appreciate creativity and love art, which is most capable of receiving and absorbing the projections of our personality core yearnings and of lifting us out of our Sisyphean drudgery.

Authentic creativity seems to release the pent-up psychic energy of the creator, so that it bursts out and is structured into a work of art. The creator projects onto his creation his sense of ontological uniqueness, as well as his existential moods, so that his work bears the unmistakable imprint of his personality configuration. For instance, the explosive originality of van Gogh's expression, his almost desperate involvement with his creation, is apparent in every brush stroke.

The creative rebel grapples with reality in a Nietzschean manner, rebelling against God by the most radical defiance possible, i.e., by his own acts of creation. The creative innovator is necessarily a rebel to a certain extent. Seeing and depicting things differently, he is automatically in opposition to the mainstream cliques in art and literature, which have a vested interest in preserving the *status quo*. Many of the greatest outbursts of creativity have been fuelled by rebellion and protest. The self-exiled American and Irish expatriates of Gertrude Stein's Parisian "lost generation" literary salon generated a most spectacular upsurge in literature and art between the world wars. Arthur Koestler, Ignazio Silone and the *God that Failed* group were spurred to new heights of creativity by the Spanish civil war, while the dissident movement in the former USSR generated forceful new currents in literature and art which vibrated with an expressive authenticity that had been absent for almost half a century.

Revelatory rebellion rejects spatio-temporality, searching for the surreal, for the world of dreams of a Tanguy or a Magritte. The Tantalic artist structures his longing for unity, his quest for understanding, in his relationship with ultimates. Other people are almost superfluous to the Tantalic rebel. Of crucial importance is his inner self and its expression through revelatory experiences, with God as audience – perhaps the sole audience. Kafka's example is well known, while Camus describes the case of the silent piano: "Ernst Dwinger, in his *Siberian Diary,* mentions a German lieutenant – for years a prisoner in a camp where cold and hunger were almost unbearable – who constructed himself a silent piano with wooden keys. In the most abject misery, perpetually surrounded with a ragged mob, he composed a strange music, which was audible to him alone."[8] For the Tantalic rebel, artistic creation is a demand for unity and a rejection of the world.[9]

Pain and Creativity

A curvilinear relationship exists between conflict, pain, suffering and creativity. Some conflicts internally felt by the creator may be projected onto his creation and lend it a personalized dimension of depth. Too much conflict, however, may stifle the creator. In a similar vein, straining to overcome pain, interference and obstacles fuels the fires of creativity, but unbearable pain and insurmountable obstacles are liable to extinguish them. Indeed, the myth of Sisyphus, as interpreted by Camus, and by the present author, envisages the creativity of man within the context of a cyclical obstacle course. We should imagine Sisyphus happy in his work if he manages to be involved creatively with his stone-object, pushing it strenuously uphill. When the stone tumbles downhill, we push it up again; we try to harness this cycle in the service of our creative energies. These are the polar alternatives to our Sisyphean continuum of object relationships. Either we transform our burden into something creative or slump under it without authenticity, confounded by a petrifying routine.

The mytho-empirical anchor of man's deprivational interaction with the object, his strife and suffering, is the curse God inflicted on man following original sin. We relate the Fall and expulsion from Paradise to the ejection of the individual from the pantheism of early orality. Hence, the creative way back to the object is through the agony of thorns and thistles, through the sweat of the brow, as ordained by the God of Genesis. Indeed, a great many creative colossi have seen their art as a sublimation of their suffering. Nietzsche regarded his creativity as "that power which voluntarily takes the pain of living upon itself because it ever newly feels within itself the creative strength to turn the pain into a means to an end in which it feels itself borne beyond pain . . . in that creative power for which even the hardest, toughest materials are not too hard or tough, because it is *nevertheless superior* to them, nevertheless capable of chiselling its god-figures out of them".[10] Ezra Pound's humiliation by the town square toughs of Pisa triggered the soaring heights of his later *Cantos*. The fires of unconsummated love fuelled the writings of Petrarch, Heine and Kierkegaard. However, the curvilinear nature of the relationship between creativity and suffering may paralyze the creator if he must endure unbearable agony. On the other hand, success, and the cosy complacency which often accompanies it, may also stifle creativity.

The stressful relationship between the artist and his object, which provides the "fuel" for creativity, makes authentic creation border on brinkmanship. This is the Nietzschean and Camusean mandate to create dangerously, and is the mytho-empirical projection of Damocles dancing desperately under the sword. The key word here is desperation. Sartre describes Tintoretto as frantically and unceasingly producing; his desperation is apparent in his difficulty in deciding "whether he was trying to find or to flee himself through his work".[11] Rimbaud draws the ferocious vigour of his poetry from his desperate longing to partake of the desert winds, the damp hell of the South Sea jungles and the searing magic of pagan gods. Rimbaud courted danger in order to provide his poetry with the irreversible lucidity of desperation.

The intensity of creative involvement makes for an artist's image of egocentricity. The paradox is that the more intense one's creative involvement with one's surroundings, the more one appears to be detached from them and immersed in oneself. Upon deeper scrutiny, this paradox resolves itself with the realization that the intensity of creative involvement immerses the artist in his creation and excludes the rest of the world from his range of concentrated attention. The exclusive resoluteness of creativity effects an *extasis*, an extrusion, of the artist from the routine of space–time and a temporary ascent onto different spheres of existence. For instance, Stefan Zweig described the total immersion of Auguste Rodin in moulding the clay of his sculpture so that he completely forgot his guests waiting for him outside his *atelier*.[12] Artaud declared that he felt a sense of total existence only when engulfed by fleeting fragmentary moments of creativity, and Proust secluded himself in his womb-like, cork-lined study, to recreate the cherished landscapes of his childhood. Such creative retreat into an unshared cocoon of private spatio-temporality has its grim aspects – causing Cezanne to absentmindedly abstain from attending the funeral of his mother and Rilke to forget the wedding of his daughter. However, whatever the effect of creativity on the artist's social interaction, its authentic intensity grants him a sense of fulfilment and self-realization. It trivializes daily trials, puts existential vicissitudes in perspective and lends the artist ontological security, even in the shifting mires of the here and now. The creative process is basically an object-involved relationship. It entails reaching out towards an object or life form in order to mould it and imprint one's visions onto it. Hence, creativity comprises the wish to communicate with external entities and oft-times constitutes the sole means of doing so. Although, for the participant, revelatory experience lends a dimension of depth to the creative act, the revelation in itself, even if structured into what seems to be a creative work, is very rarely communicable. Artaud meant to communicate his surrealistic experiences, but failed, because he assaulted his own cognition and that of others with awareness-numbing rituals. He then tried to transmit his artistic messages directly to the inner selves of the members of his audience,[13] but this proved impossible because communication is effected, if at all, by symbolic interaction between cognitions. Intuition may be the igniting spark of creativity, but in order to be communicative, a creative work must be structured, stylized and intentionally displayed. Indeed, the need to communicate through art and the ability to do so is the *raison d'être* of creativity. Many have contested this conviction, expressed, *inter alia*, by Tolstoy.[14] We hold, however, that the essence of creativity is a man-world complementarity and hence an interactive quest to reach out and communicate. Sisyphus without his stone is only half the cast of the creative drama. The dialectical strain between creator and object is what constitutes the ecstasy, enthusiasm and euphoric strife of creativity. Sisyphus *incommunicado* is a solipsistic masturbator.

As we have pointed out elsewhere, if man is unable to communicate, he is likely to become violent.[15] *Since creativity is a prime mode of communication, it might well be an antidote to violence.*

The Creative Process

Unlike the Buberian concept of reaching out towards the object as a baseline for a dialogical relationship between man and the world, we envisage creativity as a real bridge of complementarity between man and object. By imbuing the artistic medium with his mythogenes and moulding it as his creation, man the creator, *homo faber*, has entwined his psyche with the object. Authentic creativity thus provides a bypass to the psycho-physical antinomy between the self and its surroundings. The Marxists claim that man is alienated from the object because he does not own the means of its production. This is like saying that Sisyphus cannot be creatively involved with his stone because he does not own it. Authentic creativity is not related to possession. A collector may own all the items he displays, but is usually dependent on an audience to appreciate his collection. He is, therefore, petrified by a Buberian I–it relationship with his collection. On the other hand, a prisoner who does not own even the shirt on his back, and is constrained by the most stifling routines, may yet find creative outlets. Indeed, Sisyphus was a prisoner and, in his moments of authenticity, when he liberated himself from the yoke of the generalized other, managed to carve a creative reprieve out of his stone into synchronic eternity.

The creator seeks to communicate through his creation with kindred spirits who can absorb and appreciate the music in his heart, as structured in his art. Often a creator believes that only a choice elite is worthy of his art. T. E. Lawrence printed a first edition of only sixty copies of the *Seven Pillars of Wisdom*, to be sent to those who, he hoped, would be able to understand his philosophical, artistic and experiential messages. Even Kafka, who wrote "for his drawer", and Erich Neumann, who declared that he was compelled to write, even if nobody read him, wished that one day someone who could understand might pick up their writings and absorb their messages. Communication would thus be effected outside the confines of temporality.

The inability of the creative innovator to communicate with his contemporaries raises the probability of his being branded a deviant. The process of so branding the creative innovator commences with the essence of innovation, the capacity to see the commonplace and familiar from new angles. Innovation, by definition, comprises non-normative attitudes, which raise the probability of nonconformist behaviour. Indeed, genius is often not more (yet not less) than the ability to make perceptions that are contrary to normative conditioning and socialization. The ability to innovate is linked to extricating oneself from the harness of stereotypes and clichés imposed by the reigning mandates of artistic cliques. Here again the revelatory component of creativity is a crucial ingredient of innovation. The innovator is also a perpetual child, ever astounded by his own curiosity, by his perceptions and experiences, and not stultified by drudgery, normative slumber, and routine.

Creativity also necessitates a certain detachment. True, without subjective involvement there can be no creativity, but in this respect too the relationship is curvilinear. Too intense an involvement may paralyze the creator; a measure of distance and dissociation is necessary for the artist to gain the right perspective. The artist could very easily be tagged by the normative branding agencies of society as alienated, estranged and deviant. The label of deviance might be reinforced by the fact that the authentic creator is immersed in the creative process and relatively oblivious to money and fame. There might be no better way of illustrating our premise than the advertisement of the Time Life Library of Arts for its van Gogh volume, which says: "It took the eyes of a madman to see the world in a new light and to paint it that way." We may propose the hypothesis that most great innovations and creations have been made by those deemed outsiders, deviants and madmen in their own lifetimes. This is a variation on the "Kropotkin hypothesis", that all great discoveries and epoch-making research were conducted outside academic institutions and, we may add, by deviants and outsiders within academia.[16] The persecution of Galileo, the harassment of Bach and the early loneliness of Einstein are some celebrated instances.

Extreme forms of the creator–audience relationship present Scylla and Charybdis choices. The extremely isolated and non-communicative artist is embedded in the solipsism of being both creator and audience. This might be illustrated by Dostoevsky's man in the underground. At the other extreme, we have the poet laureate and court jester, who are similar in their total dependence on some relevant others and in their need to cater to the tastes and whims of their audiences. These are the extreme poles of a continuum; most artists can be positioned between them. The more the artist anchors on his revelatory inner core, the less marketable his creation; the creator can try to ensure the sincerity of his art, but cannot evaluate its public reception. He may decide that the creative process is more important to him than the peddling of his art; thus he may be "discovered" after his death or not at all.

We can only guess how many Bachs have been totally forgotten because they did not have a Mendelssohn-Bartholdy to rediscover them; how many van Goghs have been consigned to oblivion because they did not have a brother, Theo, to love and cherish them and preserve their work for posterity. Oft-times, the revelatory artist, immersed in visions of his inner self, is not willing to compromise with his audience and insists on being accepted on his own esoteric terms, not realizing that he is asking for the impossible. Usually, however, the artist receives his feedback of worth from a specific audience, or from people whose opinion he values most. This is even more apparent with the performing artist, whose art is focused on his ability to "pass over" to his audience. A prominent Israeli actress once said that the stage is her sacrificial altar, on which she prays to achieve revelatory elation. Yet even for her the audience is essential, because the actor–audience relationship is the creative unit of the dramatic performance. An actor often sacrifices his personal well-being, his health and livelihood for the actor–audience complementarity and mutual dialectical strains, which are the essence of his art and its main reward.

Thus, as demonstrated, creativity aims at communication with objects and people – this is its authentic *raison d'être*. However, when the end product is complete, it may be promoted for the achievement of recognition, fame and money. These two processes have hardly anything in common. The quest for communication in creativity anchors on the process of creation and fuels the self-expression inherent in this process, whereas the sale of the end product is a pure marketing matter depending on promotion, image-building and public relations not very different from that used in the selling of detergents and cereals. The quest for communication through creativity is an organic part of the process of creation, whereas subsequent sales are not. Writing a book in the hope that someone may pick it up today or a hundred years from now and feel an affinity with the author's ideas is a dynamic of communication inherent in the process of authentic creativity. On the other hand, the motivation to write for pecuniary ends or for recognition by the generalized other is extraneous to creativity.

A surfeit of fame and money has often asphyxiated creativity, inducing the artist to rest on his laurels or slip into a contented slumber. The bourgeois, so much despised by the authentic artist, may thus have the last word. Especially painful is the case of Jacques Brel, whose last record, which he considered his rebellious testament, was callously commercialized by the carnivorous bourgeois peddlers he so masterfully ridiculed in his songs.

Creativity is stunted by fierce competitiveness, which tends to push it into an inauthentic quest for marketable products. The authentic component of creativity tends to blunt this competitiveness, making for a more sincere anchor in the processes of creation. There is, however, enough venom and malice within ambition-crazed cliques to push many heedless creators off the achievement pyramid and into the abyss of oblivion. In the lore of the combative artistic cliques, this is expressed by the observation that the moment one starts climbing the ladder of public recognition and success, there are those ready to engineer one's downfall. This, together with what is known in Hollywood as "the curse of the Oscar" and in scientific circles as "the noose of the Nobel Prize", constitutes the self-defeating component of public recognition. A best-selling author, an Oscar winner or a Nobel laureate may be swept out of the state of mind optimal for authentic creativity and hurled into the momentarily loving, but carnivorous, bosom of the admiring public, severing them from their sources of inspiration. Such temporary creative recession, experienced by Rod Steiger and Albert Camus, is dreaded by John Le Carré with every new bestseller, and is the reason for his repeated refusals of lucrative Hollywood offers.

Mytho-empirically, we may denote such fear, or even flight from public acclaim, as the Jonah Syndrome. Apart from the realization that material success is likely to deflate the dialectical energy underlying creation, the Jonah Syndrome may also arise from the creator's agoraphobic dread of an excess of stimuli, to which he may be exposed following public acclaim.

It is quite understandable, according to our model, that a public that cannot distinguish between the artist and his art would physically and mentally devour muddleheaded performers like Rita Hayworth, Marilyn Monroe and Elvis Presley. The art establishment may also muffle the rebelliousness of creative artists by burying them in the cosiness of its soft embrace. This happened to Jean Genet. After Sartre wrote a blockbuster best seller that turned Genet into the first existentialist saint, Genet, it is reported, could not write for five years. All he did was drive around in a Rolls Royce, changing his young male companions every few days. In another celebrated case, de Sade was rendered completely normative by the academic establishment, which showered him with torrents of pompous encomiums – no doubt making the Divine Marquis turn in his grave. More disturbing, and yet a proof of the universality of our model, is the fact that Camus himself, expounder of the myth of Sisyphus, succumbed to the effects of success. Public acclaim deprived him of the dialectical strain so vital for creativity. However, most creators search for recognition and the wealth that goes with it as a reinforcement of their sense of worth. If public acceptance fails to materialize, they may bask in the *ressentiment* halo of "the genius unrecognized by the Philistines". This is sure to place our acclaim-thirsty artist under the dominion of the generalized other, whose recognition he is trying to gain, in turn further decreasing the chance of authentic creation. The course which may finally prove to be both more authentic and more politic is to immerse oneself in the process of creativity and thereby gain one's sense of inner dialectical fulfilment. If public acclaim does come, one may accept it as a fringe benefit of the authentic self-realization inherent in the process of creativity.

Talent has not been equally distributed. It does not favour the power elites of artistic cliques over the powerless. The powerful and talentless within competitive groups therefore begrudge the talents of others in the group, especially if they are powerless and hence convenient objects for stigmatization and scapegoating.[17] The talented powerless are therefore predisposed to be tagged as deviants by the powerful pacesetters of professional, academic and artistic groups. Moreover, in many forms of art and creativity, the cliques are also the *arbiteri elegantiari*. They use their power to brand as mediocre or worthless the work of the authentic creators, who reject their authority or do not conform to the clique rules. The innovative outsider is usually ill equipped to fight this judgement, because he roams somewhere on the fringes of institutionalized art, or outside it altogether. Therefore, the test of the worth of an artist and his art is outside time and place. Only in retrospect can we appreciate the excellence of a Mozart, a van Gogh or a Melville. The sad fact is that most innovative creators are recognized only after their deaths. During their lifetimes, it is the cliquish interests and power structures, averse to those who rock the boat, that evaluate them. When the creator's critics are dead, his creation can be given its rightful due in a disinterested context. Creators and their creations must effect an *extasis*, in the ancient Greek sense, in order to be evaluated in their proper perspective.

The vested interest and clique-based evaluation of the creator not only dates him, but also binds him in a stifling manner to a given place. This could be denoted as the Muhammad Syndrome, exemplified by the saying,

"There is no prophet in his own country." The people of Mecca, Muhammad's native city, did not accept him as their prophet, so he moved to Medina, where he was acclaimed as the emissary of God. Muhammed's trip from Mecca to Medina, the *Hejira*, was considered so crucial that it came to serve as the baseline for the Moslem calendar. Indeed, we might hear the gentry of Mecca muttering, "This runny-nosed epileptic, a prophet? Never" The British say that "familiarity breeds contempt", while Proust remarked that we cannot impute genius to the tablemate who picks his teeth after dinner." The deeper basis for the Muhammad Syndrome is that power elites are wary of the creative innovator and try to suppress him. The authentic creator is more likely to fulfill himself creatively without the stifling normative prejudices of the indigenous others when he leaves, in a rebellious mood, for another place. Hence, authentic creativity is not bound to a particular time or place. It is boundless, whereas clique-anchored, vested-interests-based creation is both dated and unable to "travel".

Artistic cliques are composed of a few artists, and many camp followers, lackeys, groupies, critics, managers and assorted spongers – all centred around a hard-core leadership which draws its power not from creative excellence, but rather from the control of budgets, journals, theatres, and radio and TV stations. Such people are dependent on the clique for favours, employment and for a sense of relative achievement, which comes from stigmatizing their "colleagues". The cliques, through their public-relations organs, create celebrities and destroy them. When someone has been declared brilliant by the public communications channels, the declaration becomes a self-fulfilling prophecy. Even if everybody knows, including the artist himself, that the critic responsible for his rise is a shallow mediocrity, the laudatory image receives the sanction of "public opinion"; *vox populi* becomes *vox dei*. There are, however, many instances in which authentic creators need the "good services" of cliques and institutions to reveal their works to groups and individuals with whom they wish to communicate. These are, *inter alia*, professional organizations, congresses, publishing houses, theatres and galleries. Camp followers, lackeys and groupies, as well as sincere friends and constructive critics, give the artist the feedback he so ardently needs as a reinforcement of his sense of worth and an evaluation of the communicative worth of his creation. The creator may thereby become easy prey to flatterers who exploit him, materially and emotionally. Because of his need for reinforcement, he is in a poor position to distinguish between flatterer and sincere critics. The institutionalized outlets for his creations may shower him with honours that can stifle his creativity with a thick mesh of complacency, quenching his authentic rebellion with pomposity and self-satisfaction. Creative people are usually too absorbed in their work to be willingly involved in administration and institutional power politics.

At the macro level of metaphysical programming, the power elite, artistic cliques and academia might offer an apology smacking of science fiction – that stigmatization of creative innovators serves as a guard against too much innovation, for which society is not prepared. The Inquisition, which in Galileo's time stood for stability, order, propriety and probity, and was of course the staunch defender of the universal church, had to torture him to make him recant his atrocious contentions – which might have led to cosmic, social and religious chaos. Yet Galileo could not help being a rebellious creative innovator; he could not but declare against all convention: *Epur si muove.*

Nevertheless society has a way to protect itself against too much innovation, as we shall explain below. It is as if evolutionary adjustment has formed a "leash" on creative innovators to check their galloping inventiveness. Evolution seems to allow only certain amounts and qualities of innovation, with which society can cope without being disrupted. Figure 0.1, mytho-empirical scheme, shows projections of mythogenic individual and mythological group processes, and highlights the dynamics described above.

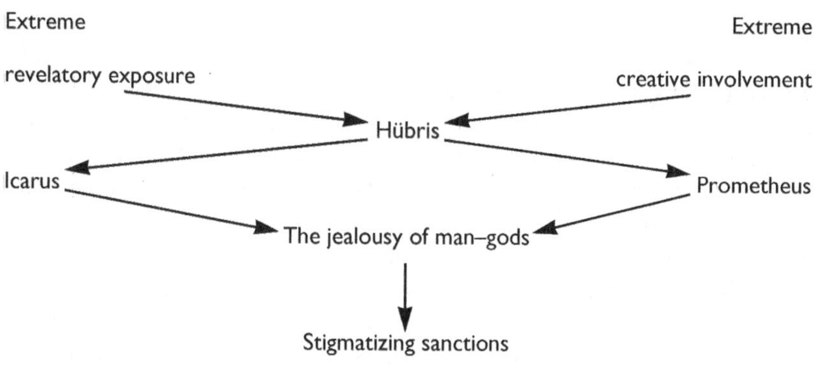

Figure 0.1 Societal reaction against innovators

Innovators try to extract or steal forbidden knowledge from transcendence. Sisyphus becomes Prometheus, stealing fire from the Olympians to give to mortals. The Faustian myth is incorporated into the life history of the most creative innovators, like Galileo, van Gogh, Artaud, Nietzsche and Joyce, to mention but a few who paid dearly for their originality. By infringing the prevailing norm of *meden agan*, "nothing in excess", the creative innovators commit the sin of *hübris*, exceeding the means, modes and medians, and hence overstepping their *moira*, or lot in life. Their extravagance arouses the jealousy of the gods, clearly a projection of the jealousy of men, kindling their wrath. The link between the normative system of a separant, competitive society and the jealousy of its man-gods has been insightfully expounded by Svend Ranulf, in his study on the jealousy of the Greek gods and Greek criminal law.[18] If a creator is too extreme in his innovations and raises the jealousy of the competitive man-gods, he is liable to be smitten by stigmatization, to be ostracized, and driven into madness and death. The mytho-empirical cycle is closed: the rock of Sisyphus becomes the rock to which Prometheus is chained.

The rule of *meden agan*, which dominated separant Greek religion, seems also to prevail in physics, evolution, the life sciences, law and sociology. Guarding the middle values, the system-in-balance between the core vectors dominating man's life, reigns supreme in all areas regulating life forms and objects. Social norms and systems of social control ensure that man does not deviate too far in his behaviour, including his creative innovations. If he does, he commits *hübris*, and the gods of creation, reflected in the Gnostic concept of the *demiurgos*, the kabbalistic stern judgement, and the existentialist hell-as-the-other, strike back to keep the creative, deviant innovator in line. The evolutionary viability of meaningfulness is also apparent in the kabbalist notion of *tikkun*. Man's theurgic function raises his stature, making him a partner in transcendence; yet in this partnership lies an inherent danger.

The seeker of revelation commits the *hübris* of wishing to become like the gods. This is precisely the kind of "knowledge" proscribed in Genesis. The Tantalic seeks not only to be exposed to God, but actually to partake of Him and thus become God. Hence, the theistic God of Genesis proscribes the actual "knowledge" of God, lest men also become gods. This proscription also contains a separate interdiction against a reversal to earlier developmental phases and non-being. In the Greek myth, Daedalus, the father of Icarus, instructs him in the perennial way of parents: "My son, be warned! Neither soar too high, lest the sun melt the wax; nor swoop too low, lest the feathers be wetted by the sea. Follow me closely! Do not set your own course."[19] We can hear our own parents warning us from their experience not to jump too high, not to stick out our necks, to abide by the rules, and to keep in line lest we get hurt.

Man is, therefore, no match for the power, arbitrariness and cruelty of the gods, but he does hold a trump card. By being victimized, abused and manipulated, he gains a moral freedom, and a mandate to imbue his own life and surroundings with meaning and values.

The link between innovation and stigma is set out in figure 0.2.

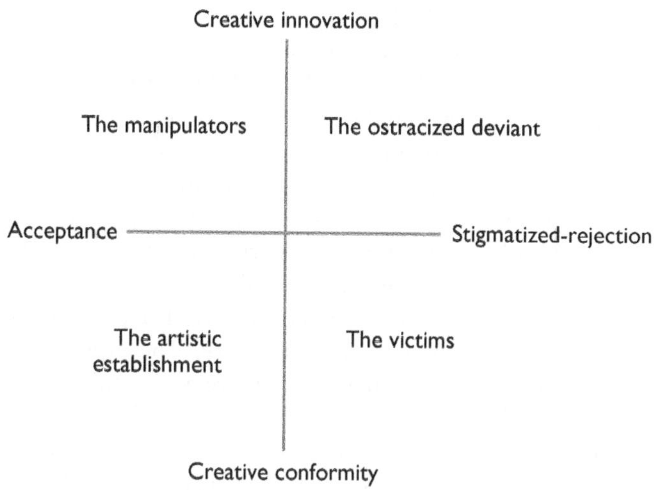

Figure 0.2 The link between innovation and stigma

The manipulators, like Picasso and Dali, can also be great innovators, but are also clever operators and merchants; hence, they can get away with their innovations and also gain money and power. The victims are the creative non-conformists, who are either deviants or belong to ethnic, religious or sexual minorities.

The next step is an exposition of the relationship between deviant behaviour and social stigma.

* * *

The Bohemians are deliberately detached from the mainstream of society, in their search for beauty, justice, or perfect theoretical structures. Intellectuals and artists, whose *raison d'être* is the expression of emotions and ideas in symbols, objects or other means of communication, are often detached from, and indifferent to, prevailing norms and values. Their creativity and methods of operation prevent them from being involved in the common rat race for social power. For deeper insight and better observation, the Bohemian divorces himself from actual social realities, so that he may gain the necessary distance and perspective to observe and analyze those realities.

Paradoxically, Bohemians have always expressed, aesthetically and intellectually, the existence, goals and ideals of the group, due to their spectator role and their deeper insight. The deviation of the Bohemian is characteristically described from the group's standpoint by Montesquieu thus, "That which shocked me most is that they [the Bohemians] are quite useless to their country and amuse their talents with puerilities. For example, when I arrived at Paris, I found them warm at dispute over the most trifling matter imaginable. It was all about an old Greek poet."[20]

Bohemians may sometimes be the nucleus of a subculture, but often such café society degenerates into pseudo-Bohemia. Such groups of very few real artists and a multitude of self-styled, perpetual would-be artists and camp-followers are an integral part of society – an institutionalized layer of social stratification. The crucial point, however, is that they are accepted as such by the other strata of society. The pseudo-Bohemians are therefore integrated in the social structure. The perennial sign of true Bohemia – the disregard of all goals that are not aesthetic – is almost non-existent in modern café-society. The latter includes the most ardent conformists in another sense: they follow exactly the middle-class concept and image of the Bohemian and outsider. The trademarks of the pseudo-Bohemian are the external and formal ones of dress, mannerism and demeanour. The pseudo-Bohemian goes no deeper than the dishevelled clothes and the unshaved face. It would seem that when a certain movement becomes institutionalized, it may either crystallize into a subculture, or sweep a whole branch of art or entertainment.

In other words, pseudo-Bohemia as a group phenomenon does not really involve deviant behaviour, and is therefore outside the scope of the present analysis; suffice it to say that we have distinguished it from and contrasted it with deviant Bohemia. However, even with the latter, the differential social attitudes ultimately decide on the label: whether to brand a van Gogh or a Gauguin with the stigma of an outcast, or enthrone (for a while) a Voltaire as a poet laureate, or a Henry Miller as a favourite court-jester of the US West Coast intellectuals. The success of a Bohemian, measured mostly by the sale of canvas or music, would elevate him by a swing of the social pendulum from the gutters of social stigma to acceptance and celebrity. This change in social attitudes would presumably affect only a meagre few. The relevant point here is that the switch from stigma to acceptance would not necessarily be linked with or caused by a change in the Bohemian's behaviour, although social acceptance might cause a subsequent alteration of behaviour.

The control of behaviour by stigma would be ineffective with a van Gogh. He took it upon himself to initiate a one-man revolution. He no doubt suffered from stigma, and his burning zeal to innovate caused many clashes with his surroundings, which eventually destroyed his sanity. But he did not succumb to the stigmatizing pressures as far as his innovations were concerned. His life as a Bohemian was determined by his inability to cope with the demands of relatives, fellow artists and critics. This was precisely the reason for his deviance. He could not possibly have conformed to the norms of his contemporary critics and preserved his *raison d'être.* For him, the points of least resistance were his social links and the reality of others. The synthetic bums, on the other hand, brandish their main stock-in-trade, powerful social antennae to detect and predict what is "in" and what is "out", what shape of toilet basin is fit for the museum and which should be placed in municipal lavatories, what pornography is "camp" and what is plain old dirt. For these, stigma is not only the most powerful of controls; it actually shapes their whole "other-directed" existence.

In order to innovate, one must see oneself and one's human and objective surrounding differently. *In extremo,* one would become a rebel. This phenomenon, of course, is not linear but curvilinear, as follows:

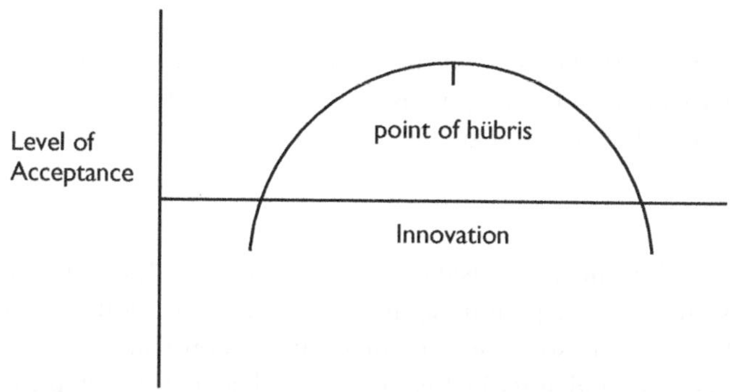

Figure 0.3 The evolutionary "leash" of creative innovators

Only slight or mediocre innovation will be allowed by the evolutionary "leash" of creative innovators, but too much innovation will bring the creative innovators ostracism and stigma. Once the creative innovator has been labelled a deviant, his ability to communicate with his contemporaries is curbed and limited. Since the creative, stigmatized deviant is ahead of his time he cannot converse with his contemporaries. Hence, he projects his innovations onto synchronicity outside history, and a Daumier, a Musil, a Bakhtin and a Gesualdo, will be "discovered" in the future. Their art will be appreciated by itself without the impediment of cliques, restraining morals and social institutions.

Since our present volume is focused on the link between creativity, deviance and madness, we shall deal in the following chapter with the structure of the human personality and its deviant, morbid disruptions.

Chapter one
The Personality and its Disruption

"Man is born with his fists clenched, as if to say 'The whole world is mine' and he dies with his hands open, as if saying, 'I have inherited nothing from this world.'" *Ecclesiastes Raba*

Our personality theory envisages two core vectors: "participation" and "separation".[1] Participation signifies the identification of Ego with external entities: persons, objects, or symbolic constructs, and its efforts to lose its separate identity by fusion with such an entity. Separation is the opposite vector. These two vectors can be best understood in conjunction with the three major phases of human development. The first developmental phase is the process of birth. The second is the crystallization of an individual ego by the moulding of an "ego boundary". The third developmental phase is a corollary of socialization, when one's "ego identity" is attained.

The urge to overcome separating pressures never leaves the human individual. If one avenue towards its realization is blocked, it surges out through another. Actual participation is unattainable by definition. The objective impossibility of participation is augmented by the countering separating vectors, both instinctual and interactive. At any given moment in life there is a disjuncture, a gap, between our desire for participation and our subjectively defined distance from our participatory aims. The coagulation of the self marks the cut-off point for this most basic developmental dichotomy.

Two separate developmental phases determine the fixation of the personality type. The first is from birth to formation of the ego boundary around the emerging individual *separatum*. This phase includes early orality. The second fixating phase is from later orality onwards. In the first phase, a potential fixation-causing trauma is registered by a separate self capable of discerning objects that are the sources of that trauma and the self as its recipient. The self that experiences such an event is a non-differentiated totality. If, however, the potentially fixating event occurs at the later oral phase, the self may well be in a position to attribute the cause of pain and deprivation to its proper source – the external objects.

The moulding process determines the nature and severity of fixation, which in turn determines the placement of a given individual on a personality-type continuum. However, the types themselves are fixed according to developmental chronology: the *participant,* at predifferentiated early orality, and the *separant,* after the formation of the separate self. The participant core vector operates with varying degrees of potency on both personality types, but the quest for harmony manifests itself differently with each polar personality type. The participant aims to achieve harmony by effacing, by annihilating, himself; that is, by melting back into an external object and achieving the togetherness of nondifferentiation of early orality. The inclination towards harmony of the self-effacing participant is denoted Tantalic, and the inclination toward dominance of the object-devouring separant, as Sisyphean.

In *Salvation through the Gutters,*[2] the author showed that the foetus at birth is fully capable of registering the enormity of the shock of its expulsion from the womb, both physically and mentally. In a publication on the psychology of childbirth, Leboyer describes the infernal experiences of the neonate during birth and just after, thus:

> Hell exists, and is white hot. It is not a fable. But we go through it at the beginning of our lives, not the end. Hell is what the child goes through to reach us. Its flames assail the child from every side; they burn its eyes, its skin; they sear its flesh; they devour. This fire is what the baby feels as the air rushes into the lungs. The air, which enters and sweeps through the trachea and expands the alveoli, is like acid poured on a wound.[3]

The transition from the womb to the outside world is violent in all respects – the need to breathe oxygen instead of receiving it directly from the mother, the need to seek food and digest it, and the exposure to changing temperature and hard objects, instead of the constant warmth and cushioned, resilient walls of the uterus. Expulsion from the womb also involves a period of varying intensity and length, of being squeezed and pushed into the narrow, inflexible birth canal, which causes the neonate pain. The shock of birth is mercifully not remembered, as a necessary defence against the intense pain and psychic traumata it involves, but it is undoubtedly registered by our sub- or pre-conscious. The newborn feels omnipresent and hence omnipotent, because at this stage of life he cannot be aware of anything or anybody but himself. Yet in his omnipresent egocentricity, the newborn experiences a disastrous catapulting from blissful self-sufficiency into painful, troubled, and hostile surroundings not far removed from the mythical characteristics of hell.

Psychologically, the pantheistic neonate learns by deprivational interaction with his surrounding objects and life forms, especially with his mother or her surrogate. They cannot fulfil all his wishes immediately and automatically, as in the womb; the neonate learns he is not "with" but "against" everything. The moment this awareness is embodied in the scar tissue of the delimiting individual "ego boundary", pantheistic, participant togetherness gives way to the loneliness and encapsulated existence of the individualized human *separatum.* This separation, the existential coagulation of the individual self, is also perceived by the organism as a catastrophe. The formation of a separate self, occurring in the midst of the oral phase of development and marking the division between early and later orality, is gradual. It is a transformation along a continuum, from a sense of partaking of a totality to a feeling of individuation.

Sexuality necessitates the crystallization of a separate self; it requires relating, by the self, to an alter or object in its surroundings. A duality, or plurality, is necessary for sexuality to achieve its affective and/or physical dyadic intercourse. The theoretical cycle here seems to be complete, in that sex is both one of the aims of, and a major factor in, the separant ejection of the nascent self from pantheistic early orality.

At early orality the "mouth–ego" interacts with the breast–mother in a binary manner. If the breast does not sprout forth milk, the "mouth–ego" suffers, but imputes the pain and "badness" to itself; at this stage, the nascent ego is not yet crystallized as a different entity, and whatever occurs, occurs within the omnipresent self. However, the "good" breast–mother who supplies food to the mouth–ego hovers somewhere on the boundaries of its omnipresence. Pain, hunger and thirst may be perceived by the infant as occurring within himself, but the milk flows from the outside and is sucked in by the mouth–ego. We shall elaborate later on the premise that the child feels sexual excitement while sucking his mother's breast, as does the mother. The mother, however, suppresses this excitement, because she conceives it as incestuous. This suppression is transmitted to the nursing child through intuitive empathy and direct, tactile, nonverbal communication, creating a severe conflict in the mouth–ego. The "good" breast–mother feeds the infant and makes him very happy indeed, because food at this stage is the early oral child's main concern. But with food comes a message of proscription and suppression of what is experienced as a very arousing sensation. Such proscription (i.e., "badness") cannot come from the "good" food itself, nor from the "good" breast–mother who provides it. Hence, the mytho-empirical projection is imputed to a vile external entity, proscribed and therefore vile, sexual experience, which accompanies the sucking of food and hence pollutes it.

Klein, Fairbairn, and to some extent Abraham, have rightly imputed an overwhelming importance to oral eroticism in the structuring of character and personality. Yet their theories and descriptions of early and later orality, sucking and biting, "emptying" the breast–mother or being deprived by it, lack clarity and circumspection, because they do not provide clear-cut criteria for distinguishing between early and later orality. This present author has done in *Salvation through the Gutters*[4] and *The Myth of Tantalus*,[5] by positing the coagulation of the separate self as the dividing line between early and late orality. Before the separation, everything happens within the pantheistic, omnipresent mouth–ego. However, after the separate ego boundary forms around the mouth–ego, the depriving breast–mother and surrounding objects are identified as such by the nascent ego and treated accordingly. Fixation at early orality then may be clearly related to a pantheistic unity of the self, others, and objects, whereas fixation at later orality is anchored on a distinct self, others, and objects.

The dynamics of harmony or congruity can thus operate either by separant inclusion, through which the mouth–ego aims to swallow and incorporate the breast–mother or external object, or by participant exclusion, by which the ego–mouth aims to efface and annihilate itself, so that it can melt back into the object and fuse with the breast–mother. These dynamics lead to the formation of a personality core continuum arising out of the deprivational interaction between mouth–ego and breast–mother along the lines indicated in figure 1.1 below.

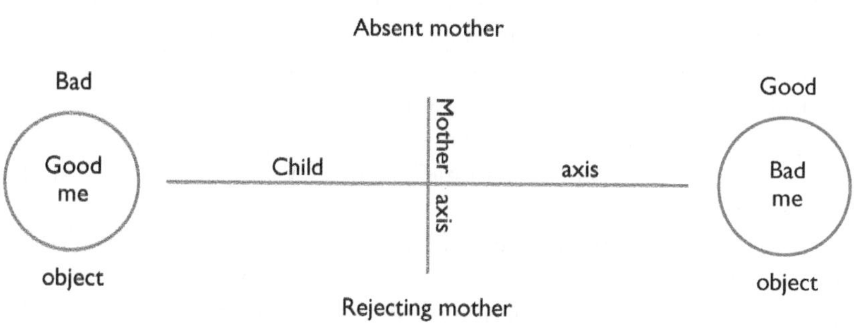

Figure 1.1 Mother and child axes

The mother axis has at one extreme the absent mother, the Genet-type foundling who grows up in institutions with very little care, where the surrogate breast is the nipple of a bottle provided erratically and sometimes carelessly, and the surrogate mother is the fleeting image of the passing nurse. The other extreme is represented by the rejecting mother. This includes a wide range of maternal attitudes: from the openly rejecting to the frustrating mother who does not fulfill the infant's needs for nourishment and comfort, and is consequently perceived by the child as hating and rejecting. The indifferent mother is one who is physically or mentally incapacitated, or one overburdened with children and work and while physically present, is emotionally detached. This mother axis represents, of course, a "skewed" and anomalous continuum of maternal attitudes, because more or less "normal" maternal care does not predispose the infant to morbidity.

* * *

To summarize, at one extreme of the child axis is the negative (bad me) ego boundary surrounded by the good object (mother). At the very early oral stage, described by Freud as primary narcissism, by Fairbairn as mouth–ego with a breast, and in this work as omnipresent pantheism, the mouth feeds on (empties) the breast and is temporarily content. However, disturbances in feeding and related irritations generate the agony of want and pain of anxiety. Consequently, says Fairbairn, the infant infers that its feeding destroyed the nourishing, comforting breast. We do not believe this to be tenable. At the very early oral stage, the "mouth-entity" is not capable of problem solving, and moreover, the "me-object" dichotomy does not yet exist. Therefore any pain, anxiety, and want that occur are in me, and only in me, because I am omnipresent; there is nothing except the mouth-anchored me. Consequently, a fixation in the early oral phase results in the registration of a painful wanting (bad) self and a nourishing (good) being somewhere in the vague, uncharted outside-of-self, which is, at this stage of awareness, outside of everything. What is present is a painful, aching self. The nourishing and soothing goodness that was previously the self is absent out there, hovering evidently out of reach. An early oral fixation is therefore a "bad me" surrounded by the "good" (nourishing) object.

At the other extreme of the child axis is the good self-surrounded by the bad object (mother). The later stage of oral development is characterized by a partial differentiation of the infant from the mother and the development of ambivalence towards her, manifested, *inter alia*, by the child's biting of the breast in moments of aggression. Here again we add an observation concerning later fixation: The emerging separation of the self, due to the deprivational interaction with the mother, creates an easily accessible source, a sequential explanation of the frustration, deprivation, and anxieties of the infant. The non-caring, non-feeding mother, who is already separate from the suffering (good) self is all-apparent and very often before the child's mouth. This location of responsibility is expressed by the vengeful bite.[6] The separation of an individual self surrounded by an ego boundary hence comports with the dialectics of a good–bad self and good–bad mother.

After early orality, man is separate from his objective and human surroundings. His omnipresent structure in pantheistic, early orality has been reduced to the size of an individual and, hence, rather insignificant separatum. This abrupt transformation from an all-engulfing unity to only another item among a myriad of pluralities contributes greatly to a catastrophic feeling of a fall. This separation from boundless infinity is absolute. The way back to it, as decreed by the separant vector, is impossible. Man is trapped within space, time, and causality and cannot even conceive boundless infinity.

* * *

The third phase of separation is socio-normative indoctrination, involving the imposition of social responsibilities and rites of passage, marking the transition from the forgivingness of childhood to the burdens of adulthood. In most cultures, the father or his surrogate is the doctrinaire figure instrumental in imposing norms and duties on both his sons and daughters, preparing them for their proper social roles. Induction of a son into the compulsion and duties of the normative social system by his father has been described elsewhere as the Isaac Syndrome[7] and will be adapted to the present context.

The first victimization of the child at later orality is maternal, blocking the free expression of its incestuous desires, whereas the second is paternal, harnessing, even coercing, the child into the normative system of society, of which the father is deemed to be the agent within the family. Usually this coercive, normative victimization is backed by the absolute authority of God, the fatherland, or the secular deity of dialectic materialism. As in the model of the offering of Isaac, there is usually a symbiotic relationship between the stern, doctrinaire father and a metaphysical source of absolute authority. It is important to note that such continuing victimization by parents, from early orality onwards, is an integral part of the separant processes of development and socialization. Maternal victimization at later orality leads to Sisyphean sublimation towards cultural creativity, while paternal victimization at a later stage leads to the separant insertion of the pubescent individual within a normative pigeon-hole sanctioned by society. At that later stage, however, the mother is the symbol of grace. She stands for the careless participant longing for the forgiveness and lack of responsibility of children within the family, prior to their being harnessed within the normative burdens of society by the doctrinaire authority of the father. In some tribes, the rite of passage from childhood to puberty (circumcision) is presided over by the elders, while the mothers join in the wailing of their aching, suffering sons.[8]

The Isaac Syndrome has been presented as the archetypal normative, paternal aggression against children, countering the Oedipal pressures of children against their fathers. The main thrust, however, of the story of Isaac is the sacrificial enmeshing of the young into the disciplinary boundaries of the normative social system. All normative initiation involves varying measures of sacrificial curbing of the well-being and freedom of the pubescent in favour of the group. In such sacrificial indoctrination, the father is seen as the intermediary between the young and the social rules, sustained through his authority, by a secular or divine transcendence.

The most striking feminine parallel to the Isaac Syndrome, replete with the gory sacrificial details and wide socio-normative implications, is the sacrifice of Iphigenia to the exigencies of socio-religious commands, through the authoritarian agency of her father, Agamemnon. Iphigenia is sacrificed to the glory of the group and its patriotic honour, an extension of Agamemnon's own, as the way the normative power of Divinity is the extension of the authority of Abraham. Unlike Abraham, who never doubts the command of God, Agamemnon waivers and rages against the need to sacrifice his daughter for the glory of the army, for the honour of the mob. This stems from the difference between the Judaic and Hellenic conceptions of divine authority. For Abraham, God's commands are the epitome of justice, not to be doubted or questioned, whereas the anthropomorphic Greek gods make no pretence of being just; they know that they are the pronouncers of *ananké* (necessity) and *moira* (fate), the prime movers of the Greek religion and normative system. The outcome, however, is the same: both Isaac and Iphigenia are sacrificed to the divine projections of socio-normative mandates. Iphegenia was not as willing a victim as Isaac, who according to the Midrash ran joyfully to the altar and bound himself.[9] Iphigenia pleaded with Agamemnon, in one of the most shattering monologues in world drama:

> Had I the voice of Orpheus, O my father,
> If I could sing so that the rocks would move,

> If I had words to win the hearts of all,
> I would have used them.
> I have only tears.
> See, I have brought them! They are all my power.
> I clasp your knees, I am your supplicant now,
> I, your own child; my mother bore me to you.
> O, kill me not untimely! The sun is sweet!
> Why will you send me into the dark grave,
> I was the first to sit upon your knee,
> The first to call you father . . . [10]

At the end, however, she accepts her fate and goes to the altar with a patriotic announcement: "Bid my father come and torch the altar. I will bring this day victory and salvation unto Greece."[11]

Finally, like Sarah in the Isaac myth, Clytemnestra, Iphigenia's mother, is the figure of grace, condemning paternal cruelty as expressed in the divine mandate to sacrifice her daughter for the glory of Greece.

The Unfulfilled Dialectic

Participation with one's surroundings is problematic, because Ego's interaction with objects and life forms is mostly conflictual and always dialectical. A non-dialogical *ity* relationship with other people is petrifying, and an I-thou dialogue, according to Buber, borders on the miraculous. A creative relationship with an object may effect an *extasis*, in the Greek sense, of the creator's spirit from time and space, and lend him a feeling of union with his object. However, such a feeling is completely within Ego's psyche, and regardless of his initial creative quests, they are bound to be different dialectically in their synthetic outcome. This is the fate of all Sisyphean endeavours directed towards the outside.

The dialectical quest of the vectors – the things-in-themselves, the prime movers of objects and life forms – cannot be apparent. Only the clashes and synthetic outcomes of the dialectical interaction constitute apparent reality – the contours and forms of matter, and the system-in-balance of life forms and personality. When the synthetic outcome of each dialectical cycle initiates another cycle, it slips again into "non-being", only to reappear in the "being" of reality as the synthesis of another dialectical cycle, *da capo*, in an endless dialectical Sisyphean–Tantalic process. Hence, the dialectical interaction of the teleological, non-realizable quests of the core vectors provide the basic energy and the prime movers of "being", as well as the systems-in-balance of life.

As we ever crave for what we are not and for what we do not have, we are living in inauthentic time. The separant vector aims for the future, while the participant longs for the past. When dominated by these two vectors, man does not exist in the present; his life is therefore a non-entity, false and inauthentic. If the quests and longings, inherent in man's core personality vectors cannot by fulfilled, there is inevitably a constant rift between his aspirations and expectations on the one hand, and his perceived reality on the other. Hence, man is ever confronted by the absurd. Such a dual impasse of inauthenticity and the absurd make the myths of Sisyphus and Tantalus so central to the human condition that they can rightly be considered metamyths. The initial inauthenticity of man's existence in the world, and his inevitable experience of the absurd, constitute his existential impasse, from which creativity and revelation are able to extricate him. Creativity thus constitutes the *modus vivendi* of Sisyphus with his stone burden, while revelation is the means by which Tantalus can go on living within his predicament. Man thus starts as a failure, yet through his ability to sublimate his unrealized quests into creativity and revelation, he is able to transform that initial impasse into authentic experience, and authentic existence. It seems that our programmer, whoever or whatever he is – God, chance, evolution, or the devil, programmed us to yearn to achieve goals that can never be achieved. To yearn to be different from what we are at a given time and place, and not to cherish the present, but to long either for earlier developmental phases, for a past state of non-being, or for the away-and-beyond of the future. Our programmer apparently intended to see how our unfulfilable Sisyphean quests, and our impossible Tantalic longings, can be sublimated dialectically into creativity and revelation.

Both the separant and participant need to sustain their quests and longings to be creative and revelatory. Both creativity and revelation are dynamic processes fuelled by Sisyphean aims and Tantalic longings that can never be fulfilled. If they are, our yearnings are extinguished, and our potential for authentic being through creativity and revelation die with them. The impasse of unfulfilled aims and the inevitable, absurd rift between our expectations and reality are transformed from a curse into a blessing. Moreover, the dialectics between our unfulfilled Sisyphean quests and Tantalic longings are our prime movers; without them we are dead.

Revelation in not transferable, but through creativity the revelatory insight of the creator becomes communicable. Moreover, a work of art becomes the vehicle through which the revelation of the artist is transferred to his audience. Such revelation, inherent in a work of art, also becomes a measure of its timelessness and hence, of its lasting value; revelation transcends the sequences of time, effecting a temporal *extasis*, both of artist and audience.

The participation vector has been conceived as the quest of the individual, at a particular moment in life, to revert to an earlier developmental phase: to the irresponsibility of prepuberty, to the grace of mother and the protection of the family fold, to the pantheistic omnipresence of early orality and the prenatal bliss of non-being. These are countered by the instinctual and deprivational quests of the separation vector, which, except in the case of death, always has the upper hand. Yet the quest for participatory non-being is ever present, and we tend to agree with the hypothesis that if a man possessed a master switch by means of which he could end his life, he would be bound to do so at one time or another. This also justifies Camus's stance that the only valid philosophical question is whether or not to commit suicide.[12]

It has been pointed out elsewhere that the quest for participation manifests itself in numerous sublimatory substitutes, both normative and deviant,[13] but actual participation is unattainable by definition. A writer such as Proust can perceive a lost childhood and graceful mother with acute sensitivity, through the hazy memories triggered by the taste of *madeleine* (cookie); yet even he cannot recapture the actual sensations of things past. We are forever looking for our lost childhood, for our narcissistic paradise, but no one can actually revert to prepuberty, reconstruct the eccentric omnipresence of early orality, or revive the sensations of blissful suspended animation in the amniotic fluid of the uterus. Participation is, therefore, a *fata morgana,* shining hazily before one's craving eyes, ever receding, never achieved. At any given moment, there is a disjuncture, a gap, between our desire for participation and our subjectively defined distance from our participatory aims. We denote this gap the Tantalus Ratio, after the Olympian demigod who, whenever he reached for a fruit, would have it whirled out of his reach by a gust of wind, and when he bent down to drink from a seemingly sparkling stream of water, saw that it turned out to be mud. Even when he succeeded in scooping up some water in his palm, it sifted through his fingers before he could cool his parched lips.[14] The Tantalus Ratio, the relationship between a longed-for participatory goal and the distance from it as perceived by Ego, is dependent, *inter alia*, on the following factors:

1. The strength of the participatory vectors, as determined by the distance in time from the developmental stages of birth, the formation of the ego boundary, and the ego identity.
2. The fixations, in the Freudian sense, that Ego might have experienced in the various developmental stages. These fixations would also be

linked to the nature and intensity of Ego's deprivational interaction with his fellows and relevant others. Such fixations would underline a personality typology continuum, denoted at one extreme as *object oriented,* and *idea centred* at the other. The continuum would, no doubt, be linked to the vast number of existing dichotomous personality continua that have been constructed and measured by personologists.

3. The culture in which the individual is reared: whether it tends to be a "tool oriented" society of doers, or a "symbol oriented" culture that encourages mysticism, meditation and quietism.
4. The residual unknown quality of variables, both on the personality and cultural levels, that affect the participatory and separating vectors and consequently, the Tantalus Ratio, which cannot be determined at this theory-building stage.

The gap represented by the Tantalus Ratio creates a strain, a tension, between the longed for participation and the distance from it as perceived by Ego. This strain, the intensity of which is determined by the factors comprising the Tantalus Ratio, is the motivating force underlying Ego's actions. It is generated within the synaptic junction of these opposing vectors; the tension is related to Ego's motivational movement towards certain participatory goals or their sublimated alternatives. In other words, the participatory and seperatory vectors comprise the crude psychic energy, whereas the gap related to the Tantalus Ratio and the strain generated by it provide the motivational direction for Ego's actual behaviour. This strain may be either conscious or unconscious, and its operation is regulated by social norms from without and by an internal homeostatic mechanism which is not necessarily linked to biological homeostatic mechanisms. Our hypothesis is that the psychic bases that underlie such mechanisms are generated by anxieties registered by each consecutive stage of development. Each developmental stage from birth onward has been experienced by Ego as a painful separation, accompanied by a deprivational interaction with his surroundings. The personality clings to its present stability, because each developmental change has been for the worse, leading to more radical separateness. The psychic homeostatic mechanisms are, therefore, "the evil I know" defences, which make the personality adhere to stable states as lesser evils.

The reversion to previous developmental stages is a practical impossibility, but all the techniques of participation, both normative and deviant, are a far cry from the intense longing for participation fuelled by Ego's memories of earlier, participatory, stages. Thus, the tension inherent in the Tantalus Ratio generates formidable energies that are constantly augmented and kindled by the impossibility of quenching Ego's thirst for participation.

As the goals of neither the Sisyphean nor Tantalic core vectors can be achieved, the only epistemic reality is the dialectical interaction between the nonrealizable separant quest and the equally unattainable participant longing. Because Sisyphean quests face the future and Tantalic longing aims at the past, man is in an absurd impasse within inauthentic time, without a present. Creativity and revelation are therefore meant to extricate man from this impasse. Those who cannot be creative or revelatory also try to escape their absurd and oppressive reality by entertainment, fantasy, or daydreaming, which feed passively, with or without the aid of alcohol or drugs, on their pent-up yearnings. The dialectics of our yearning thus provide the fuel and energy with which Ego can emerge from his inauthentic slumber and interact with objects and human surroundings. When a man is young, he still hopes to realize both his Tantalic longing and Sisyphean quests. However, with age, he realizes his quests are not attainable, and that he must make do with the dialectics between them; the very quests can sustain him without their being fulfilled. Hence, the dialectical quests that generate mental energy, the Tantalus Ratio, are most powerful at the outset of life and decrease in potency with each developmental phase, until they wane to a low ebb in old age.

The strength of the Tantalus Ratio is related first of all to the enormity of the separating forces in early childhood, which cause the participation vectors to muster contrary pressures of corresponding potency. Second, recent developmental events make for vivid memories and sharply focused images of the lost participatory bliss. The child's frantic efforts to regain that bliss would therefore be marked by a desperate surge of power to reverse the new grief of the recent developmental calamity. These efforts are not yet mellowed by the sad knowledge, which comes with experience, that direct participatory reversals are impossible. The separation of birth, registered by the neonate as a catastrophe,[15] is marked by frantic efforts to survive. The mouth–ego of the infant searches for the nipple, or anything that can spurt nourishment. This and the enormous pressures of growth at this hectic developmental phase constitute the biological vectors of separation that are at the height of their potency. And yet this is also the stage when the neonate has the strongest craving to revert to his mother's womb, from which he has just a while ago been so brutally expelled, into an experience where the mere effort to survive is painful. This is in keeping with what Schachtel has denoted as the Law of Embeddedness: "The more complete the state of embeddedness of the organism to any change in the significant environment, the less does the organism want to stir from a state of quiescent equilibrium in relation to the environment".[16] This means that the more violent the separating disturbance, the more powerful the corresponding striving for participation. And what is more violent than the separating expulsion of birth? Indeed, what Herman, Bowlby and the ethnologists have denoted as the "instinct of clinging" of primate neonates to their mothers,[17] as well as the less corporeal attachment of the human infant to his mother or mother surrogate, could be linked to his desire to regain the physical union with her, *in utero*. This could be the underlying motive for the clinging behaviour of both primate and human infants, apart from the functional desire of the young to be close to their source of nourishment and protection.[18]

The second major phase of separation we have mentioned, the coagulation of the distinct "I", the separate ego boundary, is marked by the introduction of deprivational interaction with the external objects of the oral stage, the mother, the breast, the nipple, generating the Tantalus Ratio. Indeed, we have described elsewhere how the ego boundary that separates the self from the pantheistic omnipresence of early orality is nothing but the scar tissue that surrounds the *separatum,* as a result of its deprivational interaction with its surrounding objects. The participation vectors are harnessed by the emerging self to counter the separating effects of the deprivational interaction that join forces with the processes of growth.

We have relied elsewhere on the "oralist" offshoot of psychoanalysis, which describes the mouth–ego of early orality aiming to empty the object (breast), whereas at the later, "biting", oral stage, the mouth–ego wishes to destroy, in its fits of rage, the nonobliging mother-object.[19] Apart from the need for fulfilment and other developmental connotations that these urges to empty and destroy the object have, they may be attributed to participatory functions. We have mentioned that the mouth–ego at early orality aims to swallow the object, so that its pantheistic omnipresence is regained. At the later oral phase, when the infant's deprivational interaction with the object pushes it into developing a separate self, the destruction of the object by biting – the sole weapon that the mouth–ego possesses – is aimed at countering this deprivational interaction by elimination of the object. Moreover, when the depriving object is destroyed, the narcissistic mouth–ego reigns supreme, its omnipresence regained. Consequently, the Tantalus Ratio at the stage of crystallization of the self is very potent indeed.

One of the "participation surrogates", expressed in the pent-up tension of the Tantalus Ratio, is the extreme egocentricity of the child, which is a prolongation of the narcissistic omnipresence of early orality. This egocentrism lasts, according to Piaget, up to the age of seven.[20] But here again the participatory vectors are fighting a losing battle, because egocentricity is confronted by the counterpresence of the socializers, who make it their duty to drive home to the child that "he is not alone in the world", that "one must be considerate of others". This deprivational socialization (from Ego's point of view) eventually gains the upper hand, until the young adult is extruded from the protection of the family fold by an endless variety of rites of passage to the final separation of adulthood. The participation vectors counter this separation by an intense longing for the graceful forgivingness of the mother and irresponsibility within the family fold. Most childhood memories become pleasantly idyllic, painful experiences being largely repressed.

It may be noted that we do not rely on the Oedipal process as an explanation of normative indoctrination through the introjection of the father as a source of authority. We tend to agree here with Melanie Klein and Ronald Fairbairn,[21] who claim that guilt and a conscience may be acquired at a very early stage of development; they do not point out the need for the resolution of the Oedipal complex as a source for normative indoctrination. Social separation is achieved by the enmeshing of the individual within a normative cocoon by the parents and socializing agencies, within the personal space allotted the individual by the normative system. The individual *separatum* is expected to mate and assume his proper place as a responsible citizen\subject\comrade in society. This is the social involvement decreed by every human society to its individual members. Each group either ascribes, or expects from its members to fulfil, certain positions within its structure.

Such social involvement, sanctioned by the normative system of the group and ingrained into the individual by the deprivational interaction of socialization no doubt constitutes an advanced stage of separation. Yet the Tantalus Ratio has enough tension stored to send the individual off to some arduous "participation surrogates". These are rather like Freud's "defences", i.e., modes of release of libidinal energy, the direct satisfaction of which is blocked. For Freud, most, but not all, human behaviour is "defensive", because some instinctual needs are directly fulfilled; but according to him, there cannot be any actual or direct participation, so that the ever-present quest for participation, although varying in potency, is always expressed by surrogates. We mentioned previously one such participation surrogate, i.e., the egocentricity of the child, as an alternative to the pantheistic omnipresence of early orality.

The Disruption of a Personality

Now that we have recapitulated our personality theory, we are in a position to show how a given personality structure could go wrong. We must stress that our interest at this stage is on the level of predisposition to crime; both crime and morbidity have a predisposition which can be activated by a kind of a triggering process which makes the predisposition, so to speak, "flower" into the phenomenon. This has been noted many years ago by Freud, in his *Mourning and Melancholia*,[22] where he expounded the predisposition to depression, which becomes actual depression only after loss or a severe blow. Likewise in psychosis, we also envisage a predisposition and then a trigger, which actuates the phenomenon. The same again holds for crime. We have pointed out that there is a predisposition to crime, followed by the chain process of association, learning and absorption of the patterns of crime. The predisposition and the triggering dynamics are complementary processes. Hence, we stress that our interest at this stage is only to try to pinpoint the similarities and differences between crime and madness on the personality level, concentrating on three predisposing factors and processes.

In order to ask how a personality "goes wrong", we have devised the models outlined below, which relate to the child and mother axes, as related to crime and madness.

The external manifestations of delinquency and schizophrenia are widely different. However, there is a similarity that begins on a previous level of analysis – when early socialization is still rather close to the point of bifurcation into predispositions to social deviance or functional psychosis. First of all, the aetiology schemes themselves are quite similar in their structure. Schizophrenia is believed to develop by a feedback cycle triggered by loss, deprivation or other personal tragedies in the vulnerable transitory periods of childhood, adolescence, etc. However, a predisposition to psychosis that had crystallized, presumably in early childhood, must be present for such a later event to catalyze the onset of schizophrenia. Similarly in criminology, some hypothesize that a predisposition to delinquency is incurred by a youth growing up in a broken or inadequate family, in neighbourhoods of high delinquency rates, and in societies suffering from normative disintegration (anomie). These factors, which ideally should be expressed in probabilistic terms, raise the chances that an individual will be initiated into the life of crime through later dynamic processes of role-playing and association.

The similarity becomes rather striking when we compare some of the major trends in criminology and the recent theoretical expositions on schizophrenia. The main currents in criminological theory link most criminal, or socially deviant, behaviour to learning processes.[23] One may be socialized in some cases by criminal parents, siblings or even whole communities, like criminal Indian tribes. In most cases, however, the learning of criminal and deviant patterns of behaviour is preceded by rejection of legal structures and alienation from the prevailing value system. As in criminology theory, no unequivocal physiological correlates have been firmly established as a cause of functional psychoses. The significantly high incidence of schizophrenia in families raised by the children or siblings of schizophrenics could quite readily be explained by the transmission of ego defects in early socialization.[24] That is, such defects could be transmitted by internalization through the learning of parents' faulty patterns of interaction, or even by the general breakdown in communication within a "schizophrenic" family.[25] Conversely, a boy growing up in a criminal family, such as the "notorious Jukes", would have to be disturbed indeed to become a clergyman.

A seemingly more complicated task would be to replicate to schizophrenia our second major premise, namely that crime is "normal" behaviour. Here again, the statement is more exclusionary than positive, as it aims to deny etiological primacy to structural personality defects. The normalcy contention, in this context, means that the difference in personality structure is not necessarily physiological and/or hereditary, but an outcome of the socialization process, so that personality differences between delinquents and the population at large are differences of degree and not of kind. Likewise, schizophrenia is an extreme condition, far removed from the centre of the normal curve. But by adopting Sullivan's stance that schizophrenia is not a "disease entity" but a "grave disorder of living", we are coming close to the contemporary approaches, which regard functional psychosis as a breakdown of interpersonal interaction and communication.[26]

The definition of functional psychosis as the dissolution of the ego boundary may be profitably linked to the socio-cultural explanation of psychosis. We have dealt at length with the formation of the ego boundary and its function as an imaginary dividing line between our cognitive structure and the outside world; the ego boundary synchronizes interaction between the two.[27] It is precisely this ego boundary that is destroyed in psychosis.

The dissolution here is in a reverse order, where the outer concentric circles of the ego boundary decay slowly or explode abruptly. The infantile ego core remains to take care of cognitive reality, which it is very poorly equipped to do. In severe cases of schizophrenia, the ego boundary is completely destroyed and the patient reverts to early childhood, to the pantheistic oral stage, where no dividing line exists between him and the outside world.

Our present premise is linked to solid empirical observations. We could mention Rosenzweig's typology of reactions to frustration.[28] These are measurable personality traits, which in their significant form are present throughout an individual's life and are believed to crystallize at the oral phase of development. The intropunitive type, who tends to blame himself for whatever frustrations and failures he may experience, would be more the "bad me" individual who sees only himself to blame for the disappearance (destruction) of the good object (breast–mother). *Per contra*, the extrapunitive type would be more likely to form when the frustrating mother (object) is tangible "out there" and may be blamed for any misfortune and hardship. Our hypothesis is that the intropunitive type of personality would be fixated at the early pantheistic oral stage, whereas the extrapunitive type would be linked to a later oral fixation, when the ego boundary has been coagulated and separated from its environment. This is rather important, because our highly theoretical, and conjectural, model thereby receives empirical reinforcement. It should be stressed that at this stage we are still concerned with the structure of a skewed mother–child interaction and not with its morbid results.

One of the most controversial of the skewed mother–child interactions, denoted by Bateson as "double binds", has been described thus:

> When the individual is involved in an intense relationship, that is, a relationship in which he feels it is vitally important that he discriminate accurately what sort of message is being communicated so that he may respond appropriately. And the individual is caught in a situation in which the other person is expressing two orders of message and one of these denies the other. And the individual is unable to comment on the messages being expressed to correct his discrimination of what order of message to respond.[29]

In *A Review of the Double Bind Theory,* Paul Watzlawick notes that the bind is a mutual one, binding two parties, two victims. He quotes Laing, who speculates on the early beginning of the double bind:

> One must constantly remember, of course, that the child from babyhood may put his parents into untenable positions. This may occur in the early baby-mother interaction where the baby cannot be satisfied. It cries "for" the breast. It cries when the breast is presented. Its crying is intensified when the breast is withdrawn. A mother unable to "click with" or "get through" to such a baby may become intensely anxious, and feel hopeless as a mother. She withdraws from the baby in one sense, while becoming over-solicitous in another sense.[30]

According to Bowen, the infant and mother enter into a double bind of "being for each other" – the child "being helpless for the mother" and the mother "being strong for the child". When the child is devoted to "being for the mother", he loses the capacity of "being for himself".[31] Through this symbiotic tie, mother and child try to perpetuate the highly pleasurable stage in both their lives. Any further development or growth of the child threatens this symbiosis. What is crucial here is that we attach a different interpretation to this mother–child attachment. The fixation on early orality might prolong the pantheistic fusion of child and breast, creating a double bind situation and arresting or injure "normal" development. However, as double bind situations predispose a person to psychosis, we claim that this predisposition is related to the abnormal structure of the ego boundary, characteristic of psychoses and caused, *inter alia*, by double binds. Yet this common denominator between double binds and psychosis is only a particular instance of the wider texture of participation. If psychosis, with its disruption of reality and twisting of cognition, is one of the end products of ontological participation, the double bind, with its hampering of the formation of the separating ego boundary and its prolongation of the child/mother pantheistic union, is a forceful technique of participation, of delaying the expulsion from Paradise.[32]

We have denoted as double bind type A an inconsistent, ambiguous and amorphic mother–child interaction, where the mother does not know, does not feel or does not empathize with the needs of the child; where she tends to confuse his needs with hers; and where she develops a neurotic proximity with him, thereby prolonging his early oral feeling of omnipresence. Consequently, a rather blurred and amorphic, and a very weak, ego boundary would be formed. A special case of this double bind is where the mother tends to react in an oscillating, inconsistent manner to the same basic needs and behaviour of the infant. This would result in a corrugated, fragmentary and fimbriated ego boundary.

Double bind type B is one in which overt transmission of acceptance is contradicted by covert transmission of rejection. In this case, the mother would voice and outwardly imitate the conventional gestures of a mother's behaviour towards her infant; but in her immediate attitudes towards him, as expressed by empathy, physical contact and other subtle ways of maternal transmission of attitudes, she would convey rejection of the infant and convey to him her own anxieties, which would be translated by the receptive infant as anxieties relating to his own being. At the nondifferentiated stage, the infant would regard these maternal transmissions as an engulfing, sweeping badness, which threatens to destroy everything. The resultant ego boundary would tend to be a negative one, filled with the annihilating tendencies towards the mother (breast-object) and the anxiety-laden guilt (badness) of the inadvertent destroyer. A special case of this type of double bind is scapegoating, in which the mother would send messages of rejection towards the child. His being a scapegoat makes him covertly needed as a receptacle for the scapegoating transmissions. This, no doubt, would be the major distinction between double bind type A, where the covert messages of annihilation are contrasted with the mother's cognitive attitude of acceptance, and the scapegoating, double bind type B, where the tags of badness, depersonalization and rejection conflict with the mother's need to retain the child as a receptacle for her own aggressive and sinister needs. Moreover, this subconscious attitude of rejection would clash with the scapegoating mother's overt gestures of acceptance, prescribed by her normative role of mother.

To sum up our present premise, we restate that scapegoating leads to a clash of (a) the tags of depersonalization, as internalized by the child and which form a negative ego boundary, and (b) the scapegoating dependence of the mother on the child, which makes for a forceful attachment of him to her. When internalized, such maternal need is displayed within the personality of the child as the hostile outside world. These two dissonant factors might also clash with whatever cognitive pressures the mother might direct towards the child. Such severe conflicts inherent in the scapegoating situation would result in a very strong ego boundary, separated from the outside world by many thick layers of scar tissue.

In double bind type A, some extreme maternal transmissions are contradicted in a rather consistent way, generating a conflictual *Gestalt* between the emerging self and its surrounding object-mother. Such transmissions, as we have just described, make for a very strong ego boundary, rendering the self relatively immune to the incoming conflicting transmissions of reality, letting the delusional negativistic conviction of the paranoiac reign supreme. The extreme inversion of incoming stimuli also supports our model of the conflict between the "good" me and the rejecting object, inherent in the predisposition to paranoia. *Per contra*, in double bind type B, the autistic reaction has been hypothesized to be generated by a relationship between the infant and an absent or neglecting mother-object, so that the nascent self does not have a strong ego boundary. It is fixated on predifferentiated early orality, so that its relationship with reality is detached. This makes for a weak and amorphic relationship with the object and, in keeping with our findings, its attitude towards the environment is undecided, erratic and resigned. This, indeed, is the typical profile of the autistic reaction, which is mainly characterized by a detachment from outer reality and the submerging of the self in an inner reality not readily amenable to communication.

The paradigm presented in figure 1.2 can be seen as a general guideline to our deliberations.

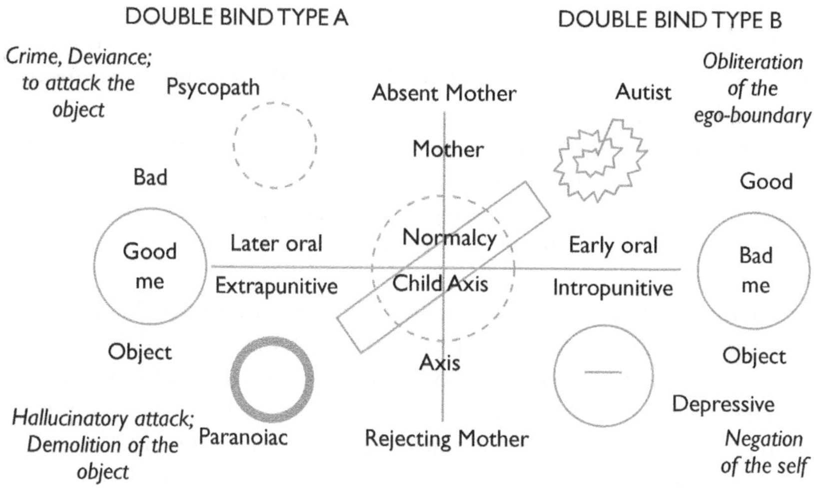

Figure 1.2 Core predispositions to structural personality defects

The autistic predisposition is related to a hazy and amorphic ego boundary, which becomes vulnerable to any outside pressure or trigger, which may catalyse the onset of morbidity. The relative indifference of the autistic schizophrenic to outside stimuli is, therefore, both a syndrome and the outward evidence for the weakness of his ego boundary. His difficulty in differentiating between himself and the object is a measure of his uncertainty concerning the strength and direction of the stimuli transmitted to him.

The paranoiac reaction is explained by the "good me" surrounded by the "bad object", linked to interaction with a rejecting mother. This is related hypothetically to double bind type A, which generates a very strong conflictual relationship, and consequently a thick, robust ego boundary. We hypothesize that the ego boundary is generated by deprivational interaction and that when a severe conflictual relationship occurs, as is inherent in double bind type A, we may expect more and stronger scar tissue to cover the nascent self, in order to isolate it from painful outside stimuli. This hypothetical model of the paranoiac predisposition is related to a later, post-oral fixation, because the coagulation and separation of the self happen here rather quickly. Because of harsher and more frequent injuries, the aggressive object is identified more readily, so that the differentiation between the "me" victim and the object as aggressor is more clearly perceived.

As for the psychopathic reaction, it may be what Cleckley calls the mask of sanity.[33] Cleckley claims that psychopathy in its true form is a morbid syndrome covered by a fragile façade of partial sanity, which collapses under pressure when the individual experiences a severe shock. Indeed, the interaction of the "good me" with an (absent) neglecting mother leaves a rather inchoate interaction with the bad object, which is not as potent as the actual deprivational interaction with an attendant mother or mother surrogate. The interaction with the bad object thus results in a partial ego boundary, in the sense that it has the outward appearances of a boundary, but is punctuated by gaps, which make it vulnerable.

Finally, we have hypothesized the depressive reaction as linked to the interaction with a rejecting mother at the early oral stage. This produces a "bad me" surrounded by a good object. This is the ideal intropunitive reaction, constantly reinforced by the aggressive object, whose authority to repress the "bad me" is legitimized by the core personality structure, which imputes positivity to its surrounding object *vis-à-vis* its self-concept.

The interaction of psychotic patients with their families in institutional settings has triggered some etiological ideas on morbidity, which are in line with our main theses and personality theory. Schizophrenia, for instance, may be envisaged as triggered by a disruption following a traumatic experience of a regulatory *ity*, the entity that coordinates the dialectical interplay between the core personality vectors, similar to Freud's ego. The *ity* is the mechanism, which sustains the ego boundary, however diffuse or traumatized it may be. However, when the stabilizing *ity* is disrupted by the onslaught of schizophrenia, the developmental predisposition to morbidity sprouts up and takes over the psychodynamics of the personality. Consequently, the mental energy produced by the Tantalus Ratio (the dynamic interplay between the personality core vectors) cathecting itself around the traumatized developmental fixations in a directionless cycle, or clogged set, activating part of the psyche and stalling the other parts, results, in extreme cases, in a complete autistic stupor or a paranoiac outburst of object aggression, depending on the personality core fixations. In paranoiac schizophrenia, the separant personality vector fixed on the object runs amok, without the checks and balances of a properly functioning participant vector or *ity*, inducing the patient to attack his surroundings with outbursts of disoriented aggression, accompanied very often by delusions and hallucinations. In the more autistic schizophrenics, the participant vector engulfs the whole personality and enforces on it disconnectedness with its surroundings. In the less severe forms of schizophrenia, the disruption and disconnectedness is fragmentary, so that the paranoiac focuses on one or more attributes of the object and inflates it into lopsided proportions, whereas the autistic schizophrenic may immerse himself in dislocated stimuli or objects, becoming oblivious to the rest of his surroundings.

Our model of morbidity, which is far removed from the existing models of schizophrenia in the literature of psychiatry and clinical psychology, does have some common denominators with a recent model of schizophrenia by Zubin and Spring, who state: "It is assumed that exogenous and/or endogenous challengers elicit a crisis in all humans, but depending on the intensity of the elicited stress and the threshold for tolerating it, that is, one's vulnerability, the crisis will either be contained homeostatically or lead to an episode of disorder."[34]

This sounds like a tautology, but it is not. It expresses the point of view, which we also find adequate, that schizophrenia should be regarded as a dynamic combination of probabilistically expressed predisposing factors and triggering mechanisms, which catalyze the morbid condition. The authors use some flowery language and bold images to describe the onset of schizophrenia:

> We might liken the occurrence of a recognized breakdown to the development of a fault in the earth's surface. Ordinarily, a brief tremor will occur before a stable formation of the earth is re-established, just as in the person's life a slight jar in the spheres of work and personal affairs will precede a new state of closure. On the other hand, if a bed of molten lava is seething below the crack in the earth's surface, the development of the fault will create an opportunity for the emergence of a volcano. In the vulnerable individual, a coping breakdown may open the way for the eruption of a psychopathological disorder.[35]

This indeed is in line with our model of the genesis, not so much of the autistic type of schizophrenia, as of paranoiac morbidity, when the coordinating *ity* crumbles down and the separant personality core vector is unleashed outwardly with a morbid fury. Indeed, when the regulating *ity* is not in control of a separant personality predisposed to morbidity, the separant personality core vector runs wild. It uninhibitedly assaults the objects and others with the later oral quest of "swallowing" them. There are no significant participant checks and counter-balances from the enfeebled or dormant participant core personality vector, or the disrupted *ity,* to make the violent separant personality core realize that it cannot "swallow" external objects in his surroundings. The paranoiac thus develops a positive feedback cycle of increasing suspicion, with augmenting hatred, of the evasive objects and people, who do not tend to be controlled. This is accompanied eventually by delusions of dominion, hazy reminiscences of early developmental omnipotence.

Finally, we wish to present a personality model with a bimodal fixation, which is the result of very harsh treatment of the patient as a child, both in earlier and later orality, by either parent. The harshness had been punctuated by short periods of acceptance and over-protection. The outcome was that, while the bimodal fixation, both in early and later orality, was effected, there was no integrated system-in-balance under the *ity*, given these extreme fluctuations and extreme erratic interrelationship. Consequently, we almost invariably have these extreme fluctuations between a "bad me" attitude surrounded by a "good object", and a hazy image of the object, up to delusive attributions to parents not only non-existent attributes but also delusions as to their basic attributes. This is generally accompanied by hatred and total rejection of the depriving mother-father object. Hence, between the peeks of this bimodal fixation there is an abyss. This "black hole" model could be as presented in the following section.

The Black Hole

This bimodal fixation and lack of coordination creates what we have denoted as the "black hole", which is constantly craving to be filled. The "black hole" model will be later applied to addiction and crime, and to predisposition to psychosis and depression. We should, however, point out that due to this disruption between the two basic personality nuclei, those of "good me" and "bad me", which are not coordinated, the drives and the mental energies can only be extreme, fluctuating between an "either or" kind of attitude towards the object. Hence, it is either total acceptance or total rejection. If one tries to fill the "black hole" – and the need is to fill it completely – and fails, a complete downfall may occur. In a sense, this is the dynamic reason underlying the internal saboteur expounded by the Kleinians, especially Fairbairn. We thus supplement the theoretical Kleinian structure when we give a deep infrastructure, in the form of a dynamic background for the formation of the internal saboteur. This internal saboteur, taken by Fairbairn to be a kind of a dichotomy, which he observed in his patients and quite amply described, does not have any "reasons" as far as the dynamics of personality described by him are concerned. In our theoretical formulation, this reason is inherent in the "black hole" and "either or" attitude, related to the polar fixations of early and later orality.

The difference between normalcy, morbidity, deviance and depression is a question of degree. If we say that the "black hole" can be filled in, so to speak, by addiction, crime, psychosis or depression, the choice of the various solutions would be related to the degree and extremity of the fixation, and the extremity of the behaviour of the mother on the mother axis. If we have both an absent mother, or none at all, and a very extreme later oral fixation, the tendency to find a solution, or in more expressive terms, to fill in the "black hole" by crime would be more imminent. If we are talking about the morbid solution, we have accepted Sullivan's idea of schizophrenia,[36] which envisages a range between inner directed mental violence, resulting in autistic schizophrenia, and the overtly outward aggressive solution, resulting in paranoiac psychosis. Hence, we envisage a continuum between the upper right property space and the lower left property space in our model (figure 1.2), which link (diagonally) the absent mother and the early oral fixation with the rejecting mother and the later oral fixation, which is the paranoiac solution, while the former is the autistic solution. However again, it is all a question of the degree of the fixation, which would be related to the type of criminal *ity or* morbid *ity*.

The same holds true for depression. If we take Seligman's definition of depression as a learned helplessness, which in extreme cases becomes a psychosis,[37] we shall confine our theoretical analysis to very severe core personality disturbances, which would predispose to manic-depressive cyclic psychosis, as well as severe drug addiction and crime. Our analysis will not deal with lesser structural personality defects like schizoids and neurotics. We shall therefore deal with the extreme "either-or" types of reaction. Autistic digression would predispose the psychotic to annihilation, with resultant autism, which actually blots out any vestiges of the ego boundary, with the "hope" of reverting to the "good object", which of course is never achieved.

The paranoiac solution would be the Promethean one – the destruction of the object. But since one cannot destroy the object without destroying oneself, one projects on it all kinds of hallucinatory paranoiac projections, which in extreme cases is expressed in the paranoiac building up of a whole new identity.

Whether a solution is criminal or depressive depends on the extent we can harness our mental energies to allow us to dwell into a psychotic breakdown, whether a criminal solution or a depressive one. In the autistic solution, if the fixation is strong enough and if the absence of any parent is extreme enough, the self, the ego-boundary is blotted out completely, with the hope of sinking back into the "good object". Of course, this is an impossible venture, and the positive feedback cycle leads to a complete psychotic breakdown of the type of autism. On the other hand, the paranoiac solution, if sufficiently extreme, aims to blot out the object completely, and if this is impossible, one envisages hallucinatory ways of blotting it out. The same goes for crime. The big shot criminal is, of course, a rare success in any illegitimate society, but in his "black hole" personality, the center does not hold; hence if he cannot achieve and become a big shot within the criminal framework, he directs all his fury to self-destruction.

In depression the dialogical solution is viable, because art is a dialogue. Art is not in the object; art is a relationship between the artist and the object. Art is in the processes of a relationship, and if the process is authentic, this viable artistic or creative interrelationship fills in the "black hole", and gives meaning to the pains of depression.

The Innovation of the "Black Hole" Model

The main asset of the present model is that it tries both methodologically and content-wise to devise a dialectic of diversity in unity. We might envisage a number of methodological dynamics related to different types of morbid solutions, as well as to crime and depression. Yet the unity relates to a model of four property spaces, so that by having the mother axis and the child axis intersect, we provide a matrix for a unified theory (see figure 1.1). Thus, the literal implication shows that the family dynamics of "double-binds" may be related to our paradigm, although its dynamics are contentwise different from the conflict situations which we have envisaged to be related to delinquent and criminal solutions.

We now make some concluding remarks, which may pertain to all four property spaces we have dealt with. This type of four-dimensional property space, which results from the intersection of the mother and child axes, may help us understand certain structural aberrations which lead to deviance, and often to crime, although they don't relate to actual core breakdowns like schizophrenia and manic-depression. We are addressing ourselves to certain sexual aberrations, which usually are in the realm of compulsion neurosis, and are peripheral, not core, aberrations.

Mother–child dialectics, in early and late orality, might result in sexual aberrations within the realm of the four property spaces. Consequently, we have provided a paradigm which may serve as an underpinning for a theoretical explanation of crime morbidity and depression, although contentwise, these phenomena are of course different. The unifying attributes are not only in the four-property space model (figure 1.2), but also in the initial bipolar fixations of all three types of aberrations (crime, madness, and depression). This results in what we have denoted as the "black hole" – the centre that does not hold between the two extreme poles of later and early oral fixation, with an abyss in the middle. This abyss can be filled only by extreme alternatives: the immediate, if momentary, subjection to the overwhelming domination by drugs and alcohol; the obliteration of the self in the autistic pole on the continuum of schizophrenia; or the delusional obliteration of the object in the paranoiac pole of the continuum.

The Kleinian internal saboteur, especially according to Fairbairn, does receive a deeper insight through our theoretical explanation, on a deep personality core level, which provides the reason why this internal saboteur would make an appearance.

As for depression, not all depressives and deviants are creative, but if one is a creative depressive, the depression may augment the energy of creativity, since here too it is an all-or-nothing kind of solution. The depressive artist goes into a frantic phase of creativity, which could in a sense be described as manic. So long as this phase carries on he is not depressive, but once it ends, the depression sets in, and may even reach suicidal extremes.

Another unifying element in our model is the idea that the morbid criminal and depressive solutions are not alternatives, but synergesic. We might well envisage a criminal who is both psychotic and depressive, as well as creative. In other words, one type of solution does not exclude the other. It might well be that a criminal-depressive and rather paranoiac artist like Caravaggio would indeed be very innovative so long as his spell of creativity lasted.

Being a criminal, one gets involved with the courts, the prison system and probation officers. Many services are harnessed to deal with him. In other words, one gets more attention being a criminal than just an unemployed welfare case.

Finally, it must be stressed that the four-property space model of morbidity, crime and depression, as well as the "black hole" model, are predisposition probability cases. The external trigger into madness and depression, like traumatic experiences such as loss of loved ones, would actuate the predisposition to morbidity. Likewise, the criminal predisposition would be actuated into crime by the processes of differential association, as expounded by Sutherland and others.[38]

Chapter two
Hübris, Suppression and Stigma

In unaccustomed comfort
Writers are traveling abroad to meet writers.

They meet with experts on writers -
On the Writer in His Time
Or in His Place
On the Writer in Society
Or in Isolation . . .

The writers do not meet with writers –
Perhaps they are not nice people to meet
Perhaps they do not care to meet writers
traveling at ease in the opposite direction –
Or perhaps they are actually writing?

In any case writers convey an untypical view
of writers –
Experts are always more dependable.

D. J. Enright, *Exchange No Robbery*

Metron ariston, the Greek noble measure (the mean), and *meden agan*, the idea of nothing in excess, are the normative safeguards against too much innovation. The innovator's transgression is denoted as *hübris*, reflected in an overweening pride, since innovation makes the innovator conspicuously different, and hence punishable. The creator's innovation, although meant to enhance the welfare of the *polis* and the individuals comprising it, could injure the delicate balance between the individual and the group, and disrupt the democratic consensus of the city-state and its social structure. Hence *hübris* was the most heinous crime in ancient Greece. It was punished by ostracism by the general assembly of the Athenians in the *Agora*, and by the god *ananké*, coercion, as well as by the Furies, who would push back even the planets that strayed from their course.

The most celebrated cases of mythological *hübris* were those of Prometheus and Icarus. The chief deity, Zeus, jealous of the increasing proficiency of man, decided to destroy the human race. Prometheus was on the side of humanity and brought down fire to earth, after Zeus deprived man of it. Prometheus was chained to a rock and a vulture devoured his liver. When he died the liver was reinstalled at night and he was resurrected in the morning, to be chained again, the process recommencing, *da capo ad infinitum*. Prometheus, by competing with Zeus to determine man's fate, committed the ultimate *hübris*. According to Aeschylus, Prometheus taught man to build houses, to write, to paint, to domesticate animals and build boats to rule the waves. The transgression of Prometheus is close to original sin and the Tower of Babel, insofar as man aspired to become "like gods". Man indeed preferred Prometheus to the chief deity; jealousy motivated Zeus' punishment of the rebellious Titan.

Prometheus is the prototype of the creative innovator. Hence, the jealousy of the gods is a mytho-empirical projection of the zealous curbing of the innovator's exploits, lest he disrupt the precarious balance of society and its institutions. The tragedy by Aeschylus ends with the moral that sin – crime against the gods – "does not pay"; Prometheus admits his wrongdoing, promises not to transgress again and is pardoned by Zeus.

Another noteworthy example of *hübris* involves Daedalus and his son Icarus, who planned to escape from their imprisonment by Minos, king of Crete. Daedalus, the craftsman, builds wings for his son and himself. While flying, Daedalus warns Icarus not to soar too high, lest the sun melt the wax that glued the wings to his shoulders. Also, he should not fly too low, since the water would wet the feathers and they would be too heavy to fly. This is a mytho-empirical projection of all parents cautioning their children not to take undue risks, to keep to the middle-way, not to deviate or to draw attention to the wrath of the agencies of social control. Icarus did not heed his father's warning. His soaring too near the sun constituted an act of *hübris*. The wax of his wings melted, he fell into the sea and drowned. This is not just a cautionary tale, but a myth of experience of innovators being destroyed by societal mechanisms of normative control, guarding the central measures as a proven security against the disruption of the social structure through excessive innovation. This is also the projection of the mythogenes of experience – cliques and power groups with vested interests sacrificing the deviant, creative innovator to the Molloch of ratings; after all, the means, modes and medians cater to a larger audience, meaning fame and money. Still, the creative innovator may pursue his authentic aims, but then he must be prepared to pay the price in suffering, ostracism and oblivion.

In Greek mythology, sanctions against *hübris* and exceeders of one's *moira* (lot in life) and *metron ariston* are administered by the Furies, the goddesses of vengeance. Plutarch assures us that ostracism was a useful measure against the jealousy of men and the anthropomorphic Greek gods; it involved "chopping off the tallest ears of corn". We tend to think, though, that ostracism, as well as present-day measures against innovation, is tied to the notion that *hübris* is a deviance from the central measures, irrespective of whether the deviance was normatively acceptable or proscribed.

Since creative innovation is bound to be deviant, as we have shown earlier, ostracism of deviants was traditionally and, to be sure, evolutionarily sanctioned. This could be related to the statistical link between innovation and deviance; if the creative innovator is also deviant, then it is a safe, normative, and in the last analysis also an evolutionary measure, to ostracize him and curb his activities. This is the "evolutionary leash" holding deviant, creative innovators in tow. It holds to reason, and is also supported by historical and institutional records, that sanction in Greece was meted out to extreme deviants and innovators.[1]

This again supports the hypothesis that social control would intervene only against extreme innovators, not the minor or modal innovators. They would be let through by normative and evolutionary selecting controls, since they do not disrupt the social system and its institutions. Kuhn's paradigm also involves control against too much innovation. Existing paradigms would cut out a Gesualdo, a van Gogh or a Melville, until a revolution (mutation), or a long enough evolutionary span would make it "safe" for the social structure to absorb their innovations without disruption. At the time of Voltaire, the Catholic Church felt that any of the ideas divulged by this arch-enemy would greatly damage it, but today the church seems to be immune to Voltaire's criticisms, and anyone who still voices them seems to be flogging a dead horse. The reason for this could be twofold: the Church became more resilient and most of Voltaire's views became readily accepted within the modern religious paradigms.

Apart from ostracism, burning at the stake, banishment and stigma, the most efficient social precaution against excessive creative innovation is indifference. Vincent van Gogh hardly sold any paintings in his lifetime.

Bach was almost forgotten, his great works discovered after his death by Mendelssohn Bartholdy. Without the vigilance of Constanza, Mozart's wife, a great many of his works would have been lost to us. Still, one almost wishes that the sentinels of evolution would have been more vigilant when the hordes of post-modernism turned the contemporary art scene into chaos, where anything goes. In the vanity fare of post-modernism, there can be no meaningful dialogue through the transmission of mythogenes embedded in artistic media, and no meaningful, maieutic communication, only solipsistic games of solitaire. Bachelard warned against this avalanche of gibberish when he said: "Facts long amassed, patiently juxtaposed, avariciously preserved, are suspect. They bear the stigma of prudence, of conformism, of constancy, of slowness."[2]

Hence, all dams were broken and the sewers of post-modern rubbish now threaten to drown us with their inauthentic flow of nonsense, meaningless to the "artists" and unfathomable to the audience. We can admire the courage of Rothko, who says: "The unfriendliness of society to his activity is difficult for the artist to accept. Yet this very hostility can act as a lever for true liberation. Freed from a false sense of security and community, the artist can abandon his plastic bank-book . . . transcendental experiences [of our authentic domain] become possible."[3] Then we can empathize with Rothko when he says: "A picture lives by expanding and quickening in the eyes of the sensitive observer. It dies by the same token. It is therefore a risky and unfeeling act to send it out into the world. How often it must be permanently impaired by the eyes of the vulgar and the cruelty of the impotent, who would extend their affliction universally."[4]

Rothko understood that he could not have been accepted by the mediocre vulgum, but most artists don't understand this. They want to be accepted by the artistic cliques and power structures, while persisting in their alienation and unacceptable innovation. Hence, they are asking for the impossible. Also, authentic innovation precedes its time and the rebellious artist would be recognized, if at all, long after his demise. Worth is, therefore, recognized only *post facto*, and the evolutionary leash will allow some innovations to be accepted sometime, someplace, in the unforseeable future. Hence, the authentic innovation hovers in synchronicity and will descend into history through a precarious combination of chance and favorable background factors. Under these conditions, Rothko opted out by suicide and we do not judge him. Yet a Camusean Sisyphus seeks his satisfaction in the process of creativity and becomes stronger than the night luring him to give in.

Authenticity Replaced by Virtual Reality

One of the scourges of the mass media is the invasion of privacy. The devouring of matiné idols by fans, the driving them to drink, drugs and suicide, is well documented. Judy Garland, Elvis Presley and Marylin Monroe are just three well documented instances. Madonna utilizes sex on the lowest non-sublimated libidinal level, but whatever she does is ascetic callisthenics compared to what is displayed on the Internet. Indeed, web-sites are not only devoid of normative reigns; they are also leading humanity towards an electronic Middle Ages, in which inauthenticity and deceit reign supreme.

A discussion on the Internet[5] is a solitary act, one which transpires in the privacy and security of an individual's home, from which he can take flight to far-off regions in search of an interlocutor. From his familiar, protected space, he moves onto another dimension, a fascinating "parallel world" in which he can expect to converse with other surfers from the four-corners of the globe. However, as Joe Blow sits in his easy chair in front of a computer screen, typing strings of electronic information into the information highway, he undergoes a thorough metamorphosis. From a flesh-and-blood being with a human personality, he transforms into a virtual entity. From now on, he is no longer a short, bald, overweight man; he can now shed his physical appearance and present himself as someone else entirely.

Pursuant to the canons of existentialist philosophy, we contend that our existence in the world and our links to our surroundings, physical and human, involve relationships of deprivation and conflict, as part of our "thrownness unto death", as Heiddegger has described life. This existence is marked by "fear and trembling", as Kierkegaard put it, which even welcomes the pain, the fear and suffering, as they are an integral part of man's lot in the here-and-now. Furthermore, only such acceptance can pave the way for the kind of authentic existence that can pose a challenge to the metaphysical design, which consigns man to an absurd existence. We accept Husserl's claim that phenomenological reduction is a means of attaining authentic existence; that is, an introspection aimed at disconnecting from the generalized other, while "peeling the layers of the onion" that surround the self.

For us, this process is an interaction within the kernel of the human personality, between the physical, experiential anchor upon which the pain of existence is etched, and the yearning anchor which propels the individual to the idiosyncratic meaning of the reality of his life. The French phenomenologist Maurice Marleau-Ponty has claimed: "Matter, life, and mind must participate unequally in nature and form; they must represent different degrees of integration, and, finally must constitute a hierarchy in which individuality is progressively achieved".[6] Kierkegaard used the phrase "leap of faith" to give expression to the authentic rebellion of one who forsakes the good things in a hedonistic, and boring, world, and leaps by force of his faith into the sphere of authentic existence.[7] A similar motif can be found in the works of Camus, who calls upon man to rebel against the forced reality of his life.[8] Further on in his writings, Camus develops the idea of the creative existence, and in *The Myth of Sisyphus* claims that man–Sisyphus must find a *modus vivendi* with his stone – the pains of being. Only then will the path to authentic existence be opened up to him.[9]

Thus, authentic rebellion is the conscious decision to calibrate all human sensory receptors, to take in the entire spectrum of possible feelings. The purpose of such reception is to experience both joy and pain as the deepest possible existential expressions, through which we may sense elevation, illumination and revelation. Every experience is non-recurring and of unique value, and without judgemental value – good or bad. The only key to evaluating an experience is by raising it to the plane of authenticity.

An individual's involvement in reciprocal social activity, most of which is anomalous, is often accompanied by feelings of impotence, embarrassment, anger and alienation, while the really pleasurable moments are few. Yet despite this, most people try to find solace in human relationships, by trying to have others view them as worthy. In many cases, when an individual is involved in a reciprocal human relationship, he must often present himself to his fellows in the way circumstances require.

Discussion rooms undoubtedly comprise a sphere in which social activity takes place; at any point in time, thousands of people are in the midst of a dialogic relationship in one or several virtual discussion rooms. Conversation channels on the Internet afford absolute freedom of expression, even permitting the user to select any identity he wishes. Since there is no possibility, technical or practical, of revealing the person punching the keyboard, a man can identify himself as a woman, or a homosexual as a lesbian, a child can identify himself as an adult, while an elderly person can revert to his salad days, the bashful can be aggressive and the modest woman can suddenly act like a whore.

When a person enters virtual space, he passes from one sphere of existence to another, and must adapt himself to the rules of the game in that sphere. Goffman claims that human interaction is something of a game, in which each participant stages his conduct in accordance with the definition of the circumstances engendered between the individuals concerned.[10] The way an individual presents himself is interpreted by his environment on the basis of a wide variety of factors, among them his facial expression, tone of voice, and physical appearance. In the virtual conversation room, the way an individual shows himself is limited to one element only, the nickname with which he chooses to identify himself. We contend that the choice of a nickname is not arbitrary, but rather reflects the normative projections of myths, of yearning, and of experience. Parents, for instance, name their children after the myths of their particular world: names such as Charity or Hope are examples of the transcendental projection of yearnings, while John or Samuel perpetuate past mythical experiences, either private or of one's group. The same principle obtains with nicknames in conversation rooms; here, though, the purpose of the nickname is to attract the amorphous other into a conversation and by means of the nickname to draw an attractive, even ideal, image of oneself as a virtual entity. Since one's actual identity has no meaning in a virtual conversation, even if one identifies oneself by one's true name, there is no way of verifying the fact.

Who is that virtual entity which lives in the fourth dimension? Is it possible to set forth an image and distinguishing characteristics, in broad outline? Is it possible to say it "exists"? The answer to these questions lies at the very point of reference from which we began this discussion – that a virtual entity is an inauthentic entity by the very nature of its existence. A conversation on the Internet is similar to a meeting of shadows in a platonic cave, only here there are no bodies behind the shadows; the entities here populate a virtual ghost community completely detached from reality. The virtual entity, which flickers across the computer screen, is at most a projection of the interlocutor on the Web, which by identifying itself by means of a contrived image satisfies some mental need. That image is usually a sharply focused and one-dimensional ideal, as identification by a nickname contributes to the construction of a set-up of expectations amongst interlocutors, a set-up that does not contain a speck of authenticity, since the images are entirely disconnected from their human anchor. The ordinary human social framework is not devoid of poses, of game-playing; presentations of the self, as Goffman puts it, are different in every set of relationships, as the persona one chooses changes in accordance with the surroundings one finds oneself in. Yet even in such circumstances, the persona interacts with the inner self. While the individual, as a bio-psycho-social composite, presents himself differently in each situation, he does not erase his previous existence, his experiences, and his real self.

Such is not the case, though, in a conversation room. Here events more closely resemble a dialogue between two or more marionettes, with someone behind a curtain, controlling them and putting words in their mouths. If that someone so wishes, the marionette will go mad, cry, laugh, or just prattle. The marionette operator, like the Internet surfer, is not responsible for what the dummy under his control does or says. The one is no more before the audience in the theatre than the other is among the participants in the discussion room. The virtual entity is thus a disembodied shadow, the projection of a shallow, kitschy illustration between which and an experiential anchor there is no connection. The important conclusion to be drawn here is that the removal of physical boundaries, the creation of an ideal image, offers a virtuoso solution to the psychophysical dilemma: a creative clash between the conflicting inner essences of the active entity is prevented from the outset. When the interaction is between banal, stereotypical entities lacking any individuality, there is no longer any room for a search for one's deeper inner essence. And neither is there room for the authentic existence of creative conflict. Authenticity remains beyond the possibilities of the new kind of technological conversation; in its place we find ourselves up against an impenetrable barrier of façades.

At this point we can say that virtual interaction cannot be considered a dialogue. One's attitude to one's interlocutor is not in the nature of an affinity. The entity at the other end is perceived in object-like stereotypical terms, which cannot be a partner in authentic dialogue. The images flickering over the screen are indifferent to one another, merely seeing each other as something to exploit for the purpose of indulging in fantasies.

Furthermore, we witness here a double estrangement: On the one hand, there is the barrier between the speakers and the images they create as virtual entities, and on the other hand, there is the estrangement between the various entities, by virtue of their being figments of the imagination. It seems we would not be off the mark if we said that Internet conversation is not even an I–it dialogue, in the Buberian sense, but an it–it dialogue. The ability to aspire to attain unique moments involving a flow of grace between man and man is beyond the realm of the possibilities of any given technological conversation; authenticity, as a value and something yearned for, simply does not enter the picture. In a world of "its", there is no need for any demands to be made of a conversation. The superficial, the it–object, does not demand particular exhaustion of our strength. Therefore, escape from the demands, of the "thou" to the easy world of the "it" is ostensibly natural.[11]

Kierkegaard wrote in *Either-Or*: "In the Middle Ages, much was told about a mountain that is not found in any map: It is called Mount Venus. There sensuousness has its home; there it has its wild pleasures for it is a kingdom, a state. In this kingdom language has no home, nor the collectedness of thought, nor the laborious achievements of reflection; there is heard only the elemental voice of passion, the play of desires, the wild noise of intoxication."[12]

Kierkegaard was speaking of an inauthentic way of life, about aesthetic existence. Aesthetic man lives an imaginary existence – what is possible, not what is real and concrete. By force of his imagination he searches for stimuli, going through life from one matter to another, without any loyalty, perseverance, or responsibility, without any inclination for binding spiritual involvement, and without real connectedness. He is a dreamer creating an imaginary world of dreams, to escape the clutches of reality.

The Internet is without doubt at the forefront of contemporary communications technology. As an information source, it is possible to reach an enormous range of sites on practically any subject of interest; as a communication channel, one may view the Internet as the technological infrastructure of the medium through which an increasing amount of human communication will be conducted. Ultra-modern interactive technology, which is presented as a means of contributing to human dialogue, can at most provide the illusion of dialogue. Authentic dialogue, the foundation stone of all cultural and spiritual creativity, cannot derive from the medium under consideration. By its very definition, this medium shatters the subject–speaker to bits with a broad sweep of the hand, which basically negates the authentic existence of the individual; without such an authentic existence, we may not strive for authentic dialogue. According to Buber, creativity is speech, dialogue; the teacher who engenders dialogic contact with his students, the painter who leaves his imprint on canvass, the author who spins words and sentences on paper, are all creative by means of dialogue.

Beethoven is an example of the process of creativity as dialogue: he listened to notes in his mind's ear. When he wrote the scores, he would listen to what came next, and write again.[13] The process of creation is a revelation within the souls of men, through an internal discourse, without boundaries. James Carey proclaimed that the structure of cognition is moulded by the structure of communication; eventually, he contended, we might become the thing which we have created.[14] This assertion has an important bearing on our argument: the disruption of dialogue is consequently the disruption of culture. Buber writes, "When a culture is no longer centred in a living and continually renewed relational process, it freezes into the It-World . . . ".[15] The Internet, as a cultural engine, drags behind it a long line of cultural cars toward the world of the "it". The result is likely to be that we "crash the train" and lose the spiritual existence embodied in the reflection of the "I" in the "Thou". In a reality in which the chance of attaining dialogue is denied in advance, we cannot expect rich cultural life, a fact manifested on a number of levels.

First, it appears that the technological overlapping of the Internet's role as a source of information and as a communication channel puts it in position to inherit the roles of school and teacher. Sites purporting to be virtual schools, in which various subjects can be learned, have already been established. Such modern trees of knowledge cannot supplant education as an undertaking in human creativity or the creative educator. A distinction should be made between the imparting of knowledge and education: the former is a basically technical matter, while the latter is an art. The task of the educator is not to force knowledge, but rather to engender an affinity with his pupil. This is a maieutic, Socratic dialogue, in which the educator scatters the seeds of knowledge on the virgin soil of his pupil, and on which trees of knowledge unique to him will grow. It is a process both complementary and mutual, involving affinity, without coercive, one-sided persuasion. The educator is indirectly midwife to the inchoate ideas in the mind of this pupil. Thus, both are likely to experience the sensation of revelation.

The end of a cultural era is also likely to be felt in another way. The Web holds an enormous number of sites and conversation channels devoted to sex. This state of affairs derives, *inter alia*, from the anarchic character of the Web, which permits it to answer man's natural inclination towards voyeurism. The Web is a medium that offers new ways for sexual release (or rather the illusion of such). The virtual world takes fantasy to the threshold of realization, and at the same time negates real existence. Culture, Freud tells us, is the sublimation of man's sexual impulse. So what will come of it if man can no longer attain a refining of his urges, and instead directs his libidinal energy to the creation of virtual visions?

Internet culture is well integrated into the post-modern age. In a culture where "everything goes", even the antinomy of "virtual reality" does not raise an eyebrow. Post-modern schools of thought, such as deconstructionism, have shattered the connection between what signifies and what is signified. Likewise, they have erased the referent behind phenomena, exactly as the virtual existence of entities in conversation rooms erases the concrete existence of those who actually speak. The Internet is the ultimate post-modern instrument – it is based on the relative and temporary nature of relationships, creating an impenetrable barrier between phenomena and their representations.

One of the most popular figures on the Internet is the American anarchist poet William S. Burrows, and one site named for him displays the slogan, "Nothing is true, everything is permitted". In reply to that slogan, which so well reflects the spirit of our times, all we can do is invoke Ivan Karamazov: "If everything is possible, then nothing is true."

We have already mentioned the role of chance in the discovery and in the recognition of some major art works. If not for van Gogh's sister-in-law, Mozart's wife, and Bach's rediscovery by Mendelsohn Bertoldi, many of their *chef oeuvres* would have been lost to us. Also, the fact that Tolstoy, James Joyce and Graham Greene did not receive the Nobel Prize supports our contention as to the lack of correlation between the intrinsic value of a work of art and its acceptance.

Indeed, the mere creativity of a Mozart constitutes an affront to the mediocre Salieri, yet as Milos Forman shows ingeniously in his *Amadeus*, the misery of a mediocrity is in the recognition of the genius of a Mozart; Salieri refused to be himself and strove to be what he was not. Eighteen publishers rejected the wonderful *The Leopard* by Di Lampedusa and no publisher wanted to publish Melville's *Moby Dick*. Melville had to publish his masterpiece himself. Yet who remembers Bougereaux, the president of the Parisian painters' association, who laughed at van Gogh's sunflowers. The basis for these very often tragic, but almost universal, phenomena of no one being a prophet in his time and place are that revelation and creativity are an individual affair, whereas groups and institutions have a vested interest in stability, social control and safeguards against innovators who "rock the boat". Hence, innovators would be more likely to be accepted in other times, in other places, where the cultural developments and background factors would be more amenable to their work.

For the cliques of the power and economic structures, art is a commodity to invest in, to show off, to sell or barter. Since usually the work of the creative artist is as yet unrecognized, and hence of little commercial value, it usually is of no interest to art galleries, museums and publishers. Dubuffet aptly states: "Art hates to be recognized . . . if it is greeted by its name it runs away immediately . . . it leaves in its place a prize stooge marked Art . . . which everybody immediately showers with champagne, and which the lecturers lead from town to town with a ring through its nose. That is the false Art."[16]

The philologist Papirianus, who had been reproached for agreeing with an erroneous view of Caesar, replied: "It is absurd to refute the view of a person whose stance is backed by 30 legions." Hence it is equally absurd for the creative innovator to clash head on with the social systems and institutions who reject him. The "system always wins" in any head-on collision. He will be accepted, though, by other individuals whom he reached through a maieutic dialogue. Bosch understood the mindlessness of social institutions, and the indifference of the power structures to the struggles of the suffering innovator. He painted Christ surrounded not by hatred, but by disregard, stupidity, and self-serving egotism. One has to find the relative calmness of the eye of the storm and try to achieve a creative *modus vivendi* within it. Being creative in spite of demiurgic societal adversity is the only way to combat such adversity. Head-on wars with mindless, cruel and power-backed social institutions are a waste of precious energy. Hence, the only way to deal with societal adversity is to be creative in a relatively sheltered niche. This roundabout way would assure both survival and meaningful life-sustaining creativity. Otherwise, Ibsen's *Enemy of the People*, who found noxious bacteria in the tourist resort's baths and hoped to be acclaimed and rewarded by his thankful hometown, would be hunted down, even by his own brother.

There are talentless aspiring artists, who sense the relationship between deviance and artistic innovation. Hence, they develop the external forms of the "Bohemian life". They try to lure the naïve tourist to their worthless "art" by their demeanour, their long hair, in blue denims frayed in the "right places". These are fakes, who often become president or functionaries of the artistic cliques. A T. S. Eliot can compose his *Wasteland* in the suit and tie of a bank teller; Manet can paint his *Dejeuner sur l'Herbs* while sporting an impeccable attire of a middle-class French bourgeois.

An important instance of the curbing of artists' authenticity and their individual styles is totalitarian regimes, especially in the twentieth century, which allowed only forms of creativity which served the right political and economic aims. All other forms of art were declared illegal, and their creators persecuted.

According to Walter Benjamin, communism politicized art, whereas fascism aestheticized politics. However, Benjamin, being a gentle soul and somewhat of a Marxist, couldn't bring himself to state the blunt truth that Communism and Zdanovism crushed art altogether, by depriving it of authenticity. The Nazis also declared all art which did not depict the glory of the Germanic, Nordic Arian race as Jewish-degenerate and treated it accordingly. Alfred Rosenberg, Hitler's *arbiter eleganriarum*, stated: "In the metropolis [the antithesis of the wholesome Germanic Blut and Boden – S.G.S.] began the race annihilating work . . . A race-chaos of Germans and Jews created the anti-natural street race resulting in mongrel 'art' claiming that its bastardized progeny, nurtured by spiritual syphilis and artistic infantilism, was able to represent 'expressions of the soul'. One should gaze long and hard upon something like Kokoschka's self-portrait in order to gain a halfway understanding of the monstrous inner-nature of this idiot art."[17] Hitler himself, in his tirade against "degenerate art" decreed: "The artist . . . just like everyone else, creates for the people. Hence, National Socialism has made it its aim to rid the German people from all the influence which are fatal and ruinous to its existence and which putrefy its culture."[18]

Those responsible for the putrefaction of German art, argued Hitler, are the Jews, who usurped their power position in the press, and through the ineffable and confusing concepts of art criticism destroyed the whole domain of wholesome German art.[19] True to his word, Hitler geared German art according to the trajectories of Germanic mythologies, as ordained by the older Eddas, which he knew by heart. When he realized in 1945 that all was lost, he ordered his chief of staff, General Keitel, to conduct a scorched earth policy: to burn all factories, fields and houses from which the German army retreated. Also the *Wehrmacht* should open the Eastern Front to the violently destructive and vengeful Soviet armies, and block the advance of the more humane Western Allies. This *Götterdämerung*, the twilight of the gods, was also practised in the realm of art. Hitler ordered Speer, his court architect, to construct buildings which "dignified ruins". Speer had to show his *Führer* how the buildings would become delapidated after 500, 1000 and 2000 years. The prophesies of the Elder Eddas came true with the Berlin Philharmonic playing Wagner's *Götterdämmerung*, while Russian heavy artillery was tearing Berlin apart.

As for communism, Lenin's draft resolution on "Proletarian Culture" (October 1920) states: "All educational work in the Soviet Republic . . . in the field of art should be imbued with the spirit of the class struggle to overthrow the bourgeoisie by the proletariat, for the successful achievement of the aims of its dictatorship."[20] The manifesto of the Red Group, the German Communist league of revolutionary artists, declared: "Art is a weapon, the artist a warrior, in the peoples' struggle for freedom from a bankrupt system. Socialist being determines consciousness."[21]

Communist art should express the ethos of the revolution. "Down with art as a beautiful patch on the squalid life of the rich".[22] The Soviet regime declared war on disinterested art. Art should serve the material goals of socialist realism and be subservient to the manufacture of machines and artefacts. That was a death sentence to art as an authentic, maieutic dialogue between artist and audience, by means of the mythogenes ingrained in the artistic medium.

Stalinist–Zdanovite dictates were also enforced in science, and decreed that it should not be conducted by methods designed to test refutable hypotheses. Hence, Lysenko's "creative Darwinism", proclaiming the inheritance of acquired traits, became the official doctrine of Soviet genetics. Likewise, Heisenberg's uncertainty principle and Bohr's complementarity principle were rejected and labelled as "deviationist". Many "deviant" scientists and artists were imprisoned, some even incarcerated in mental institutions, implying that anybody who deviated from the official doctrines of the normatively monolithic Soviet policy and planned to get away with it was surely mad.

The presently-available records of the KGB reveal that almost the whole of the Soviet hierarchy, including the Politburo, was harnessed in the effort to destroy Solzhenitsyn. He was first expelled from the Soviet Writers Union, and then publicly abused, harassed by the KGB, imprisoned and exiled. Viktor Grishin, one of the top spokesman for the regime, said:

> In Moscow we need to pay particular attention to ideological work, and weed out the kinds of phenomena mentioned in the report, because Moscow is where we have the largest numbers of tourists, various delegations, and conferences... Leonid Ilyich was correct in saying that among these renegades there is not (and indeed there is no way there could be) a single working person, not a single member of the intelligentsia who is distinguished or significant in any way . . . And who is Solzhenitsyn? Solzhenitsyn is a true degenerate.[23]

The possibilities of twisting or disrupting interpersonal communication are inherent in each component of the stigmatization process. The outlet of aggression for stigamtizers and their defensive projection outwards of their guilt and frustrations seems to be the main fuel pushing them to smear their fellow man. Some of the author's colleagues, who never added the names of their assistants as co-authors of their papers, although they did most of the work, were ever accusing somebody of plagiarism; others, who were less than honest in their financial dealings, had many stories about Professor X or Dr Y who were improperly appropriating research funds. One colleague, who used to bring his mistresses to conferences abroad, always had stories about his "adulterous dean". In a similar vein, Simmons and Chambers found that people who were more liberal tended to resort less to negative stereotyping (stigma) than conservatives. The latter had to project outwardly through stigma their repressed aggression against the normative system.[24] The stigmatizing projections operate by some of the principles of the projective measurement techniques. In the Rorschach and TAT tests, for instance, one must keep the objective stimuli at varying levels of ambiguity in order to induce the testee's projections to soar outwards. In like manner, the projections of stigma would be more prominent in cases where the predisposing factors within the configuration are amorphic and ambiguous. In mental illness, the venting of aggression and the projection of guilt in the form of stigma usually result in an extremely biased communication, because it provides a subconscious basis and a righteously indignant support for our numerous Archie Bunker-like bigotries.

Defensive displacement through stigma is apparent in the very common practice of labellers to slander people they do not know or who could not possibly have had any connection with the facts attributed to them by the stigma. The author has recently been labelled a nihilist by one person and a paranoid by another. Well, sometimes a good dose of paranoia in our rat-race world is a sign of sanity. Besides, international politics on the eastern shores of the Mediterranean indeed make the world seem a tragicomic mistake. However, both stigmatizers have admitted not to have read any of the author's books, nor attended any of his lectures, or for that matter ever having met him.

The scapegoating of outsiders, pariahs, the bizarre, misfits, as well as the creative innovators, usually involves some form of stigmatized ostracism, which entails some blocking of communication with the stigmatized. Those who were ostracized in ancient Greece and the "outlaws" in medieval Europe were actually cast out from the community. In modern society, the non-communication with the stigamtized may take other forms. For example, an "office politician" telling a colleague: "Nobody in the office likes Tom so you are better off not having anything to do with him, if you know what I mean." Or a gossip offered to a hostess: "Dick is such an awkward fellow, he doesn't know how to behave. He'll just stand in the corner, and stare at your guests embarrassing them. If I were you, I wouldn't invite him to the party." In all probability, the hostess will not invite Dick, even if she usually distrusts the gossiper, because she does not want to take any chances with the success of her party. The gossiper knows that all he has to achieve by his stigma is to cast a slight doubt as to the desirability of inviting or of communicating with the stigmatized. Professional gossipers know that the effect of casting a doubt on the integrity, propriety or desirability of the stigmatized is rather effective because of the "reasonable man's" maxim, "if in doubt, out".

In the *Mark of Cain* and in *Society and the Absurd*, the author traced man's anxiety relating to the dissident, the strange and the deviant concerning his congruity-based quest of concordance. In the *Myth of Tantalus,* the author linked this congruity principle to man's core personality quest to regain togetherness with the object. The relevance of this to our present context is that the stigmatized constitutes a direct or symbolic source of danger to the stigmatizer, so that he evades encounters and avoids communication with him.

The powerless stigmatized and downtrodden are often unable to communicate freely with people outside their social structure. Very often ethnic minorities and the politically oppressed are notoriously cut-off from communication channels outside the immediate structures in which they are enmeshed, confined and oppressed. Even if they are exposed momentarily to these channels, they prefer to be silent, fearing the backlash which is certain to be wrought on them later by the power structure. In like manner, there can be very little candid communication with creative people within a given structure or group by people outside it. The stigmatized and downtrodden within a given institution very rarely come to the attention of the official spokesman of the organization, nor are they "plugged in" to the proper channels by which modern public relations are manufactured. Visitors to countries, organizations and institutions are towed towards the more desirable scenes and led to communication with the "right" people. In totalitarian regimes this is done blatantly, whereas in pluralistic societies trained PR personnel do it with polished sophistication, but the selectivity of exposure is similar.

Many of the stigmata adapted to fit pejorative communication are related to what we have denoted in the *Mark of Cain* as "relative achievement".[25] By derogating Alter and belittling his achievement, Ego raises himself by his own bootstraps of stigma. Ego's derogating description of Alter is rarely related to a material issue of achievement. Mostly it is in the form of: "What? Harry, an academy award winner? I went to school with this schnook and his nose was always running." In academia, "explaining away" a colleague's achievement by means of stigma is a favourite vocation. Smith developed a new field of research; so along comes the campus gossip and assures his eager listeners that Smith did academic market research and ascertained that nobody wanted to deal with that specific area so he decided that that was his opportunity to become a lone shining star. If Taylor publishes too much, the labeller's verdict is that he must be shallow. If he publishes too little he is surely sterile and suffers from "writer's block".

Before proceeding to the next chapter, however, there is one important aspect of stigma-communication which has to be covered – the labelling of mental illness.

The Labelling of Mental Illness

The sociological approach to the genesis of mental illness, with its stress on the importance of the breakdown of human communication as a predisposition to mental aberration, highlights the importance of stigma in the formation of the self-concept roles and images of the mentally ill.[26] Moreover, some scholars find a close similarity between the core mechanics of social deviance and mental illness. Scheff, for instance, regards social deviance as the main dynamic underlying mental illness. "The culture of the group," says Scheff, "provides a vocabulary of terms for categorizing many norm violations: crime, perversion, drunkenness, and bad manners are familiar examples. Each of the terms is derived from the type of behaviour involved. After exhausting these categories, however, there is always a residue of the most diverse kinds of violations for which the culture provides no explicit label."[27] Scheff illustrates his point by the rather amusing yet apt illustration of Ego, who insists on gazing during his conversation with Alter at the latter's ear. The author has tried it with one of his colleagues and indeed the word was spread that "Shoham has become clinically mad far beyond his usual eccentricities".

In so far as some forms of madness involve a breakdown of the sensory encoding of messages and of interpersonal communication, and infringe a residual mass of social norms which generate a value-laden societal reaction and control, the mechanism of labelling social deviance applies, *mutatis mutandis,* to mental illness. The role of stigma in accelerating and deepening mental illness, analogously to its role in forming the deviant career, has been pointed out by Scheff, thus:

> In a crisis, when the deviance of an individual becomes a public issue, the traditional stereotype of insanity becomes the guiding imagery for action, both for those reacting to the deviance and, at times, for the deviant himself. When societal agents and persons around the deviant react to him uniformly in terms of the traditional stereotypes of insanity, his amorphous and non-structured rule-breaking tends to crystallize in conformity to those expectations, thus becoming similar to the behaviour of other deviants classified as mentally ill, and stable over time. The process . . . is completed when the traditional imagery becomes apart with the deviant's orientation for guiding his own behaviour.[28]

Nunnally has demonstrated that the mentally ill are regarded with fear, distrust and dislike. As with social deviance, their whole person is engulfed with a negative "halo" effect. Their public image is that of being "dirty", unintelligent, insincere and "worthless".[29] Scheff artfully demonstrated how the patient who is confused, insecure and powerless is totally influenced by the "Great White God", the omnipotent and omniscient therapist.[30] As psychiatrists and clinical psychologists are notorious labellers, the patient is more willing to oblige "the Great Man", adopting the labels of mental illness and acting accordingly. Such stigmatization effects the production of the symptoms of mental illness in an even more pronounced manner than in the covert stigmatization of the young Genet by the peasant family at the Le Morvan region, as we shall show later *in extenso* in chapter five.

Of special importance is Temerlin's study, which had psychiatrists, clinical psychologists and graduate students in clinical psychology diagnose a sound-recorded interview with a normal man. Just before listening to the interview, they heard a professional person of high prestige, acting as a confederate of the experimenters, say that the individual to be diagnosed was "a very interesting man because he looked neurotic but actually was quite psychotic".[31] The results were that the suggestion by the prestigious person had the greatest effect upon the clinicians, biasing them towards diagnosing the normal person as psychotic.

Rosenhan's study reports the adventures of eight sane (whatever this means) psychiatrists, volunteers who gained admission to different mental hospitals by feigning symptoms of mental illnesses. After being admitted, they dropped all pretences of madness, yet found it difficult to be released from the institutions. He puts the matter thus:

> Despite their public "show" of sanity, the pseudopatients were never detected. Admitted, except in one case, with a diagnosis of schizophrenia, each was discharged with a diagnosis of schizophrenia "in remission". The label "in remission" should in no way be dismissed as a formality, for at no time during any hospitalization had any question been raised about any pseudopatient's simulation . . . the evidence is strong that once labelled schizophrenic, the pseudopatient was stuck with the label . . . It is clear that we cannot distinguish the sane from the insane in psychiatric hospitals. The hospital itself imposes a special environment in which the meanings of behaviour can easily be misunderstood. The consequences to patients hospitalized in such an environment – the powerlessness, depersonalization, segregation, mortification and self-labelling – seem undoubtedly countertherapeutic.[32]

A recent court case in Israel revealed that a person was institutionalized in a mental hospital for five months by the order of a district psychiatrist (a government appointee) who never examined the patient, but made his decision on the basis of a complaint by the patient's wife, who was herself institutionalized in a mental hospital. A general practitioner also wrote a letter stating that "the patient is a sick man who disturbs the family's life". When investigated by the judge, the district psychiatrist testified: "Sometimes there is no choice and I have to commit a person to a mental hospital without examining him. Sometimes I issue four committal orders a day and I cannot examine everyone of them." The judge wrote in his verdict against the district psychiatrist, who was sued by the patient for damages: "I tremble with fright as to what could happen to every one of us if the district psychiatrist is not aware that he has to get clear evidence as to a person's mental illness before he commits him to a mental hospital." But the sad moral of this and many other cases is that there are no clear-cut and unequivocal definitions and syndromes of mental illness.

The author recently had a long talk with a very perceptive and intelligent young woman who spent many years in a mental hospital and managed to pull herself out of the vicious cycle of institutionalization, remission, stigma and breakdown by sheer willpower. In conclusion, she said: "I received all the so-called therapeutic shocks and have been diagnosed by all the diagnoses in the books. I don't believe in any of these. They are just words." One may conduct as many aetiological studies of schizophrenia as one wishes with the same worthless or amorphic results, because the dependent variable, schizophrenia itself, is a "blanket", nondescript construct. The most visible, and to be sure most concrete, aspect of mental illness is the labelling of the patient as ill and his committal to an institution. This is linked to the general dynamics of stigma, the projective nature of which is more apparent with phenomena which are amorphic and ill-defined, so that they are more readily tagged by the projections of the stigmatizers.

Some critics, like Walter Gove, reject the extreme labelling approach to the genesis of mental illness, on the grounds that societal reaction, in and by itself, cannot explain the aetiology of schizophrenia. Says Gove:

> In summary, the available evidence on how people enter the mentally ill role indicates that the societal formulation, at least as stated by Scheff, is false. The evidence is that the vast majority of persons who become patients have a serious disturbance, and it is only when the situation becomes untenable that action is taken. The public officials who perform the major screening role do not simply process all of the persons who come before them as mentally ill, but instead screen out a large portion. If the person passes this initial screening he will probably be committed, and there is reason to assume the process at this point frequently becomes somewhat ritualized. But even here a number of persons are released either through the psychiatric examination or the court hearing.[33]

Here again the fault lies in the extremity of the labelling approach, and the exclusiveness which its proponents claim for stigma as the main or even sole dynamic of mental illness. As with deviance and crime, the more realistic approach is to see the societal reaction as one dynamic within a configuration which also includes behavioural disturbances and functional maladjustments as predisposing factors towards morbidity. In the study referred to in *The Promethean Therapy*,[34] we show the importance of familial double binds in predisposing a child towards schizophrenia, in the same way that conflict situations in the socialization process predispose a child toward deviance and crime. However, the predisposing factors to morbidity are not so readily perceptible as in crime and deviance, so that the role of stigma in the ultimate definition of mental illness is bound to be more pronounced than in social deviance and crime.

The stigma of mental illness is also used as a device of relative achievement. Among the author's academic colleagues, a scholar's esoteric yet brilliant book is often dismissed as the "hallucinations of a madman". The author was present recently at an excellent lecture by a scholar who was known to be a dull lecturer. The author overheard one of the lecturer's colleagues explaining away the brilliance of the lecturer by the fact that he had undergone intensive psychiatric treatment. "So much treatment and money", winked the friend of the lecturer, "should produce at least one good lecture."

Labelling of madness solves many conflicts. For example, a third party may intervene in a fight and pacify one of the combatants by saying, "Leave him alone, don't you see he is mad." The most revolting instance of labelling with mental derangement as a weapon of power politics was experienced recently by a close friend of the author whose two sons were killed in the Yom Kippur War. He tried his hand at politics and his political opponents confided to everybody that he was totally unreliable and should not be elected to the Knesset (Israeli Parliament): "You know, of course, the terrible blow he suffered", they whispered with a tragic intonation. "Well, this has pushed him off the rails. It is a great shame, but one cannot vote for him because his lack of mental balance is sure to endanger the party."

The labelling of mental illness involves an extreme disjuncture of communication. The basic assumption underlying some forms of mental illness is that they constitute a severe breakdown of the patient's communication with his surroundings. But even in cases where such non-communication is not so extreme, as in some psychoses, the patient is apparently labelled for infringing residual social norms, which he might not even be aware of contravening. In social deviance and crime, the infringed norms are more conspicuous and not as residually amorphic as in mental illness. Consequently, the patient is often confused, anxious, disoriented and totally unclear as to what has happened to him, or what abominations he has committed in order to incur his declaration as a mad non-person. It is probable that this total confusion, more than other factors, is responsible for the patient's further retreat into an *incommunicado* stance *vis-à-vis* his incomprehensibly hostile surroundings. Mental health professionals utilizing the medical model of diagnosing mental illness are probably not aware of a crucial point: labelling behaviours which infringe residual conventions and norms with the amorphic and ambiguous psychiatric labels constitutes another distorting dimension in the interrelationship between such professionals, their patients and the public.

The Stigma of Madness as Social Control

Howard P. Rome, former President of the American Psychiatric Association, declared some time ago: "We appreciate that in a very meaningful sense, society can be sick too . . . Actually, no less than the entire world is a proper catchement area for present-day psychiatry, and psychiatry need not be appalled by the magnitude of this task."[35] Two Australian authors have stated that "mental health services do in part perform a legitimate social control function (because) some mentally disordered people create intolerable burdens".[36] Nicholas Kittrie expounded in his volume-length thesis that the functions of the administration of criminal justice and social control are more and more being vested in the organs and institutions of the modern state.[37] If indeed some, at least, of the custodial and therapeutic measures against the mentally ill are initiated by overt or covert aims of social control, then the stigma of madness attached to these measures has also a function of normative sanction and control. Khrushchev declared in the late 1950s that "there are no political prisoners [in the USSR], only persons of unsound mind".

Sidney Bloch and Peter Reddaway recently published an account of 200 cases of political dissidents, social outsiders and intellectual nonconformists who were labelled mad and treated accordingly.[38] At the 1977 meeting of the World Psychiatric Association, a former Soviet psychiatrist, Marina Viokhanskaya, presented a "white list" of Soviet political victims in mental hospitals and a "black list" of psychiatrists who committed them to these hospitals. She pleaded with the delegates to "help hundreds of psychiatrists in the Soviet Union who have been drawn into crime only because they lacked the courage to say no".[39]

Psychotherapists, treaters of aberrant human behaviour, do indeed aim to tow "crazy" individuals back within the limits of acceptable social standards of a given society at a given time. The pressures of the therapeutists on individuals to behave in conformity with the normative system becomes apparent if we bear in mind that unless a person seeks treatment voluntarily, he may constantly suffer, yet he may not be considered mad if his outward behaviour falls within the margins of accepted social norms. There is, therefore, a levelling element in psychotherapy, because "successful treatment" involves bringing the patient back within tolerable limits of the mean, mode and median of normative behaviour. Many creative innovators whose singular outlook was necessary for their novel perspectives and insights have been victims to the adjustment-based levelling pressures of psychotherapy. A particularly sad instance was the experience of Antonin Artaud, who was virtually reduced to a vegetative existence by a succession of electric shocks.

Artaud states that "a lunatic is a man who has preferred to become what is socially understood as mad rather than forfeit a certain superior idea of human honour . . . a vicious society has invented psychiatry to defend itself from the investigations of certain superior lucid minds whose intuitive powers were disturbing to it".[40]

Psychiatry as a prime tool of the cult of mediocrity, adhered to by the organs of social control, was denounced by Karl Kraus, the *enfant terrible* of Vienna: "nerve doctors who ruin genius for us by calling it pathological should have their skulls bashed in by the genius. One should grind one's heel into the faces of all rationalistic helpers of 'normal humanity' who give reassurance to people unable to appreciate works of wit and fantasy."[41]

It is relevant to the present context that Ego's striving to assert his ontological uniqueness as programmed by his specific psychosocial *Gestalt* will be stifled if he wanders out and beyond the mesh of normative controls.

There is also a marked element of subjugation of the patient to the therapist, because the powerlessness of the patient is almost total in a mental hospital, where he becomes a non-person. The therapist is the one who decides when to release the patient and many times his decision is influenced by the patient's family, which often has a vested interest in his remaining institutionalized. Greenly reports in his study:

> In the informal interview, most of the psychiatrists confirmed what the structured-interview data appear to show: patients' families had the ability to effect a discharge or prevent a release. As one therapist put it, "It's hard to stand up to a family, which is quite funny, since we are supposed to be a professional group." Only a small minority of the psychiatrists interviewed denied consistently that families were sometimes more influential in release decisions than they themselves were.

As a far-fetched hypothesis, based partly on the author's own observations, he suggests that therapists are attracted to and choose their profession because of their own psychic problems, which they project by prodding into the patient's mind, which "opens up" to them trustingly and willingly. The mechanism of transference enhances this symbiosis, which creates a skewed form of communication, and dependence of dubious value between therapist and patient, except that the patient gets a captive audience to listen (for a consideration) to his troubles. The therapists, however, have most of the trump cards, both lucrative and mental. The gist of our argument is that unless the patient suffers from organic nervous system damage, relatively minor problems can be "sold" to the therapist. These may be coped with by the individual's recognition of his inner potential as determined by his personality core vectors and by trying to implement his quest of authenticity by a Camusian revolt against his stifling surroundings, including the labels of maladjustment, deviance and madness. We offer no philosopher's stone or cookbook recipes for instant authenticity.

Chapter three
Don Carlo Gesualdo – A Murdered Love

"He who loves the more is the inferior and must suffer."

Thomas Mann, *Tonio Kroger*

The exact birth date of Don Carlo Gesualdo, Prince of Venosa in the Kingdom of Naples, is uncertain. Some say it was in 1560, others in 1562.[1] One authority puts his year of birth as 1564.[2] All authorities agree, however, that he died on 3 September 1613. In between, he murdered his first wife, Maria d'Avalos, a patrician beauty and his first cousin, and her lover, Fabrizio Carafa, Duke of Andria. He then entered into an arranged, political marriage with Donna Eleonora d'Este, cousin of the illustrious Duke of Ferrara. He lived a life of sado-masochistic misery, and wrote the most powerful and painfully disturbing of madrigals.[3]

We hardly know anything about Don Carlo's formative years. The adult prince, however, was a sexual pervert who derived pleasure from being flogged by a group of twelve young men, kept especially at his court, three times a day. He even could not defecate without being violently beaten beforehand.[4] Socially he was a recluse, an outsider, who fitted no social or artistic paradigm. Yet he was a musician of genius, whose innovative use of the five-voice unaccompanied madrigal and unaccompanied motets made him unacceptable in a musical climate which advocated the instrumentally accompanied monody and dramatic cantata.[5] We may, however, try to reconstruct his personality and some of its developmental phases by the admittedly problematic method of *ex post facto* inference. Don Carlo's personality was presumably doubly fixated, both at the early and later oral stages of development, so that a "black hole" was structured within it. Gesualdo tried to "fill" this abyss by unrequited love, both sadistic and masochistic, and after he murdered his wife, by guilt and self-inflicted pain.

We may hypothesize the pattern of child–parent relations in Gesualdo's case as follows. He was seriously abused by his father, or surrogate father, and consequently experienced severe fixations both in early orality and later orality. Since his mother was also abused, she was largely absent emotionally; hence, apart from abusing the child, there was no strong integrating, socially interacting *ity* to synchronize between the two divergent core personality components. The result, as explained in chapter one, was a "centre does not hold" syndrome. An early oral fixation makes for a longing for the object, the movement of warm milk, food, well-being. The nascent core personality at this pantheistic stage would perceive the deprivation and abuse by the parents as reinforcing the "bad me". This "bad me" would be cognitively perceived later on with the crystallization of the personality as an abysmal lack, a non-satiety which longs to be requited and filled. Hence, this black hole of hunger and thirst, to satisfy the ever augmenting longing for the absorption of the "good object", is ever augmenting with the strength of the fixation. However, the later oral fixation on a bad object would also effect a paranoid part of the personality. Therefore, we have a combined insatiable quest for a "good object" to flow in the ever-augmenting "black-hole", coupled by a distrust and hatred of all relevant others. Hence the non-coordinated personality, with extremely fixated polarities with the gaping black hole in between, is predisposed from infancy to long for the relief of the intense want, pain and deprivation generated by the "black hole".

Gesualdo's obsession with love and his longing to "fill" the "black hole" of his personality by passive love, submissive love, and, if unrequited by pain, agony and guilt, may be hypothesized as outlined below.

The separant way of loving is to include, to incorporate or "swallow" the other into oneself. The implementation of this Sisyphean aim is impossible by definition, so that the surrogate inclusionary techniques of the separant lover is to subjugate, manipulate, tyrannize, oppress and patronize his objects of love and sex. The dialogue below in Henry Miller's *Sexus* is aptly illustrative:

> "You never wear any undies, do you? You're a slut, do you know it?" I pulled her dress up and made her sit that way while I finished my coffee. "Play with it a bit while I finish this."
>
> "You're filthy", she said, but she did as I told her.
>
> "Take your two fingers and open it up. I like the color of it."
>
> . . . With this I reached for a candle on the dresser at my side and I handed it to her.
>
> "Let's see if you can get it in all the way . . . "

"You can make me do anything, you dirty devil."
"You like it, don't you?"[6]

Norman Mailer, in *An American Dream,* envisages an even more far reaching inclusion. Mr. Rojack, the hero, projects on his sexual object Ruta a total compliance with his separant aim to incorporate her within himself. Rojack proclaims that Ruta "was becoming mine as no woman ever had, she wanted to be part of my will".[7] The Sisyphean ever looks for new sexual objects to conquer. However, once the object has been conquered, a new target of subjugation is sought. The Sisyphean may also focus, not on the whole person, but be enamoured of the eyes, the lips. He may be mesmerized by the breasts of his love object. This stems from the nature of the Sisyphean's emotional attachment to a person or parts thereof, as targets for absorption, manipulation and mastering, not as partners in a mutually satisfactory emotional and physical encounter.

The sado-masochistic dyad of the passionate torturer and the voluptuously tortured is also Sisyphean in essence. The infliction of mental and physical pain has always been a prime mode of subjugation, manipulation and control. The sadistic ego may devise subtle and sophisticated modes of painfully manipulating its alter, so that the latter may see no choice but to willingly submit. Pure and courageous heroes, who always manage to outwit and vanquish their sadistic tormentors, are in the exclusive domain of pulp magazines. In real life, and especially within the confines of monogamy, man and woman may devise such ingenious devices of mutual torment that the gory cruelties of the Divine Marquis would seem amateurish. Moreover, the masochist is also bound to manipulate the sadist into providing the type of torment suitable to his specific gourmet palate for esoteric pain. Even if the partner in a passion dyad is no masochist, he is very quick to realize that his sadistic partner needs him much more than the partner is needed. Once he realizes that, he has a trump card with which he can, and often does, manipulate him into a Sisyphean interdependence. The sado-masochistic dyad is, therefore, an extreme Sisyphean interrelationship, one in which one party objectifies the other and manoeuvres him to cater to his own separant whims and aims.

The Sisypheanism of the sado-masochistic dyad is also apparent from its cyclic conflictual nature: the masochist creates conflicts, so that he may be abused and tormented, whereas the sadist provokes conflicts in order to be able to inflict pain and torment. This may eventually lead to a self-defeating deadlock; we can envisage Leopold von Sacher-Masoch kneeling in front of the Marquis de Sade begging to be whipped, while the Divine Marquis, although brandishing his whip, says No, with a sadistic smirk. The ultimate in Sisyphean possessiveness is to kill for love. This is what Oscar Wilde meant in the *Ballad of Reading Gaol,* when he lamented that "each man kills the thing he loves". The master of this genre of amatory Sisyphean possessiveness is Jean Genet, the self-confessed murderer, who writes from his experience of the ecstasy and elation of killing a man: "I would like to kill a handsome blond boy, so that, already united by the verbal link that joins the murderer and the murdered (each existing thanks to the other), I may be visited, during days and nights of hopeless melancholy, by a handsome ghost of which I would be the haunted castle . . . "[8] This is the ultimate possession of the murdered by the murderer, the irreversible acquisition of the beloved victim by his passionate executioner.

In his *Romantic Agony*, Mario Praz comments on the various works by Pushkin and Gautier based on the account of the *Liber de Viris Illustribus,* in which Cleopatra used to kill her lovers after having sex with them:

> Cleopatra, like the praying mantis, kills the male whom she loves. These are elements which were destined to become permanent characteristics of the type of Fatal Woman of whom we are speaking. In accordance with this conception of the Fatal Woman, the lover is usually a youth, and maintains a passive attitude; he is obscure, and inferior either in condition or in physical exuberance to the woman, who stands in the same relation to him as the female spider, the praying mantis, etc., to their respective males: sexual cannibalism is her monopoly. Towards the end of the century, the perfect incarnation of this type of woman is Herodis. But she is not the only one: the Helen of Moreau, of Saiman, of Pascoli (Anticlo) closely resembles her. The ancient myths, such as that of the Sphinx, of Venus and Adonis, of Diana and Endymion, were called in to illustrate this type of relationship, which was to be so insistently repeated in the second half of the century. The following point must be emphasized: the function of the flame which attracts and burns is exercised, in the first half of the century, by the Fatal Man (the Byronic hero), in the second half by the Fatal Woman; the moth destined for sacrifice in the first case the woman, in the second the man . . . [9]

Without going into Praz's argument concerning the alterations between the passionate male and female murderer, it is worth mentioning that his comments and descriptions aptly illustrate our premise. The extreme Sisyphean lovers, both *femme* and *homme fatale*, prey on their paramour as an act of exclusive possession. His dominance of his miserable partner must be so complete that no one else must be allowed to share the passionate favours of his lovers after he has shared the fatal bed. The possessive lover/killer is not content with a mere subjugation of his beloved, body and soul; he insists on his lover's immolation on the altar of his passions.

The participant desire to annihilate the self and fuse with one's beloved may be linked to self-destructive tendencies, which are instrumental to Ego's Tantalic goal of self-effacement and of being absorbed by his or her lover. It is not physical death or suicide that is the aim of the Tantalic lover, but the continuous, strenuous (depending on the intensity of his love) efforts to be debased and humiliated. Such stripping of the infatuated ego's self-esteem, and hence the obliteration of his identity, facilitates the obliteration of his separate self and its being engulfed by the lover. It should be stressed that this is the description of the amorous self-destructive infatuations of the polar participant type. As this course of emotional involvement was mostly determined by an early oral fixation and the dynamics of the inner personality, Ego's amorous behaviour would largely be motivated unconsciously. As his self-debasement would be unlikely to be reciprocated by the coveted emotional acceptance by the beloved Alter, such self-destructive Tantalic binges are not very likely to be terminated by nervous breakdowns or suicide. Usually, the Tantalic lover is jolted from his "bad trip" by traumatic abuse by his paramour. He would then emerge from what is seen retrospectively as his nightmare, and recuperate for a while. But not for long, because he is destined by his core-personality dynamics to ever look for the "great consuming love" of his Tantalic dreams.

The subjugation of the Tantalic lover is the most consummate. He yearns for the total submission of his body and soul in his lover, while desiring passionately that his wilful sacrifice be graciously accepted. Oscar Wilde, in *De Profundis*, written in the form of a letter to Lord Alfred Douglas, describes his carnivorously separant paramour: "Having made your most of my genius, my will-power and my fortune, you required in the blindness of an inexhaustible greed, my entire existence. You took it."[10] Wilde was well aware of his Tantalic subjugation to his greedy lover, yet the self-annihilating trust of his love was so overpowering that he could not help but plunge headlong to his ruin. He then recounts that he knew that to apply for the arrest of the Marquis of Queensberry, Lord Douglas's allegedly libellous father, was a fatal error. But Wilde found himself coerced by the duties of his consuming love, and was hence unable to resist the disastrous demands of his lover. In *The Ballad of Reading Gaol*, Wilde describes how he totally sacrificed his dignity, will-power and freedom not to Douglas but to his love for Douglas. Wilde's professed abject slavery was not to a person but to a Tantalic infatuation. Douglas sponged Wilde shamelessly, ultimately bankrupting him. The most fantastic revelation by Frank Harris, Wilde's controversial biographer, but corroborated by G. B. Shaw, was that they both tried to dissuade Wilde from suing Queensberry. Wilde was convinced, but then Bosie (Lord Alfred's nickname) Douglas changed his mind:

> At Oscar's request I repeated my argument and to my astonishment Douglas got up at once, and cried with his little white, venomous, distorted face:
> "Such advice shows you are no friend of Oscar's."
> "What do you mean?" I asked in wonderment; but he turned and left the room on the spot. To my astonishment, Oscar also got up.
> "It is not friendly of you, Frank", he said weakly, "it really is not friendly."
> I stared at him; he was parroting Douglas' idiotic words. "Don't be absurd", I said, but he repeated:
> "No Frank, it is not friendly", and went to the door and disappeared.
> Like a flash I saw part, at least, of the truth. It was not Oscar who had ever misled Douglas, but Lord Alfred Douglas who was driving Oscar whither he would.[11]

We have here the sacrifice of dignity and the forfeiture of a sense of choice, the twin frameworks on which an ontological self-concept may support itself. By sacrificing these, Oscar Wilde sacrificed his self. The question of whether Bosie was worthy of this ultimate sacrifice is beside the point, because the essence of total Tantalic submission is that it becomes a goal in itself, ordained more by the lover's core dynamics than by the identity and characteristics of the loved one. When Ego is in the grip of a Tantalic carousal of self-sacrifice to an idol, the lover discards normal recognition of time and reality, and rushes after his glittering projections on to his beloved. Such self-sufficiency of Tantalic involvement in a self-destructive love is also portrayed by Truffaut's cinematic story of Adele H., Victor Hugo's love-crazed daughter. Adele falls in love with Pinson, a British lieutenant who is consistently indifferent to her. She follows him to Halifax, Nova Scotia, and to Barbados. She pays his debts, feigns pregnancy and procures a whore for him, as proof of her love. When she finally catches up with Pinson, she looks through him as if he was so much hot air, and continues to chase the projected inner vision of her romantic will-o'-the-wisp.

We hypothesize that a person's quest for a "pure" sacred love is related to the degree of his participant early oral fixation and an exclusionary longing to partake of the "good" mother–object. Per contra, the separant quest to control the object is linked to a wish to objectify and manipulate the partner in the sexual dyad. This profane love is related to a later oral fixation on the "bad" object-mother and the inclusionary aim to dominate. Our hypothesis, as stemming from the continuum described in chapter one, envisages a predisposition of the early orally fixated male to seek an immaculate Madonna-like love. If, in addition to his fixation, the male's incestuous oral sexuality has been harshly suppressed, he might find a combination of large breasts (an over-inflated reminiscence of his early oral fixation) and restrained demeanour quite irresistible. This might have been one of the main reasons for the popularity of the girl-next-door-idol, with the accentuated bust of the 1940s created by Hollywood, to cater for mother-longing, home-sick soldiers of the Second World War.

Early orally fixated girls are bound to dream about the proverbial virtuous knight on the white horse, many times to the detriment of her – and especially her parents' – matrimonial plans. A later orally fixated girl would pursue sex in a truly Sisyphean manner. She would aim to subjugate her sexual partner and use him for the satisfaction of her hedonistic passions. Both love and sex are conceived by her as conflictual – an ever recurring battle of wits, stamina and sexual potency. Her amatory exploits recognize only victories or defeats – nothing in between. Mutually satisfying encounters and intersubjective rapport are outside her range of emotions and conceptual contexts. The Sisyphean woman is also bound to use sex and love as a means of achieving personal, matrimonial and social ends. In such cases, a strict suppression of incest by the mother might have brought about a bipolar predisposition towards sex and love. The strict Catholic upbringing of a Fellini, for instance, contributed to the cinematic creation of the extreme bi-modality of the ascetic saint and the whore – the fragile and sexless mother–woman–lover and the vulgar, sinful female sex object.

The beauty of ugliness is the affective, often sexual, attraction to the maimed, the deformed, the hideous, the unclean, all of which is just a more extreme form of an attraction to the "dirtiness" of sex. This may range from paraphiliacs who are sexually aroused mostly, or solely, by cripples, to a Genet, for whom the more ugly and disfigured a person, the more magnificent he was.[12] The most ardent troubadour of the beauty of ugliness was perhaps Baudelaire, who sang the praises of beggar maids, the seductiveness of hags, and the loveliness of brothels and skeleton-like women.

A mytho-empirical support for the nature of "dirty" sexual passion is the evil Circe, who turns the men who desire her into swine. Moreover, Circe, the bad-mother–woman, sends Odysseus to Persephone, the mytho-empirical post-oral, sexually-defiled transformation of the early-oral "pure" maiden Koré.

All authorities attest to the sado-masochistic nature of Don Carlo, both in relation to women and as a basic attitude towards his life and object-relationships. He was unable to perform his daily routines unless flogged.[13] He was also, quite probably, homosexual, as attested to by Spaccini, who wrote in his diary in 21 September 1613: "He (Don Carlo) could never sleep unless someone stayed with him, embracing him in order to keep his back warm. And for this purpose he had a certain Castelvietro of Modena, who continuously slept with him when the princess was away."[14] There are reports that he maltreated and physically abused his second wife, Leonora d'Este. We may find support for Don Carlo's sado-masochism in the courting of death, and above all the agony of love, to "fill" his "black hole". If the longed for love to requite the bottomless abyss within his personality, which could not be filled, or is murdered by his own hands, agony, pain and suffering may be a perverse substitute to cram the "black hole".

We find ample evidence for Gesualdo's agony, his masochistic courting of death and his delight in pain, as well as his tortured love for his dead wife and guilt for her murder, in the lyrics of his madrigals. He did not write the lyrics; most were written by Guarini and Tasso. The latter, a paranoiac poet, was frequently a guest at the Gesualdo court, and he might have written the lyrics to suit the prince's morbid desires and moods. Also, the choice of the other lyrics may point to the preference of Gesualdo for poems, phrases and words expressing his perverse inclinations, painful guilt and the pangs of a lost love. In the text of the madrigal *Resta di Darminoia,* we read thus, "Dead is for me all joy; and never may I hope to know what gladness is."[15] He chooses lyrics which extol and revel in sin, death and guilt. Gesualdo uses the chromatism of a succession of two half tones to create a disturbing, harassing sense of violence, when applied to such phrases as *miserere mei* (have mercy on me), *lacrimis meis* (my tears) and *dolor meus* (my sorrow).[16]

Gesualdo sings the pangs of love like singeing arrows in lyrics by Tasso, thus:

> Little by little you have broken
> and loosened and extinguished
> the arrows and bonds and fire
> which pricked, which tied, which
> inflamed my heart.
> O Love, my blessed one,
> I feel without pain
> another dart, other chains,
> another flame.

Tasso, knowing the prince intimately, catered to his sado-masochistic whims in writing for him with such perverse lyrics as:

> If from so noble a hand
> should come sticks for my wounds,
> Love, why do you not inflict
> my breast with a thousand blows?
> Do not blame yourself for it

because nothing wounds the heart
as seriously
as the mild wrath
of a beautiful hand.

Love, I seek not peace,
I do not ask for shelter or shield,
but against the naked breast,
if she is the enemy, you are the
warrior.

Exaltation of pain, delight in wounds, are also in the text of Gesualdo's fourth book of madrigals:

Clear, sparkling eyes,
You set me on fire, you, but my heart
feels
Delight in the blazing fire, not pain.

Sweet, dear words,
You wound me, you, but my breast
feels
Only delight in the wound, not pain.

O miracle of love!
The soul, all fire and all blood,
Is consumed without pain, dies
without languishing.

The mad paranoiac Tasso thus provides the lyrics to which the morbid sado-masochistic Gesualdo provides the chromatic music, which lifts his art by stormy waves onto unprecedented heights of innovation. There probably was never a better indication of the link between innovation, deviance and madness.

The pivotal event in his life, which of course strongly affected his music, was the murder of his first wife, Maria d'Avalos and her lover the Duke of Andria, on the 26 October 1590. So much so that Denis Arnold terminates his short essay on Don Carlo by saying, "Perhaps without the murder some great music would have not been granted to the world."[17] This inference of causality might seem rather rash, but the guilt, the agony and Gesualdo's wish to join his beloved wife in death, are indeed linked to his magnificently expressionist and tortured music. The art of Gesualdo may be linked to the myth of Don Juan which generated so many works of art related to the pangs and mourning for a dead love.

The myth of Don Juan presents the archetypal Tantalic lover who longs to be immersed in universal womanhood, to be absorbed by the eternally feminine. Nothing short of complete grace can satisfy him, so that his amatory exploits are bound to disappoint him. Don Juan longs for an *amour sacré,* for an ethereal "Eternal Woman masterpiece of the male".[18]

Don Juan is a participant pursuer of pantheistic grace who in order to achieve it is ever ready to be annihilated, even at the price of the fire and brimstone of hell. Don Carlo is indeed a Don Juanic lover who extols the anguish of an unrequitable love for his dead wife, murdered by his own hands. Tasso laments the death of Donna Maria D'Avalos and her lover, thus:

On the Death of Two Most Noble Lovers

Weep, O Graces, and you too bewail, O Loves,
the cruel trophies of death and the cruel spoils
of the beautiful couple whom death enviously
takes from us, both the funeral blossoms and the shadowy horrors.

Weep, O Nymphs, and strew blossoms on this couple,
their moist leaves painted with old lamentations;
and all you who vie with each other in distilling
the piteous anguish and the scent of tears.

Weep, Erato and Clio, for this horrible event,
and scatter, with mournful sound (your) bitter complaint,
henceforth, instead of sweet water, (O) Parnassus.

Weep, sad Naples, clothed in mourning,
for the dark fate of beauty and of virtue,
and may the song address its harmony to grief.[19]

On the Same Subject

O souls, marvellously lovely and beautiful,
who suffered in dying bitter torment,
whether it was death, or love, or fortune, or heaven that united you,
nothing divides or uproots you any more.

But like rays conjoined, or even torches
of immortal splendour in the third circle,
you already flame, and the serene stars shine more
brightly because of your gentle desire.

Nay, Heaven is even adorned by your sin
(if ever there is sin between two courteous lovers),
it is made more lovely by your amorous disgrace!

Whoever blames you for straying among the sad sighs (of love)
Let him accuse the sun which brought forth the day
when wandering stars so erred.[20]

Gesualdo sings about his cruel love in Book VI of his madrigals, thus:

Alas, how in vain are my sighs,
Alas, how in vain are my looks at you
Since, cruel one, each gives you a joy
And me only death!
Unhappy is my fate,
That life for me becomes Death.[21]

The cruelty of his love gives him sado-masochistic pleasure, but also the hope, à la Don Juan, that his love unto death will help him join his beloved in the ever after. Hence, he courts death, *O dolce strana morte* (the sweet and strange death),[22] which will join him to the eternal existence of his murdered beloved. Such courting of death is expressed in a paradoxical manner in the second madrigal of Book V:

If I do not look, I do not die
Not looking nor do I live
So if I am dead, I am not deprived of life
O miracle of love, ah strange fate
That to live is not to have life, and being dead not to have died.[23]

His dolorous, temporal life is not life and his death is not death, since he thereby joins his beloved. In one of Guarini's texts, Gesualdo sings the paradoxical delight in dying while still sighing "*Mora e Mentre sospiro*", welcoming a languishing death, "*Languisco e mora*" until sweet death (*dolce e'l morire*) overtakes him.[24] With death he may join his dead beloved, but in his miserable life his perpetual agony turns his temporal existence into a prolonged death, as expressed in Book VI:

A thousand times each day I die
And you, oh cruel sighs,
Alas, you let me not die of sighing?
And you unkind soul, if my sorrow
Afflicts you, why do you not take to our heels?
Death alone takes pity
On my harsh and loathsome pain, and kills me!
Thus, neither sighs nor my love
Do show me mercy, but Death is charitable.[25]

The Myth of Don Juan – A Scaffolding for Understanding Gesualdo

Let us investigate the possibility of a connection between our protagonist and the myth of Don Juan.

Don Juan is a true myth and there is mytho-empirical value in the various plays based on it because they utilize the basic scaffolding of archaic realities, *in ille tempore*. The lover infatuated with the unattainable ideal of feminine perfection cannot be satisfied with artless flesh and blood imitations. In the chasing of the woman of his dreams, Don Juan destroys everyone and everything which stands in his way, and in the end he destroys himself. This myth is simple, strong and real, because while it has occurred endless times in real life with many variations on the basic theme, the core of the myth remains constant. The various playwrights who have utilized the Don Juan myth might have changed settings and subplots, but the core myth is still at the basis of the drama, to serve as an anchor to their own archetypal and mytho-empirical projections. The myth of Don Juan is archaic and universal, because it represents the archetypal unquenchable thirst for a participant love. A recent survey of literature and works of art based on Don Juan has brought to light no less than 500 plays, novels, critical works, operas and films.[26] These have been classified, analyzed and taxonomized by scholars into periods and styles. For example, there are the classic *commedia dell'arte*, the romantic and the modern Don Juans.[27]

Myths have many layers superimposed on the archaic core, layers which might be variations on the theme of the core myth, as projected on it by its various dramatic, literary and artistic interpretators. However these variations do not interfere with our purposes, so long as the core ingredients of the myth are present in a given interpretation. These, as recorded in the first version of the play in the first half of the seventeenth century, by the Spanish monk Gabriel Tellez, alias Tirso de Molina, are more or less as follows. Don Juan impersonates the fiancé of a duchess in a king's palace, to seduce her. He is caught but manages to escape. During his escape, he is shipwrecked and is saved by fisher girls. He promises marriage to the most beautiful of them, seduces her, but after one night escapes again. When he reaches his hometown, he seduces the daughter of an illustrious commander on the eve of her marriage. Don Juan is caught and the commander comes to avenge the honour of his daughter, but Don Juan kills him. He is exiled, but on his way he manages to seduce another bride and stays with her his customary one night. When he returns to his hometown again, he enters a church in which he finds the statue and tomb of the murdered illustrious commander. He tweaks the beard of the statue and invites it to dine with him. The statue accepts the invitation for dinner in the course of which he flings Don Juan to hell.

This is a Christian myth of love, sin and damnation. Love may be both the longing for purity (for the sacred archetypal mother–woman), yet when it alternates with vile sex, it leads to hell. Nevertheless, the romantic agony of longing for an unattainable love makes the quest of love by itself the saving grace. Indeed in some versions of the myth, the unreachable beloved is instrumental in transferring the sinning Don Juan from hell to heaven. We have here a myth in which damnation and salvation alternate, and sometimes intermingle. The damning component of the myth is overt – the libertine Don Juan is hurled to hell; the saving layer of the myth is more subtle – the unachievable love effects a saving grace, because the unquenchable longing lends the love a Tantalic permanence.

Grabbe, who produced the most ambitious, elaborate and profound Don Juan play, has his black knight assure Faust, Don Juan's alter ego: "Everything possible has been done. But you love the impossible – the infinite."[28] Don Juan's love is infinite, boundless and timeless, and thus unreal and out of reach.

"Love is the only creative omnipotence", declares Don Juan. Tantalic love is a quest to revert to early orality, when the self and the graces of mother–woman are still united in omnipresence and omnipotence. Tantalic love is impossible, because it concentrates exclusively on a projected perfection of woman. The transcendental nature of the projection reduces all mortal imitations to insignificance. Don Juan's dilemma is either to make do with an endless succession of surrogates for the feminine ideal, each of which rejects or annihilates him in a crescendo of *Götterdämmerung,* which hopefully would reunite him with the absolute and perfect womanhood, a course to which he ultimately succumbs.

Don Juan defies death, because his Tantalic love makes him seek the annihilation of his temporal existence, to reunite with the absolute, which contains in its engulfing unity his perfect love. In most of the versions of the play, Don Juan displays a suicidal courage, as if he actually courts death. In the play by Tirso de Molina, Don Juan gives his hand to the commander's statue and assures it that he is not afraid; he expects challenges and even if it were hell itself, he would give him his hand.[29]

What makes the sacred love of Don Juan a romantic agony is that his approach to his beloved is barred by the impossible. The Don Juan portrayed by Flaubert laments the "impossibility of perfect communion, however adhesive the kiss. Something hinders and makes a wall of itself."[30] This barrier between himself and his perfect love is sealed tight; it cannot be passed. All Don Juan can do in his temporal existence is to move from one woman to another, while fixing his gaze upwards towards his sacred love, or else aim to unite with his pure love in the immaculate infinity of the ever after through perdition.

Yet it is not a woman that is loved, but rather love itself. It is the longing for the absolute, the wish to solve existential riddles, and the escape from ontological loneliness, which his programming has directed him to anchor on a particular beloved mortal, knowing only too well that she is no match for this awesome burden. Don Juan's participant longing for a woman is unattainable; the archetypal mother–woman who bears for him the sole hope for the graces of partaking of unity is beyond his grasp. The paradox and tragedy of Don Juan is that his Tantalic self craves to partake of unity, through his love for an unreachable and pure *amour sacré*, while the amorous encounters that are within his reach quickly become distasteful.

Don Juan seeks his way back to a lost God through the love of a woman, the one and only all-consuming infatuation which will serve as a vehicle to revert to his early oral omnipresence. When he embraces his great lady, he will fuse with her in "silent bliss"[31] and thereby, ultimately, "share God's Throne".[32] In the same vein, the impossible love for Donna Anna is a prototype of a Madonna – a spiritual and rather sexless, yet all-embracing, love reminiscent of Robert Graves' *White Goddess*, the Judaic *Shechina* and the Gnostic *Sophia*. This archetypal good mother–woman is the harbinger of Tantalic grace and the forgiveness inherent in the partaking of unity. Indeed, Donna Anna chooses to stay in purgatory and wait for Don Juan, to allow him a chance for salvation.[33] After the statue of the commander stretches its stone hand to hurl Don Juan to hell, the spirit of Donna Anna stretches her hand and offers the dying Don Juan a forgiving ascent to heaven, proclaiming, "Love saved Don Juan!"[34] This love was not profane or sexual, but innocent and devoid of all sensual passion. This saccharine happy ending was, of course, aimed at the church and the simple tastes of the common people.

On a deeper level, the offer of salvation has a mytho-empirical significance.[35] Don Juan, the Christian knight, is saved by the immaculate, spiritual and sexless love of the pure mother–woman, in this way proclaiming all the worthlessness of vile and profane sex, in which he wallowed all his temporal life. The beatification of the innocent, spiritual love implies the condemnation by Don Juan himself of the vileness of carnal sex.

For the present context, Don Juan's agony may be interpreted in terms of the projection of his participant core longing for non-being on the love of an ethereal ideal woman. Yet at the same time, he strenuously tries to quench this spiritual longing by feeding on a succession of female bodies. He thus attempts to achieve his Tantalic amorous goals by Sisyphean means. This basic Don Juanic dynamic is not only self-defeating, but wrought with unbearable suffering. The daredevil Don Juan seems to be almost relieved by his temporal death – he actually stretches out his hand freely to his stony executioner. In some versions, the play ends by demonstrating that only after being relieved of his temporal misery, does Don Juan have any chance of being saved, by the forgiving mediation of his wholesome perfect love, out of reach in the here-and-now. Don Juan's is a mytho-empirical *mourir d'amour* – a self-annihilation for love.

This indeed is the aim of our grief and guilt stricken Don Juanic prince. In Book VI of his madrigals, Gesualdo wails:

> If you desire my death,
> Cruel one, I happily die;
> And after death shall still love only you.
> But if you desire me not to love you,
> Ah, merely on thinking of it,
> The pain kills me and my soul takes
> flight.

But ultimately his dolorous joy is to die a sweet death,[36] which to him is life in the ever after, the abode of his beloved; yet he does not wish to be cursed by his wife's hatred. He wants to die forgiven:

> I languish and die, oh cruel one!
> But you, wicked cause of my fate,
> oh, for pity's sake, console
> such a sorrowful death
> by at least one tear,
> so that I might say
> with my last breath,
> "How merciful you can be,
> sweet it is to die."

Yet like all Don Juans, Don Carlos is asking for the impossible.

Gesualdo loved his first wife, killed her in a fit of jealousy and lamented her with excruciating remorse. His second marriage was political, yet he hoped for marital peace. If not bliss, he expected at least some peace and quiet; but even that did not transpire. To include Gesualdo's second marriage into our theoretical framework requires recourse to a previous work of the present author.

In *The Violence of Silence*, we expounded at length our thesis that whenever two people engage in a dialogic encounter, both expect to achieve a deeper level of communication than they actually achieve.[37] There will always be a gap between the aspired and achieved levels of encounter, as defined by each party of the dyad. The different biological predispositions, personality fixations and cultural imprints of Ego and Alter make it statistically very remote, or well nigh impossible, that both parties aspire to reach similar levels of encounter, let alone to be able to achieve them. Moreover, there are bound to be fluctuations in the willingness and ability to enter into a deep encounter of both Ego and Alter, varying with place and time.

Love is a special case, and to be sure an extreme one, of a dyadic encounter. Precisely this extremity of emotions and goals, which in many instances is nothing less than a longing for the fusion of body and soul, makes the differences of the expectations from the amatory dyad far reaching indeed. The resultant discrepancies between aspirations and levels of achievement of emotional communion, as sensed by the lovers, are bound to be correspondingly more pronounced in the amatory dyad than in other types of encounter. This may account both for the emotional violence inherent in the amorous dyad, and its greater vulnerability to rupture. The different expectations on the Sisyphean–Tantalic continuum between the parties are also bound to be initially greater, because the primary predisposition of woman is to contain her lover in a Sisyphean manner, whereas the man is predisposed to be tantalically contained. The initial anticipations of man and woman from their encounter of love are bound to be complementary in form, yet contradictory in content.

Unequal involvement in an emotional dyad may sometimes result in cases where the love-lorn Ego may try to control his torrential emotions to be more palatable and acceptable to the less involved Alter. The relationship may proceed for a while in a socially sanctioned ritual, rather like a stylized minuet, but then tortured Ego will more often than not burst out with a torrential lava of passion, and the less enamoured Alter may retreat in confusion, embarrassment or dismay. Alter expects a subdued and pleasantly soft-hued presentation, such as depicted by Ingres in his *The Turkish Bath*, but is exposed to a nerve-racking shriek of a Munch. If Ego wishes to reach a deeper level of amatory encounter than Alter is ready or willing to reach, he exposes his innermost sensitivities and is liable to be hurt by the lack of Alter's response, or his indifference and sometimes callous exploitation. Paraphrasing Sartre's closing lines in his play *No Exit*: an emotionally less responsive Alter is the loving Ego's hell.

In a few cases, the submissive Ego may carry on his masochistically abject yielding to the bullying Alter, because his overt or covert goals are self-destructive. In such cases, the emotional dyad is liable to be disrupted by the breakdown, madness or even death of the participantly self-destructive party, or by the final loss of interest of the separant bully in his downtrodden victim.

Sartre has already pointed out that in amatory relationships, there is always one who subjugates and the other who is subjugated.[38] In our context, this means that in the dyad of love, the one who is more involved has power over the one who is less enamoured. We have pointed out earlier that because of bio-psycho-social factors and contextual considerations, Ego is bound to have different expectations from an amatory dyad and to be differently involved in it than the intensely involved Alter. This in itself has the seeds of disruption, which are bound eventually to break up the dyad. The more involved Ego will demand reciprocation from Alter, but because of "the least interest principle", he is liable to get less reciprocity of emotions, precisely because he longs for it and displays his intense quest for it. The less involved Alter is liable to feel bored or fed up with Ego's imposing emotions and disengage himself, either abruptly or gradually from the dyad. The less involved, separant Alter might also feel that the over-eager Ego has already been won, so that further targets for conquest have to be sought.

Moreover, as there is no intersubjective communication, Alter may not even be aware of the nature and intensity of Ego's emotional or other expectations. When Alter inevitably fails to fulfil Ego's projected expectations, Ego feels cheated, betrayed and disenchanted; yet Ego rarely realizes that it was not Alter, but his (Ego's) own projected expectations concerning Alter that have betrayed him.

Each party projects on the other expectations the other not only cannot fulfill, but often cannot be aware of. This is the main reason for love being mostly a self-defeating passion. The essence of Don Juanism is the infatuation with the projected expectations on to one's beloved; when such expectations fail to materialize, which they invariably do, one focuses one's Tantalic longings on another love-object, *da capo*. Indeed, at the height of our emotional involvement, we hang on to every twist of our beloved's eyebrows and anchor on each minute change in the hue or glow of his eyes, as proof and reinforcement that one's projections are well placed and are being fulfilled. The disjuncture, alas, sooner or later becomes evident. The cracks widen and the ruptures cannot be patched any more. A marriage may go on and the family thrive and multiply with children, grandchildren, feasts and rituals; a certain rather durable friendship may even develop between the former lovers, but their love is dead.

An easily complying Alter does not fit the ideal image of a strong and superior lover worthy of Ego's total submission. This is why a participant lover may still be infatuated with a beloved who rejects or is indifferent to him, whereas the separant lover relates to his beloved in a curvilinear manner. Some rejection may spur his amatory interest, but a total rejection would convince the realistically separant lover that his chances of making a conquest are meagre, and it would be more expedient for him to invest his efforts in someone more promising.

In his sado-masochistic fluctuations, our prince opts for one of the extreme alternatives, thus:

> My lady, I ardently wish
> that you might show such gracious
> mercy

> or such cruelty,
> that the one will grant my heart's
> desire
> or the other will end my life!

The infatuation of love, says John Money, may last at most around two years, but usually wanes much earlier.[39] Like all life processes, a love affair is conceived, erupts and grows, blooms, flowers, dims and dies a natural death. But mostly it breaks down violently, because of the fierce emotions it invokes. Because of gender, personality type and cultural role differences, the amatory goals, as anchored on the core vectors of the lovers, are bound to be conflictual to begin with, so that the violent disruption of the dyad is even more inevitable.

Once Ego falters or is temporarily engaged in concerns other than his burning love, the pitch of his infatuation lowers and the amorous flame perishes; Alter will not, or cannot, feed it. Its sole source is Ego; Alter provides only a reflector image. When the flame is extinguished, its mirror image is blotted out with it.

Hence our disenchanted prince sings bitterly of his disillusionment:

> My lady has frost in her heart
> and fire in her face,

Whatever pain and suffering one incurs in one's amorous encounters, one is baited to ever engage in them by the Sisyphean desire to possess, or by the Tantalic longing to be possessed by, love.

Our prince indeed laments his rejection by his consort:

> I do not like your unpleasant
> voice,
> my lady said to me,
> and with stinging darts
> of sorrow and suffering she
> pierced my soul.
> Yet I lived and live still.
> Ah, one cannot die
> of sorrow and suffering

Indeed, like in Sartre's hell his wife rules his life, petrifies his emotions and kills his hope, which alternates with suffering.

Gesualdo declares bitterly:

> I will never change
> my condition, desire and thought
> for the cruel enemy of my heart,
> with sweetest authority,

rules my life, my days and my hours
and tempers my desires
now with hope, now with joy,
now with suffering.

"Is there any sorrow like unto my sorrow?" Gesualdo asks in his *Sacrae Cantione*. We tend to agree that the cups of his torment are full when he reproduces a variation on the theme of some of the domestic repartees in Book III of his madrigals:

"I do not love you", (O hateful words),
My Lady said to me,
And with piercing darts
Of pain and torment transfixed my soul.
Alas, even though the wound was bitter and
deadly,
Yet I lived and still live. Ah, one cannot die
Of pain and torment!

If love is agonizing, frustrating, unattainable, illusory, subjugating, petrifying, and well nigh impossible, then what kindles its fires? What induces us to indulge in the amorous cycles of involvement, infatuation and disenchantment? We contend that our very yearning for love, be it the Sisyphean covetousness of possessing our beloved or the Tantalic longing to fuse with him/her, is the essence of love. The process of involvement, not the attainment of our goals, kindles our amorous fires; the goals as such are as unachievable as the aims of our participant and separant core vectors. Nietzsche laments not so much his lost love for Lou Andreas Salome as the destruction of his illusions of love and his ability to long for it.[40]

The essence of love is but the longing to unify with another. Who amongst us has not experienced the thrill, the elation, the quickening of the pulse when revisiting the place of our first kiss and embrace. The yearning for an amorous encounter is enough to fill our hearts, even though its realization is remote or even impossible. The craving for love takes us out of our daily routines, our drudgeries, lending a dimension of elation to our Sisyphean quests, infusing revelation into our Tantalic longing. Such independent potency of the yearning for love, which has an essence and dynamic of its own, irrespective of the object of love, might well be the reason for our being baited by it to mate and reproduce. Love songs, tales, myths and drama are anchored on the yearning for amorous union, not on the processes of mating, reproduction and growth.

Man is in love with love. The objects of our amorous involvement, however, are transitory. What is permanent throughout life is our yearning to love and be loved. Tantalic longing has been projected onto religion as the pure mother-of-God, the graceful Sophia, the Shechina. The timelessness of love is a function of the longing for it. A sacred love is a love for an inaccessible object. The rebellion of the participant lover is to immerse himself into his longing for his beloved, however unattainable he or she may be, and however impossible the love might be. The rebellious lovers' motto is to love at all costs and to hell with the consequences.

Kierkegaard performed his metaphysical rebellion together with his renunciation of the consummation of his love for Regina Olsen. By so doing, he elevated his love to the stature of permanence. He extruded it from the precariousness of spatio-temporality, rendering it timeless. He also prevented it from souring and waning through the levelling down and petrifying routines of matrimony. To yearn for a love, irrespective of the possibilities of its realization, and even being certain that it is unattainable, is to render it absolute. By the same logic, but for diametrically opposite ends, Sade aimed to destroy the longing for love and thereby annihilate love itself. He realized that the prime mover of love is the yearning for it. Hence, the destruction of the longing for love will bring with it as a necessary corollary the extinction of love. This fits Sade's radical nihilistic design of killing sex through boredom by repetitive perversion. Sade wished to be society's ultimate executioner, because without a yearning for an amorous encounter, without a longing for an emotional dialogue, man enters a state of indifference and loneliness, and hence a lack of empathy and desire for involvement with his human surroundings.

Without the longing for union, the act of sex becomes a mere banality, which eventually destroys erotic passions. Without the Tantalic longing for grace and the Sisyphean dreams anchored on sex, the contours of flesh, the texture of skin, the glow of eyes, lose their baiting value and love peters out. By killing erotic desire and the yearning for love, which sustain the human core vectors, Sade meant to halt reproduction, dissolve the human family and disrupt the normative system which he hated. Sade knew that by depriving man of the longing for love, human life, which he despised and aimed to annihilate, would become not only unbearable but totally meaningless and hence not worth living. His negation highlights the basic assertion of life inherent in the longing for love.

Our prince takes the opposite but complementary road. Tasso, knowing his friend and master's masochistic affliction, wrote the following madrigal for him:

> Is this not the hand which
> thrust so many sparks and such

deadly darts into my heart?
Yet here it is found
restrained in my hands,
neither force nor wiles help
 it escape.
It holds neither torch nor
 thunderbolt
to protect itself from me.
It is indeed just that I do not
take revenge on it, love, tho'
it wounded me, I kiss it.

Gesualdo forwent any possibility of the requiting of love, expressly preventing and forbidding its feasibility, so that the woes of its lack would be forever unassuaged. His live-wire chromatism had a violent, disturbing effect when combined with the tortured sado-masochistic texts of his madrigals. The combination of his themes of anguish, death and betrayed love, when expressed with dissonant chromatic music, shakes us to the core. Likewise, his dense ecstatic, sacred music catapults us into painful clashes with transcendence.

The basis of Gesualdo's innovation lies in his introduction into Mannerism (the artistic movement in Italy following the Renaissance and Baroque), the sublimation of his personal torture and agony in the normative themes of the Counter Reformation. Watkins says: "The erotic, secular fantasies of the madrigal are transformed by Gesualdo into ecstatic visions of Marian worship, the dolorous sighs of unrequited love into the mournful cadences of the passion story, the amorous agonies into scriptural utterances which reflect a personal sense of quiet and an unspeakable desperation".[41] His sado-masochistic and manic-depressive alternations could account for the innovative contrasts in his music between diatonism and chromatism, and the overloaded style of his expressionism. The genius of Gesualdo lies, as Einstein points out, in stylistic dualism and in oxymoronic music,[42] in trying to link life and joy and agony, which is our conceptualization of the complementarity between his painful Sisyphean mythogenes of experience and the Tantalic mythogenes of longing. This could only be accomplished by a disrupted personality, with a gaping abyss dividing it into sado-masochism and mania-depression. The Prince of Venosa, the painful recluse, the deviant pariah, made Gesualdo the brilliant madrigalist and innovative expressionist genius.

Chapter four
Caravaggio – The Violent Enlightenment

Washed and laundered
by the rain.
Dried and blackened
by the sun.
The flesh we fed
too much
was long ago devoured.

Francois Villon, *Epitaph for a Hanged Man*

Michelangelo Merisi da Caravaggio was born either on 28 September 1573, as one authority has it,[1] or between September and December 1571, as others claim.[2] Either way, he was Gesualdo's contemporary. Since he was very fond of *madrigalli* and *canzoni*, he quite probably played, or sang, some of the madrigals of the prince of Venosa. Caravaggio spent his early childhood in Lombardy, and about age 12 was apprenticed to a mediocre Milanese painter, Simone Peterzano, from whom he learned the rudiments of mixing paints, the choice of brushes and the construction of frames.

After some years of apprenticeship in Milan, Michelangelo da Caravaggio left for Rome. The first years in the capital were hard and grim. At first, he was employed by a Sicilian painter, Lorenzo, for whom he worked long hours for a pittance. Afterwards, Caravaggio was engaged by the miserly Monsignor Pandolfo Pucci, whom he nicknamed "Monsignor Insalata", because all he fed his employee was vegetable salad.[3] At about that time he became seriously ill and was hospitalized in Santa Maria della Consolatione, where he stayed quite a while; it was there that he painted some of his earlier works, including quite probably *Bacchino Malato*, the sick Bacchus, with himself as model.

Towards the end of the sixteenth century, Cardinal Del-Monte bought his painting *The Cardsharps* and subsequently invited Caravaggio to join the homosexual menagerie of young musicians and painters in his mansion. Caravaggio's homosexual preferences are evident from his paintings, and are also known from independent sources. We also have ample evidence of the painter's quarrelsome, violent nature and predilection for brawling. He had the psychopathic trait of ever looking for stimuli, be they creative or merely sensation-rousing. He would throw stones at his landlady, hurl artichokes at a waiter, and duel a notary at Piazza Navona over the amorous attentions of a woman.[4] In 1606, Caravaggio killed one Ranuccio Tomassoni, his partner in a ball game, and was banished from Rome. In all likelihood, his journey from Milan to Rome in 1592 was actually a flight following a murder he committed. His short fuse and pathological need to seek disputes landed him in trouble all his life. Oftentimes he abused and assaulted his benefactors. Consequently, he was frequently obliged to flee from one place to the other; his death was also caused in a skirmish.

In August 1603, the painter Baglione sued Caravaggio for disseminating defamatory poems about him. The courts decided for the plaintiff and Caravaggio was jailed. He was released by the intervention of the French ambassador, since he was engaged in painting the side wall of the Contarelli Chapel in the church of San Luigi dei Francesi. In October 1604, he was arrested again for assaulting a police officer; in 1605 he injured a lawyer in the face and fled to Genoa. After his banishment from Rome, following the murder of his ball-game partner, he fled to Naples and thence to Malta. He was made a Knight of the Maltese Order of St. John, only to be expelled from it following his offending the Grand Master. He fled to Sicily, was fatally wounded in Naples, and died in Civita Vecchia on 18 July 1610. We hypothesize, by a rather problematic *post facto* inference, that Caravaggio suffered from an ever hungry, insatiable "black hole" personality, as described in chapter one.

This "black hole" of hunger aims to satisfy the ever augmenting longing for the absorption of a "good object". Caravaggio's father died when he was six, an event which could also effect a later oral fixation with a bad object; in such cases, the paranoid part of the personality would also be apparent. Caravaggio's mother was left with four children, the eldest barely six, for whom she had difficulty providing. She could well be described hypothetically as either a physically or mentally absent mother. Therefore, we have a combined insatiable quest for a "good object" to fill in the ever-augmenting "black hole", coupled by a distrust and hatred of all the relevant others. Hence, the non-coordinated personality, with extremely fixated polarities and a gaping black hole in between, was progressively predisposed from infancy to absorb all stimuli, which momentarily relieve want, pain and deprivation, until stimulus-hunger is generated again. This biological predisposition is, of course, complemented by the psycho-cognitive one, since the oral attachment of all young primates to their parents, as shown by ethnologists, is so strong that its deprivation by the parent exacerbates the "black hole" longing initially generated by the biological pre-disposition.

Having assumed that Caravaggio had a later oral developmental fixation, which effected a "black hole" personality with an interactive *atzmi* component and an early oral pure-self participant *ani* component, without the coordinating *ity* to hold them together, the symptomatology of our protagonist's character amply vindicates our assumption.

One can hardly find clear evidence for oral fixations even with contemporary cases, yet the outward manifestations of Caravaggio's "black hole" personality are solidly attested to by his many biographers. He was constantly aggressive, even at great harm to himself. Whenever things were going for him, an inner disrupter, or as denoted by Fairbairn an "internal saboteur", would "decide" that they should not go for him, and he would get into a brawl, offend the powerful or hit a police officer, so that he would be arrested, banished, or had to run for his life; yet all the time he was conscientious with his work, brilliant in its execution and quite punctual in meeting completion and delivery dates.[5] Indeed, there seem to have been two persons within his body. One vain, uncontrollably aggressive, ever ready to start violent escapades; the other an authentic artist, scorning publicity and the aesthetically "in". *Niente belloto*, nothing embellished, was his motto.[6] Whenever he could, he would strive for self-expression in his art as against the expectations of rich and powerful others, even if they were his patrons. This accounts also for his extreme originality, and for his extremism in whatever he did. His early paintings were in the Lombard tradition, but even then he rejected the manneristic style and made nature his model, for which he was severely criticized by members of the mainline trend, who advocated the imitation (mimesis) of the classics. He always rejected artistic convention, fads and fashion, following his inner convictions. In Rome he was influenced by the Venetians, Titian and Giorgione, but he was bolder in the expressionistic presentation of his models. He expressly exaggerated the foreshortening of his subjects, like the horse and the fallen apostle, so as to convey the tumultous *psychomachia*, the inner struggle leading to the conversion of St. Paul. He despised the elitism of Raphael, and painted saints and apostles as common men. He enraged the church hierarchy and the artistic cliques by painting the dead Virgin modelled as an old, drowned whore, her body inflated in *rigor mortis*. He empathized with the explosive violence of Tintoretto and admired Leonardo's *Last Supper,* which he might have studied in Milan. Yet, his *chiaro-scuro* (light and dark alternations) is more extreme and dramatic than Leonardo's *sfumato* (contrasting technique). Caravaggio's starkly contrasting shadows and the light flooding his accentuated subjects are extremely innovative, since the illumination seems to come from nowhere, as if it sprouts from the inner self of the artist to maieutically trigger, a torrent of light within the viewer's *psyche*.

This technique helped Caravaggio to achieve a most innovative effect in his religious paintings. The Counter Reformation developed the powerful methods of practical mysticism, the sacralization of routines and the deification of everyday life. One can see in the religious paintings of Caravaggio one such attempt at *enthousiasmos,* in the classical Greek sense, of imbuing holy revelation into the vicissitudes of history. This was ordained by St. Ignatius de Loyola's *exercitia spiritualia*, and interpreted by Filippo Neri, a contemporary of Caravaggio's, in Rome.[7] The notion that one can seek salvation even through sin, provided one *sincerely repents*, is depicted repeatedly in his art. We have mentioned Mary, the mother of God, depicted in death as the swollen cadaver of a whore (*The Death of the Virgin* [Louvre, Paris]).

Caravaggio's repentant Mary Magdalene, indeed, conveys the excruciatingly painful transformation of a whore into a saint (*The Penitent Mary Magdalene* [Galeria Doria Pampleili, Rome]).

The Crucifixion of St. Peter depicts the dazed pain of an old peasant who cannot bear his torture, showing the peasant's bewilderment at his own martyrdom. Nobody had before painted martyrs with such a humane and down-to-earth credibility, yet with a sublime resignation, which lends an immediate aura of holiness to their suffering (*The Crucifixion of St. Peter* [Santa Maria del Popolo, Rome, Italy])

Caravaggio depicts Christ as a peasant, which the historical Jesus most certainly was. The horse in the painting of the dramatic conversion of St. Paul, which takes up most of the canvas, is a coarse plebeian peasant horse. The first version of the inspiration of St. Matthew shows a proletarian, barefoot peasant or artisan, visibly illiterate, since an angel guides his hand with the writing instrument on the open book. The exertion of writing is evident both in the heavy grasping of both the writing instrument and the book by the saint, as well as the painful twisting of the toes on his left foot (The Conversion of St. Paul [Santa Maria del Popolo, Rome, Italy]; and [Odescalchi Collection, Rome, Italy]); (Matthew and the Angel [destroyed in 1602; panel, San Luigi dei Francesi, Rome, Italy]).

This conception of St. Matthew's revelation was violently criticized and rejected. Indeed, it was seen as an affront to the apostle to present him as an apparently illiterate peasant. Caravaggio withdrew this painting, and evidently had it destroyed. Later, he painted a more acceptable version of St. Matthew and the angel. Yet this first version is the more interesting and a better clue to understanding Caravaggio and his art.

We have described Caravaggio's personality as disrupted by a "black hole", so that it has two non-synchronized core parts: a participant "bad me" surrounded by a "good object", and a separant "good me" surrounded by a "bad object". These two non-aligned components represent two different cognitive orientations. The separant stands for the experiential mythogenes of history and the participant for the mythogenes of longing for transcendence. The process of creativity, for Caravaggio, was also a therapeutic "mending", a "tying up", of his disrupted personality components into meaningful coherence, at least for the duration of the creative process. Hence, the historical figure of St. Matthew – the coarse simpleton – subject to the vicissitudes of the here-and-now, is aligned with the angelic mythogenes of longing for *enthousiasmos*, the descent of grace which would, eventually, transform the illiterate peasant into an apostle of God. Indeed, the light coming from "nowhere", from transcendence and, of course, from the painter's inner self, highlights St. Matthew and the angel, flooding both figures in a synchronic harmony which stands for the painter's own longing to patch up the violent rift in his personality.

Of special importance is Howard Hibbard's observation that Caravaggio must have subscribed to the Pauline and Augustinian theology of divine grace and mercy being determined by God alone, irrespective of man's deeds.[8] This view was prevalent in sixteenth-century Rome, and was suitable for Caravaggio, who could murder, injure, insult and engage in pederasty, and yet believe he would receive God's grace. Moreover, the Counter Reformation ascribed supreme importance to conformity to church authority. *Perinde ac cadaver*, "obey like a corpse", was the motto of the Jesuits. This mandate, decreed for political reasons, was again quite useful for the Borgia, Medici and Berberini popes, who were all highly immoral, as well as for Cardinal Del-Monte and his homosexual entourage. One need not be moral, righteous, or of good deeds; the acceptance of the authority of the church is enough to fare God's grace. It would follow that God, too, need not be moral or righteous, or even comprehensible to humans, since grace would by necessity be mediated through the authority of the church, which is through the pope, the infallible entity. Hence, God may be, and is, arbitrary. Therefore, the crucifiers of St. Peter performed their tasks in cold disinterest, serving an arbitrary

God, who has forsaken His only begotten Son to die on the cross. "All my sins are mortal", uttered Caravaggio after having painted the beheading of St. John,[9] implying that in the eyes of God, he is not a sinner and may yet obtain grace. What with God being cruel, harsh and arbitrary, as depicted in the sacrifice of Isaac, who knew that he is to be slaughtered, with no happy ending in store for him. Caravaggio's attitude towards transcendence is one of distrustful acceptance. One may achieve revelation, therefore, through a creative dialogue, but disaster may be meted out, time and again, without warning. This might well be the meaning of the horse's hoof aimed at St. Paul's head, coincidental to the saint's revelatory conversion.

The swashbuckling image of Caravaggio, as the cad about town hunting for his next victim, is skin deep. The inner Michelangelo Merisi was driven, frightened, sad. His self-image as Medusa, the snake-coiffeured queen of the Gorgons, shrieks fright and the excruciating pain of the stifling judgment by generalized and specific others. The same agony exudes from the severed head of Goliath, another self-portrait, debauched and reflecting an inner rot (*Head of Medusa* [Uffizi, Florence]); (*David with the Head of Goliath* [Gallery Borghese, Rome, Italy – as used on the cover of this book]).

This is Caravaggio's inability to ward off the stigmata hurled at him from all sides, a good part of which he knew to be justified; his fractured personality could not but cope with these stigmata in the only way possible: passing judgment on himself by means of his art. The compassion of David holding the severed head of Goliath, while looking at the debauched self-portrait, is an appeal for mercy to assuage his infernal agonies.

Never has there been a more desperate attempt to bridge over an inner abyss by an artist through an attempted dialogue between his disrupted core personality components (*Martyrdom of St. Matthew* [Contarelli Chapel, S. Luigi dei Francesi, Rome]).

Caravaggio must have considered himself a victim of hostile circumstances beyond his control, and hence stemming from transcendence. This is reflected in the martyrdom of St. Matthew, in which the old apostle lies on his back and his hands, stretched in incomprehensible horror against his tormentor, while the painter himself peers from behind a column at this arbitrary cruelty. There are just a few steps from seeing oneself martyred by the depriving others–objects to perceiving oneself as the chosen, the anointed, the Christ as self-image. The notion of Christ as self-image is the most powerful role model for projective identification. Our self as Christ being ever crucified in our daily tribulations is especially apt for the fiercely competitive, separant Occidental societies where indeed

Christianity has been more readily adopted than in the participant, and less competitive, Oriental cultures. In the rapid rat-race of achievement-oriented cultures, the Christs are both the Sisyphean *arrivistes* and participant self-effacing individuals. The separant achiever is constantly crucified, because there is an ever widening and inevitable gap between his insatiable appetite for "swallowing" the world (controlling his objective and human surroundings) and his actual achievement. Hence, the extrapunitive orientation of the *arriviste* is to claim betrayal and blame it on specific or generalized others. These betrayals legitimize his identification with the betrayed Christ.

The participant, on the other hand, is constantly taken advantage of. His self-effacing orientation *vis-à-vis* the carnivorous others, make him a natural and ready-made victim, yet his identification with Christ enables him to reinforce his sense of uniqueness and perceive the assaults of the surrounding others as proof of it. The participant suffers the abuses of the others, while constantly carrying his saving cross as a dignifying force field guarding his sense of uniqueness. Moreover the image of Christ carries the separant's unrealizable quest for omnipotence in Christ's kingdom to come, when the betrayed – "the meek – shall inherit the earth". This is the epitome of the achievers' wish fulfilment! "Here I suffer but wait, I'll show you yet! When He comes I am going to overcome and prevail and subjugate all my betrayers." The participant may also identify with the suffering Christ, because his self-effacing is an apt precursor to partaking of the Godhead. This fantastic appeal of Christ as a self-image in separant cultures, where everyone could find solace in identifying with Him, irrespective of his personality type, may account for the almost universal prevalence of Christ and his symbols.

The church was quick to realize Jesus' universal function in reinforcing both separant power and participant self-effacing meekness. Hence, His image lends credence, authority and benediction to all social institutions, churches, courts of law. Fighting knights and competing sportsmen, all bear his image. At birth He is the first one to bless the newborn and He is the last one to accompany the soul and body back to their origin.

The need to be martyred has both separant and participant connotations. The separant achiever, creative artist or scientist, when persecuted, hurt or blocked in his professional endeavours, can always reinforce his sense of election by his martyrdom, stating that his enemies persecute him because they are jealous of his excellence, which they may well be. The creative innovators, when martyred by the institutional cliques, as they are hunted by the power structures and blocked by individuals or groups the vested interests of which are hurt by their innovations, may find solace in History. They will bring to mind the cases of Galileo, Jordano Bruno, van Gogh and many others whose persecution partially derived from their genius, because their innovation was far-reaching enough to rock boats. The martyrdom of the creative innovator thus reinforces his self-image as a creator of worth, and supports his claims to excellence by identifying with the martyrdom of other innovators and with that of Christ, the archetypal religious innovator. The *Kiss of Judas* (Betrayal of Christ, [National Gallery of Ireland, Dublin]) portrays a gripping drama of the inevitability of betrayal by the other. Yet, this betrayal is a necessary step in the process of beatification. The embrace of Christ by Judas, and the clutching of their hands, is a partnership in the creation of a saviour through betrayal. Jesus and Judas are partners in the creation of Christ, and Caravaggio peers with approval on the fatal embrace from the upper right-hand corner of the canvas.

Caravaggio's inner revelation is effected by the painter, peering à *la* Narcissus at his reflection in the water. This self-contemplation makes for at least a temporary synchronization of his fractured self into a functional unit to carry out the creative mediation between self, artistic medium and viewers. Especially effective are Caravaggio's revelatory scenes depicting an *enthousiasmos* from transcendence *via* the inner self into objects, others and life-forms in history. The most striking example is the calling of St. Matthew (*The Calling of St. Matthew* [Contarelli Chapel, S. Luigi dei Francesi, Rome, Italy])

Christ stretches out his hand in a stylized, limp gesture, not unlike Michelangelo's God stretching out his hand to the newly created Adam on the ceiling frescoes of the Sistine chapel. This limp gesture forms a synaptic junction which allows for a maieutic flow of dialogue between God and man, transcendence and history, rather than a tactile, epistemic directive, which is authoritarian and does not leave an independent, innovative leeway by man and within man. The incredulous "Who, me?" gesture of Matthew is both a sign of humility and unequivocal acceptance, since doubt is a dialectic which might lead to a higher awareness following a process of soul searching. Matthew's call for authentic *enthousiasmos* does not permit a negation, only a short, inner conflict to come to terms with the flooding, revelatory light, which seems to emanate from the upper right-hand corner; one feels it shine from the glow on the saint's face; the illumination seems to sprout from within. There is probably no better portrayal of the synchronic, sacred time flowing from Christ through the mediation of St. Peter into, and mingling with, the profane diachronic time of Matthew, who is not yet beatified, since he has not yet accepted his divine calling.

However, the most innovative works of Caravaggio are reflexive, in which the painter is both observer and observed, object and subject, within history and outside it. We shall comment on two such paintings: *St. Francis in Ecstasy* (Museo Civico, Cremona, Italy) and *David with the Head of Goliath* (see below).

In the first painting, both St. Francis and the angel have the same facial features, very similar to Caravaggio's. This is a depiction of a dialogue between the painter and his tortured self. It is a sublime effort of *enthousiasmos* of the infusion of angelic grace into the agonized face of the saint, aiming to extricate himself from his sore, inflicted body, and join his sacred alter ego in divine bliss. In this painting, Caravaggio lets us know that his only chance and, to be sure, only way of bridging over his internal abyss, his "black hole", is through the inner "mending" of his art, linking miraculously history and transcendence with himself, as the arena in which this *coincidentia oppositorum* takes place. With *David with the Head of Goliath* (Galleria Borghese, Rome, Italy) we have a fusion of the two types of time. There is the diachronic time of Caravaggio, with Goliath ravaged by the temporal hazards of drink, drugs, sex and violence; and the pure sacred time of Caravaggio's David, exuding a longing for compassion, grace and salvation for everyone, including his corrupt decapitated alter ego. Caravaggio the artist is the anthropic site within whom the mortal conflicts are resolved, momentarily at least, while engaging in the art of creativity; he becomes the mediator, the son of God passing the barrier between the agonies of the here-and-now and the bliss of the ever-after. In the process, his inner "black hole" is patched, glossed and bridged-over for another cycle of Sisyphean creativity, until the stone-burden rolls down in another binge of violent self-destruction, only for the artist to bend down and start pushing the Sisyphean rock upwards in a creative dialogue, *da capo*. The artist, through his dialogue with his object via the artistic medium, creates a new reality which is not only his own and within history, but also divine through the creative, authentic domain.

Michelangelo Merisi da Caravaggio, the painter whom Burckhard denotes as "of low taste", appears today on IL 100,000 bills. The painter whom Bellori called "the destroyer of the art of painting" is considered today the most important artistic innovator of the seventeenth century. He joins van Gogh and Gesualdo in delineating the horizons of artistic possibility, even at the price of their own self-destruction.

Chapter five
Jean Genet – A Criminal Manifesto

> I shall allow myself a certain coquetry and say that I was a clever thief. Never have I been caught red-handed in *flagrante delicto*. But the fact that I know how to steal admirably for my earthly profit is unimportant. What I have sought most of all has been to be the consciousness of the theft whose poem I am writing.
>
> Jean Genet, *The Thief's Journal*

The Set

Jean Genet, the thief–playwright–philosopher, can be considered the mouthpiece of the brotherhood of criminals. The aim of our analysis is to delineate patterns in Genet's writing which illustrate the genesis and mechanisms of stigma, crime and social deviation. In a devastatingly sincere manner, Genet has succeeded in portraying his self-image as a criminal, as well as the ideology of the criminal group. Genet, the thief, deviant and outcast, will serve as the prototype illustrating the stigma theory of crime and deviation expounded in chapter two. He professes to be a perfectionist: "It is because an action has not been completed that it is vile."[1] He records in minute detail his self-image as a criminal and vividly describes the underworld, its norms and values, establishing a diametric negativity to the legitimate world and its institutions.

Genet proclaims the criminal manifesto with the voice of authority and experience; as Sartre says: "Genet the novelist speaking of Genet the thief is more thief than a thief."[2] Genet is an exaggerated instance – almost a parody of the stigmatized criminal and his self-image; but it is precisely this extremeness and exaggeration which make him invaluable to us. He illuminates every step of the stigmatization process and delineates the borders of a seemingly amorphous theoretical premise.

An exaggerated case is valuable for highlighting features, but it gives a very poor image of the middle ranges. We should therefore bear in mind that Genet is far from being a model of the common thief, and is many standard deviations from the mean, mode or median type of the underworld.

Moreover, we must take into account Genet's obsessive and ideological homosexuality, which prevents us from trying to generalize from his self-image and view of his own group, and society at large, to other members of the criminal subculture.

Genet's pederasty can be attributed to his satanic orthodoxy in behaving in a manner diametrically opposed to that prescribed by cultural mandates: If most men are heterosexual, he is homosexual. In addition, homosexuality is part and parcel of the criminal world: ample evidence exists that most long-term prisoners have, to varying degrees, homosexual experiences. Close proximity to a totally male world, long abstinence from heterosexual contact, and the grim routine, press most prisoners to some kind of relationship with their fellow convicts. The intensity of these relationships ranges from the profound homosexuality of a Genet to the anxiety and fears of pederasty that are a mild form on the same continuum of homosexuality. Homosexuality is an organic part of the criminal's world, his folklore and value system, though Genet turns it into an obsession.

The perspective of the observer is all-important in the social and behavioural sciences. Psychology, sociology and mental health devoid of values do not exist. Conclusions, observations, hypotheses and concepts are inevitably dependent on one's standpoint. An industrial psychologist studying "conflict" and "strain" with a view to finding the best ways of preventing them is obviously opposed to conflict and strain in worker–management relationships. A sociologist or criminologist studying the criminal and his group is clearly against crime. On the other hand, a habitual criminal like Genet, who spent a considerable part of his life in prison, describes himself, his colleagues and "the other", i.e. legitimate society, as they are seen from his side of the barricade. This legal and social barricade between "our" criminal world and "your" legitimate world is institutionalized by Genet; he perceives it – as indeed he should, according to our stigma theory – as a normative iron curtain. The criminal is, of course, aware of this barricade, because he bumps into it, to his detriment, almost constantly. Genet, however, perceives the individuals on the "legitimate side" of the barricade as equally preoccupied with being normatively opposite to criminals. The guard in *Death Watch* assures Lefranc that he has to be the very opposite of the criminals and thugs[3] not of the good or bad. This is the recurring theme in our stigma theory: The law-abiding person is defined by exclusion as a non-criminal, and vice versa; definition by opposites contrasts "good" with the "not-good".

The central idea of Genet's play *The Blacks* is this definition by tagging: The blacks, who are the non-whites, are on the opposite side of the "right" side of the barricade. The blacks are the tainted and have been assigned by society the roles of prisoners, criminals and outcasts. In the words of Archibald: "On this stage, we're like the guilty prisoners who play at being guilty."[4] Genet is no doubt "the foremost prince in the lineage of the French *poètes maudits*".[5] He is more profound than Villon and more outspoken and sincere than de Sade. However, the present analysis is solely concerned with Genet's work insofar as it illustrates our stigma theory of crime and deviation. Sartre[6] has established Genet as a saint of existentialism, unearthing new vistas of art and philosophy.

Self-image

Genet's self-image is, no doubt, one of a thief, an "ex-con", a member of the criminal sub-culture. His writings are very personal. Although fact and fiction intermingle, most of the episodes happened in one way or the other, with Genet as participant, resulting in a *mélange* of personal experience, feeling and reminiscence.

Genet was born out of wedlock. His mother abandoned him in his cradle and he was cared for in his formative years in an orphanage of the *Assistance Publique.* He never succeeded in finding out anything about his background. Later he imagined his mother as a thief just out of prison, "an old thief with a pale shifty-looking face".[7]

The state orphanage in due course entrusted him to a foster home – a peasant family in Le Morvan. At first he was happy there. He lived the peaceful life of a village youngster; as a child he was led to believe, as Sartre says, that his soul was white, without sin, without malice.[8]

However, he soon realized that he was not like the other village youngsters. He was a foundling, he had no mother, no father and therefore no clear identity to internalize. The village was a closed community and he soon found out that in the peasant family he was "Jean, the little bastard". The other children in the family attributed any mishap or misdeed to "the little bastard" from the orphanage. He thus became the receptacle for all the unwanted and despised attributes of the family and the small peasant community; his self-image, or inner anchor of identity, consisted of definitions, images and characteristics tagged on him by the relevant others. Young Genet, in a state of "other-directedness", complied with the image built for him by his immediate surroundings. The self-branding and tagging in Genet's case derived from an inner-directed alternative image – from his need to become what he was accused of being: "I owned to being the coward, traitor, thief and fairy they saw in me."[9]

We are, in fact, connecting links in the chain which are not necessarily arranged in a causal sequence; what we are doing could be better described as drawing imaginary lines between the visible peaks of an iceberg. The gaps in our analysis are to be attributed to lack of information or to the fact that Genet's accounts do not necessarily correspond to the actual process which took place. We have the facts of illegitimacy, the initial stay in the orphanage and the upbringing at Le Morvan. We then encounter a youth in an extreme state of other-directedness, who does his utmost to comply with the negative images branded on him by his adoptive family and village. We do not have enough information to formulate a comprehensive account of the process, but we may describe it from the facts we do know, as a typical positive feedback cycle of being rejected by a group and rejecting it in turn; this could be traced to the initial stigmatizing process triggered by the primary fact of being born illegitimate. Genet says:

> The uncertainty of my origin allowed me to interpret it. I added to it the peculiarity of my misfortunes. Abandoned by my family, I felt it was natural to aggravate this condition by a preference for boys, and this preference by one for theft, and the preference for theft by one for crime. I thus resolutely rejected a world which had rejected me.[10]

This is the perpetual vicious circle. The cognitive rejection and counter-rejection could be more of a rationalization by Genet of his inner compliance with the image with which he has been tagged. The "other-directedness" of Genet, his being branded as illegitimate, as "bad" and a thief, and consequently obliging the alters by realizing their image of him, is a display of acquiescence and submission. He wilfully, almost joyfully, plunges into the depths of negativity. He finally knows who he is, he has been given an image he never had – and if the image is that of a pederast and a thief, it has to be honed to perfection. This subconscious process is one phase of a cyclic ambivalence towards the stigmatizing group. The acceptance phase of submitting to the image, and compulsively over-conforming to it, alternates with the cognitive counter-rejection of the painful rejection by the group. This, incidentally, might afford a partial explanation of the "outsider's dilemma", the agonizing, unsuccessful efforts of the outsider to be accepted by society. Our thesis is that the outsider striving to be accepted and acclaimed by society fails because he never wishes to adjust, conform or integrate himself normatively into the group – all he wants is to be accepted as an outsider, thereby asking for the impossible.[11] Such an expectation is somewhat naïve and undoubtedly shallow. The stigma premise seems to afford a deeper insight into the "outsider's dilemma".

Outsiders like Genet, who comply with the images of evil imputed to them by the surrounding "alters", feel that by assuming the role, they serve the group; by being evil because he has been defined as evil, the outsider feels he has fulfilled a mandate – he has been submissive, has conformed to the tagged image, and society owes him, if not acclaim, at least acceptance. Disillusionment is bitter if he is not accepted. Many convicts have personally reported similar feelings to the author. They are accused of committing a crime and against all common prudence they are seized with an urge to confess, a wish to expiate themselves, to turn over a new leaf, to repay their debts in order to be reaccepted – and all this by one magic act of admission, of compliance, of redemption. Some confess even when the prosecution has scant evidence against them, and they subsequently feel a sense of ease; they have been "good" for once by admitting their badness: "You, judge, jury, attorneys, the world at large, you say I am evil; right, I am, but now we are quits. You have to accept me – you owe it to me." The inevitable rejection quickens the cycle of stigma and counter-stigma; this is the meaning of the "outsider's dilemma".

Indeed, being rejected by society, despite his compliance with the image cast on him, Genet feels cheated. He has what seems to him a justified grievance and becomes thoroughly negativistic, with a dual purpose. The first is to perfect the vile image; perhaps his contrariness was not thorough enough, maybe he has not yet achieved the requirements of the relevant others, so that he has to pursue more evil and greater vileness. "When I undertook to accomplish Evil," Genet writes, "I knew it was the only thing that had sufficient power to communicate enthusiasm to my pen, a sign in this case of my perfect allegiance . . . that will, that daring to pursue a destiny that is against all rules."[12] Genet's other purpose is his cognitive rationalization of his rejection of, and counter-rejection by, "your world". This contains more than a tinge of *ressentiment* in it because he never really relinquished his desire to be accepted by conventional avenues, rather than through sordidness and crime. "I wanted", he says, "to give my body and arms an opportunity to assume conventionally beautiful poses which might integrate me into you world."[13] But to no avail!

Nor was his normative transformation instantaneous; he had his inner struggles with the remnants of the conventional morality he had managed to internalize. "I had to combat . . . to abolish what is called remorse."[14] These may have been intermediate stages of an incomplete negation of the normative system of "legitimate society". The exaggerated reaction-formation against these "square" norms indicates an inner struggle, an ambivalence, towards the norms he attacked. However, these stages were passed very quickly, and from his first proclamation as a thief, he seems to pursue his inner identity and salvation furiously. His inner identity longs to fulfil an image: "In children's hells, in prisons, in bars, it was not heroic adventures that I sought. I pursued there my identification with the handsomest and most unfortunate criminals."[15] This identification with criminal images and the desire to play criminal roles are in line with a current theory of criminal behaviour,[16] which presupposes an inner identification with the criminal image prior to outward delinquent behaviour, but does not try to explain why some people identify with criminal images and others with non-criminal ones. The stigma premise can provide a partial explanation: A person tagged with the stigma of a thief will eventually seek the proper criminal images with which to identify, in order to comply inwardly with the image thrust upon him. For Genet, this crystallization of his identity with the ultimate in crime, the perfection in vileness and satanism, became his personal idea of salvation:

> The greater my guilt in your eyes, the more whole, the more totally assumed, the greater will be my freedom. The more perfect my solitude and uniqueness. By my guilt I further gained my right to intelligence. Too many people think, I said to myself, who don't have the right to. They have not paid for it by the kind of undertaking which makes thinking indispensable to your salvation.[17]

Genet would pursue his salvation through the gutters together with his mother, who, he hopes, would be more degraded than himself – proof of her higher saintliness in the dimension of sanctity through degradation: "Had I met my mother and had she been humbler than I, we would have pursued together the ascension, though language seems to call for the word 'fall' or any other that indicates a downward movement, – the difficult, painful ascension which leads to humiliation."[18] This saintliness through filth would be quite similar to St. Jerome's sense of the Medusan beauty in the observation that the filthier a penitent is, the more beautiful he is.[19] In his striving for a diametric reversal of everything which belongs or relates to "your [legitimate] world", Genet even advocates an inversion of connotations. He realizes by intuition the gist of our stigma theory, that name-calling, defining, and tagging do not stimulate reality, *they are reality itself*. He therefore builds a novel, reversed, system of adjectives to exchange the derogatory meaning of theft, cowardice and fear in "your world" with their commendable opposites in "our" world of crime and sin.[20] Treachery, theft and homosexuality are Genet's sacred trinity, which he raises to the rank of a theology (*The Thief's Journal*, p. 149), contrasting them with the cherished bourgeois virtues of loyalty, the sanctity of private property and heterosexuality.

An entire, splendidly inverted *Weltanschauung* is constructed to serve both as an internal mirror and a negation of "your world". Beauty is of the Medusan genre – the more an object is ugly, dirty and disfigured, the more it is magnificent and attractive (*The Thief's Journal*, p. 91). Genet revels in and adores filth (*The Thief's Journal*, p. 24) – he reveres it as the counterpart of the Protestant "cleanliness is next to godliness" ethic. Shame is great, marvellous, magnificent; he applies these adjectives to the Carolinas, the transvestites of Barrio Chino in Barcelona, whom he lovingly calls the Daughters of Shame (*The Thief's Journal*, p. 65). He would have accepted with shame (an emotion he cherishes) that his soul was rotten, since it emitted "an odour that makes people hold their noses" (*The Thief's Journal*, p. 72). He takes pleasure in shame not out of a "sour-grapes" resentment, but as the inevitable corollary of stigma. "Jean, the young bastard, whom I gave shelter to, cared for like a son, and the thankless treacherous thief started to steal from us", they said about him. Whatever they said became reality, the plain truth, the only reality known to Genet himself. He fulfilled their wish, he performed his duty. By becoming the deserved receptacle of their scorn, he earned their praise. If "your world" is delaying the payment of commendable recognition and acceptance, something is apparently wrong with the system of values, the adjectives are upside-down, and connotations should be reversed. Eventually we shall trace this reversal of the normative system of "your world" as the basic link unifying the stigmatized and rejected into underworld groups, initiating the processes of association into criminal subcultures.

Young Genet was sent to reform school, which proved to be the cornerstone of a career which included begging in Spain, thieving in France, deserting from the Foreign Legion, being a male prostitute and smuggling drugs all over Europe. After several years of this, Genet and "your world" could have no love for each other; their contacts were thenceforth belligerent through the gaps in the legal and social barricade which separates them. Genet, the little bastard who obliged his relevant alters by becoming what he was tagged to be, gave way to a belligerent outsider whose own cherished evil is contrasted with the fake evil of "your world". The prime meaning of theft for Genet is its being diametrically opposed to the legitimate world: "For half an hour I shall be operating (committing a burglary) in a world which is the reverse of the customary world. I do not think specifically of the proprietor of the place, but all my gestures evoke him" (*The Thief's Journal*, p. 155).

The adroitness and literal-mindedness of the criminal world is contrasted with the hypocrisy, smoothness and double standards of "your world". Apparently the two different brands of evil, the personal satanism of Genet and the monstrosity of "your world", were conceived by him as force-fields combating and repelling each other. He likens himself to the mother who reared and guarded her monster daughter. "Within herself she ordained an Alter where she preserved the idea of the monster. She set herself up against the world, and against the world she set up the monster, which took on the proportions of the world and its power. It was on the basis of the monster that new principles were ordained, principles constantly combated by the forces of the world which came charging into her, but stopped at the walls of her home where her daughter was confined" (*The Thief's Journal*, p. 28). Here we have a consecrated inner monstrosity to offset the monstrosity of the world. The world of evil is taken for granted. The relationship between the ego and the generalized alter is constant war and combat. The way to defend oneself against the greater evil is by an internal shield of evil. This is something quite different from the Hobbesian *Homo homini lupus*, the Sartrean "Hell is other people". For Genet, the foundation, the very heart of human society, is evil in every possible sense, and the individual's inner evil is a writhing, struggling part of it. This is no controversy involving ethical judgement, of good or relative good against evil. It is a fight between a greater evil and a lesser one.

We shall deal later with Genet as a member of the criminal group; at this stage we wish to analyze the state of mind of Genet, the individual criminal. He professes to be happy in his despair; his ecstatic adoration of destruction borders on a love affair with Thanatos. Perhaps this is proof of the psychoanalytic contention that crime is fuelled by a self-destructive urge, by a wish to be punished for unresolved subconscious guilt. This does not seem to be the case if we rely on the evidence gleaned from the present study. The act of crime for Genet means vigour, freedom and fulfilment. Vigour, because one puts a lot of energy and concentration into an act of stealing; it has a "terminal oneness", a combination of sacrifice and damnation which for Genet is the epitome of moral vigour. Freedom, because the commission of a crime or a betrayal gives one a sense of ease without any moral preoccupation, a feeling of expiatory detachment (*The Thief's Journal*, p. 215). Fulfilment, because the inner violence of the act of theft gives it a ritualistic and religious aura – a sacrifice, an offering;

Genet literally used to dedicate his crimes to various persons and objects. Crime is therefore an expiating sacrifice, a black satanic sacrifice. This is borne out by the fact that the flowers seemed black to him when he laid them on the alter of a church whose collection box he had stolen that morning (*The Thief's Journal*, p. 79). It was a black mass offering at night in a dark and empty church. The ritualistic black offering inherent in a crime brings expiation and fulfilment. This combination of vigour, freedom and fulfilment associated with the act of crime, seems to fit the stigma premises rather than the "guilt – quest for punishment – crime" formula.

When Genet commits a crime he is in a state of "ego-diffusion", to borrow Erikson's concept:[21] Of unknown origin, no parents, no past, a precarious present and uncertain future, he at last finds his coveted ego-identity, one that is not only cast upon him, but is his alone; nobody is going to challenge him to it or take it away from him, as they did other things. The compliance with the image of a criminal not only gives him an individual ego-identity, but also makes him eligible for entry into the group of other thieves and homosexuals, thus affording the opportunity for group identity and a sense of belonging.

Empirical confirmation of this hypothesis was provided by Lewin, who showed that the emotional tension of adolescents was greatly diminished when they finally became members of a criminal gang, where they presumably found their coveted "ego-identity".[22] The crucial point, however, is that every new act of crime reinforces this ego identity with a resultant feeling of accomplishment, elation and vigour. But the sense of fulfilment accompanying a criminal act is more complex and conjectural, possibly owing to the sense of pollution ingrained into the criminal stigma.

The black religiosity of Genet induces him to apply rituals to each step in his evil transformation. Each negation is a triumph. Murder should be performed as a human sacrifice to the accompaniment of a black mass. Being a criminal as a vicarious obligation to others, as a sacrifice to others, insofar as one complies with an image tagged on him by others, is a sacrifice worthy of fulfilment. The salvation through the gutters here is apparently not confined to Genet himself; it is a sort of cleansing vehicle for the pollution of others. He is the scapegoat, the damned. As with stoning, all the evils of the community are cast off and transferred symbolically to him. By receiving these stigmatizing stones he is ritually expiated: he cleanses them of their sins by taking them upon himself. This is the basis of his claim for ritualistic fulfilment – the beatitude of a thief. However, there is no hope of resurrection for him; he knows by now that his vicarious expiation of the evil of others by being their scapegoat will not be paid for with social acceptance in this world or by heavenly love in the hereafter. The dilemma of the outsider emerges again in full force. Genet once had a gaze filled with love which did not perceive "the striking features which cause individuals to be regarded as objects".[23]

Genet, the existentialist criminal saint, ceased to love because other people invariably became objects incapable of giving love, or apparently of receiving it. The fulfilment, therefore, is to destroy this love built with sin.[24] This previous love of others should be transformed into a ritual of destroying "your world". The previous joyful obedience is transformed into fires of hatred of "your world". Love of others is carnivorous and greedy.[25] It should be feared and destroyed. Eros should be transformed into a ritual of Thanatos, for which every new crime against "your world" is an act of expiatory fulfilment. A thief actually appears to Genet in the image of a destroying angel.[26] For psychoanalysts, punishment is the subconscious delegate of guilt which presses the individual towards crime.[27] The present case study does not uphold this hypothesis. For Genet the primary essence lies in the act of crime and the existence of a criminal in the group. Punishment is a drudgery, a necessary evil regarded as a professional risk. It has no grandeur, nor is it desired; all it evokes in him are the reminiscences of prison smells, paint, formaldehyde and urine.[28]

The Group

Genet describes the structure of the criminal group as a loosely organized band. The leaders, the "directors", choose the location of the "job", draw the plans, supervise the performance and sell the stolen property for a considerable commission.[29] Social status within the gang is difficult to determine, because criminals usually magnify their exploits. Thieves have an innate need to boast of their successes after a theft, and they persist in doing so even if they know that their bragging is frequently the cause of their apprehension. The main assets of a leader are not unlike those of a company executive: "brains", know-how, charisma, or, in Genet's words, mysterious brilliance and scintillating magnetism (*The Thief's Journal*, p. 25). The younger members of the group are the bold performers, the daring lackeys, who carry out the job; the old-timers offer advice, professional hints and reassurance (*The Thief's Journal*, p. 59). The criteria for mobility in the group include the reputation of a "bruiser", a "tough-guy", a record of spectacular jobs involving dare-devil stunts, a rich criminal career, and years in prison.[30]

The king of them all, however, is the murderer. A thief is a beginner; if somebody is called the "slasher" and has a dozen armed robberies to his name, he is fine, but in order to reach the top, to achieve the peak of status and prestige, "you need a murder with all the trimmings. Nothing else'll do."[31] The group is held by a crude but severe normative system, "a rough-and-ready morality", which regulates relations between its members and very often determines their fate by prescribing sanctions. There is a strong norm for comradeship and mutual help among the members of the group. "Squealing" and "ratting" to the police are the unpardonable sins. Pimps and homosexual prostitutes often betray their mates to the police and are therefore despised as the scum.[32]

Certain norms are actually rules of professional ethics. Amongst criminals, one must not murder without financial motive; a burglar who killed a mate "to settle an old score" took a five-franc note from the scene, so "nobody'll say I committed murder without getting something out of it".[33] The techniques of crime and the pressures to join the criminal group, as described by Genet, uphold some of the sociological theories as to criminal subculture formation and the manner of operation of its members. The social pressures to join the group of criminals and deviants serve as an appropriate ground for stigma premises, affording a perspective as to the place of stigma in the other social pressures towards crime and deviance. The planning of an operation and its execution by the group involves the integration of several individual functions and complex skills. This would support Sutherland's basic axiom that crime is largely a group phenomenon, transmitted and acquired by association with the criminal group, and the learning of patterns of criminal behaviour and techniques.[34]

An operation is conceived first of all on the basis of information from "the intelligence service". A night watchman tips the gang as to worthwhile places for burglaries. The operation must be carefully planned, in order to allocate the right tasks to the appropriate gang members, and to allow for the unforeseen, the surprise element.[35] The techniques of crime are many and varied, and success depends mostly on applying the right method to specific "mugs". For instance, when stealing from homosexuals, one "should let the guy come up to you, keep him dangling, act a little surprised when he suggests that you do it".[36] One should recognize the right time to strike and with whom to act dumb. An example of the complicated and elaborate technique employed in property offences is the method of stealing from jewellers' showcases. This involves teamwork; one distracts the attention of the detective, another flirts with the salesgirl, while a third examines a piece of jewellery and quickly replaces it with a similar counterfeit piece. A "quick snatch" of goods on display is more dangerous, but more spectacular and daring.[37]

The actual initiation of group members into the life of crime fits the three theoretical components of the sociological exposition concerning the pressures towards criminal behaviour previously mentioned. These are:

1 *Differential Identification*: Daniel Glaser[38] contends that prior to a person's actual criminal behaviour, he adopts criminal values and roles, and sees himself as a criminal or law-violator. When his self-image is deviant, he is ripe for association with criminals.
2 *Differential Opportunity Structure*: After the identification with criminal images, there must then be access to illegitimate social structures for the actual criminal association to take place. Cloward and Ohlin[39] describe the way in which an individual becomes aware of the availability of illegitimate opportunities and finds access to them.
3 *Differential Association*: This is the process of actual initiation into criminal or deviant behaviour, by means of association with a criminal group, and learning the criminal techniques and patterns of behaviour. Unless an individual is mentally deranged and the manifestations of his mental aberration constitute the offence, delinquency is deemed a group phenomenon, the patterns of which are transmitted to new members by learning and association.[40]

The differential identification process is illustrated in the role-playing of Stilitano, one of Genet's criminal mates. He used to invent roles of criminals and "big shots"; he also invented gangster attitudes and cherished his image as a dangerous outlaw, and constantly acted the role.[41] Darling, one of the thief–pimp–homosexuals of *Our Lady of the Flowers*, dresses up as a "big shot" to impress his mates, to appear as the "big-time" criminal he imagines himself to be. Darling actually dresses up for prison. He imagines the effect of each new set of clothes on his past or future prison mates at Fresnes or La Santé.[42] Access to illegitimate structures is sought at a tender age. Members of juvenile gangs engage in petty pilfering while they wait for the chance to join the big fellow, whom they revere and who commits real crimes.[43] The young beginner longs to be accepted by the "real man" of the criminal group and to win his friendship; then he feels that he "has made it".[44]

The differential association process is clearly depicted by Genet when he describes the learning process by which the more experienced criminal, "the chief", the "liege lord", would divulge the secrets of the trade to novices. The bosses instruct new recruits how to steal from churches, the techniques of robbing villas and the ways of prostituting themselves with sailors.[45] In one prison, where a school for pick-pockets had been organized, the "pupils" had to practise on sleeping prisoners; they had to empty all their pockets and replace the contents without waking them. The gist of the operation was to tickle the victim in the right places so that he would turn over in his sleep to reveal the required pockets.[46]

Having studied some of the sociological processes leading to crime and deviation as background for our main concern with the elements of stigma inherent in Genet's work, we shall proceed to analyze those elements as reflected in his criminal menagerie.

The exclusive function of stigma, definition by negatives, operates according to Genet by the label "thief" itself. It determines a man's identity, the chief essence of which is theft. An antisocial label simplifies the image of a person: by calling a person a thief, you reduce to irrelevance all his other roles and attributes.[47]

Stigmatization by tagging, defining by symbolic elements of dress and behaviour, is the starting point of the process of segregating the criminal from the rest of society. Even a seemingly unimportant detail, a single pocket on the left side for convicts in Devil's Island, can suffice to distinguish these convicts from the rest of the world.[48]

A more basic element of the stigma premise is the classic instance of a child's behavioural compliance with the image branded on him. This is the pressure exerted by the group on an individual. Genet the child became a thief because he was stigmatized as such. When the child was caught stealing by the mother superior in charge of his school and asked why he had stolen, all he could answer was: "Because the others thought I was a thief."

Once an individual has been labelled a thief, many other derogatory attributes stick to him quite easily. The labels of outlaw and outcast make him more susceptible to other tags: he becomes a sort of "fly-paper" attracting offensive adjectives. "First they'll say that he's a thief, therefore his feet stink, and his teeth and his mouth; that he sucks his thumb, and talks to himself when alone."[49] If somebody has been cast out of the community, he must be made as different as possible; a thief or an outsider cannot possibly remain a normative or legal outcast, and the stigma process piles on him label after derogatory label in order to make his apartness more and more conspicuous. Once this process has really pushed the stigmatized person out of all possible legitimate roles and statuses, he actually has no choice but to operate within the confined boundaries of his stigma. If we have been painted black, we might as well act as complete cannibals. In the words of Archibald, a masterfully portrayed combination of satanic preacher and black Muslim:

> I order you to be black to your very veins. Pump black blood through them. Let Africa circulate in them. Let Negroes negrify themselves. Let them persist to the point of madness in what they're condemned to be, in their ebony, in their odour,

> in their yellow eyes, in their cannibal tastes. Let them not be content with eating Whites, but let them cook each other as well. Let them invent a criminal painting and dancing. Negroes, if they charge toward us, let it not be out of indulgence, but terror.[50]

The whore in *The Screens* is another instance of stigma portrayed by Genet. She points out that the real essence of prostitution is compliance with the image cast on her by her clients.[51] The particular role of the whore is what she gets paid for; whims, unfulfilled desires and perversions are projected onto the prostitute, who caters thus to her stigmatizers' frustrations.

One cannot run away from the stigma with which one is branded. Green-Eyes, the handsome murderer in *Death Watch*, tried at first to shake off his mark of Cain, but to no avail. "I didn't want mine", he said. "It chose me. It fell on my shoulders and clung to me. I tried everything to shake it off".[52] It just stuck; there was no choice but to accept it with fatalism. The stigmatized person has very little choice but to mould himself according to the cast set by his entourage of alters. The mother of the thief, for example, knows that if he goes to jail, it is not just to pay for his crimes in the past or in the present, but to receive his just deserts for the thefts he is sure to commit in the future. The judges and public[53] have already determined his future for him: "once a thief always a thief". He stops being an individual, and becomes a prototypical thief roaming the collective mind of "public opinion".[54] Genet proceeds to rely on his peculiar brand of gutter psychoanalysis when describing the safety-valve function of stigma: The thief receives all the soddy, slimy and larcenous cravings of "your world", of good, law-abiding citizens. "Your world" projects it onto him, and he has to accept this transference. You have to be thankful to the thief for taking your criminal cravings upon himself, albeit without choice, but complacently; otherwise, you respectable folks "will steal cutlets and chickens in your dreams every night".[55]

The finality of stigma, the pressure to act like the murderer one has been branded as being, has the power of destiny and finality of Greek Fate. Green-Eyes was crazed at first: He tried to back out, to adopt any other image but that of a murderer; he tried to be a dog, a cat, a horse, a tiger, even a rose, but he could not: even his body was tuned to the act of murder.[56] Murder was for him as inevitable as it had been for Oedipus.

Concerning the stigma of conviction, Genet is even more final, almost disinterested. The stigma of conviction is the prime mover towards more crime and deviance. Proof of guilt of subsequent offences is unnecessary. Having already been convicted of theft, one is guilty as far as the stigmatizing public is concerned forever and ever. The presumption of innocence is mere make-believe. Every casual accusation results in conviction. If one has been convicted, it means that one is capable of the deed[57] and will perform it again and again. A man may come out of prison, having served his sentence, but he is still a thief.[58] He may even be innocent, but if people think that he is guilty, guilty he is. "With a mug like mine, I can do anything I like. Even when I am innocent, people think I'm guilty."[59] This segregation and definition, tagging and separating the stigmatized criminal and deviant from the rest of "your world", results in a class of outcasts who must unite for sheer survival, creating a normative system of its own. This system is based on the common denominator of apartness, but also needs a common value system and an apology.

Criminals and deviants must find justification for being criminal; "otherwise how could one live?" (*The Thief's Journal*, p. 10). Like everyone else, they must create a coherent self-image and determine for themselves the essence of their reference and membership groups. Criminals and deviants envelop themselves in a garment woven of rationalizations and explanations used to build and define their image as members of a criminal and deviant group, and to protect themselves from the corroding attacks of "your world".

The novice criminal looks for value rationalizations to account for his criminal deeds. Not so the hardened professional – he has no illusions. His ambivalence towards legitimate norms is a thing of the past; he knows that the immediate aim of his crime is gain, pure and simple. The trinity of moral vigour, freedom and fulfilment imputed by Genet to his own crimes is inevitably related to the criminal and deviant existence of the group as a whole. Moral vigour is also inherent in the acceptance of its destiny (*The Thief's Journal*, p. 101). In terms of stigma, we may interpret this feeling of right and propriety as the group's fulfilment of the role forced on it. Its members have finally become what "your world" has destined them to be, an isolated group for whom a certain space has been allocated outside the borders of legitimized norms. By accepting the roles of criminals or outsiders in a special group, they have been institutionalized within the social structure, albeit the "wrong" side of it. They have performed the functions expected of them and are therefore "entitled" to a feeling of rectitude, propriety and moral vigour. Genet also describes the liberating ecstasy of the act of killing:[60] Green-Eyes feels calm and relaxed after the murder that would eventually lead him to the guillotine,[61] because the confusion as to his identity and self-image has been clarified; he is a murderer now – how could it be otherwise? Nobody had ever doubted that he would eventually end up under the guillotine. The sense of liberation is incidental to the dispersion of the confusion as to one's self-image. Being a criminal clarifies every subsequent criminal act, which in turn reinforces the resolution of inner conflicts. The thief in the group defines himself by his crime; he delimits his social contours, liberates himself from confusion and sets himself in order.[62]

The fulfilment inherent in the criminal existence of group members is the consequence of the ritualistic nature of their crimes. Murder is to be performed by a "noble gesture".[63] Murder should be a ritual with the solemnity of a Black Mass; it should be a rite of hatred.[64] The fulfilment in murder also stems from the pollution "earned" by it; this is the final and irredeemable "badness", the point of no return, social damnation. The positive feedback cycle of mutual rejection and counter-rejection has culminated in the sacrificial flow of blood.[65] The polluted have passed judgement both on themselves and on "your world". Murder is considered the most noble of crimes, because more than any other, it has the ritualistic finality of severing its perpetrator from "your world", the society of legitimized fakes.[66]

The murderer holding the knife, the gun or the poison phial, is in the super-human and extra-lucid state of the damned.[67] He has begun his descent (or ascent). The outcast pollutes himself for the sake of others. A self-willed scapegoat, he hurls himself to the bottom of the pit, ritualistically damning and polluting himself in full compliance with his stigma. He thus achieves expiation and fulfilment. For good measure, he dreams that he ejaculates into the toothless mouth of the old man he has just strangled.[68] Members of the criminal group quite often do not mind, and are sometimes even glad, to go to prison. This is not, as the psychoanalysts claim, because of an inner urge to be punished which makes prison the *raison d'être* of their crimes, but because they feel a sense of belonging to the inmate world and/or have high status in it (*The Thief's Journal*, p. 111). Genet himself displayed many traits of "prisonization" – prison being for him a place of relative security where lovers could be procured in abundance and with ease. The members of the criminal group, through Genet their spokesman, felt a morbid affection for the world of prisons and penal colonies. They would not have wanted to transform them into a "your world" kind of life. The disheartening message to penologists would be that the hard core of the underworld retain their nostalgic affection for the world of criminals and prisoners; this world is a part of "our world", and is not a tool for reforming the criminal into a boring, nauseating member of "your world" (*The Thief's Journal*, p. 136).

Genet feels that the prison leaves an imprint on the convict's external features, the signs of the penal colony being cropped hair and heavy muscles; the personality of the convict also radiates hypocrisy, violence and fierceness (*The Thief's Journal*, p. 252). These signs, taken by many criminologists from Lombroso to the modern Sheldon as casual factors in the genesis of crime, are identified by Genet from his own experience as the traits acquired from prolonged incarceration and violent interaction with the society of inmates.

"Your world": The Image of Society

To the members of the criminal group "your world" is surrounded by a glass wall. This is the wall of laws, norms and mores for criminals and other outsiders to crash against (*The Thief's Journal*, p. 88). The overwhelming image of "your world" is one of a force field, a branding and degrading mechanism which operates by brute power and whose prime movers are geared to everything, except the so-called morality and justice as defined by "your world".[69]

Another feature of legitimate society, as perceived by the criminal group, is its preoccupation with forms, outer shells, empty gestures, rather than content and inner meaning. "Your world" consists of image-makers for whom the picture of an object is more important than the object itself.[70] External appearance above all is cherished by Mr. Blankensee in *The Screens*, a bizarre cross between a bourgeois Gentilhomme and Babbit. He is very upset about losing his padded clothes: "Without my pad on my belly, what would I look like? My pad is the chief element of my glamour. So are my boots . . . ". [71] "Your world" renders impossible any sincere and open-hearted communication between individuals: It is mortally afraid of any direct flow of emotions among individuals, who rely heavily on the separating effects of pomp and insolence (*The Screens*, p. 123). The outwardly righteous and scrupulous bourgeois conceals within his murky brain "treasures of duplicity, hatred, meanness, cruelty and lust" (*The Screens*, p. 230).

A paradox and a dilemma result: If "your world" on the legitimate side of the legal and social barricade consists largely of a bunch of thieves who are hypocrites to boot, how can an "honest" thief assert his criminal identity? He is, alas, inside the normative boundaries of "your world" when he steals. A conscientious thief, laments Genet, is bound to be forever frustrated because in a society of thieves, he conforms to the norm, he commits a model act when stealing. "If I steal here", Genet contends, "I perform no singular deed that might fulfil me. I obey the customary order, I am not committing evil. The outrageous is impossible, I am stealing in a void" (*The Screens*, pp. 96–7). The confusion here might stem, if we ignore Genet's vitriolic sarcasm, from an overlapping of roles; a thief's role of complying with the expectations of his stigma is marred by the fact that the stigmatizers themselves are thieves. The conspicuousness inherent in stigma is levelled down by the comradeship in larceny between criminal and victim. Genet leaves no doubt as to the criminal group's attitude and his own towards various social institutions.

The one institution close to Genet's heart and to the welfare (or misfortune) of the underworld is, of course, the police, which represents legitimate society and its institutions. As the official delegates of "your world", they are crooked by definition: they are always willing to have "their palms greased" (*The Screens*, p. 197) and collaborate, for a consideration, with the underworld. Genet himself feels a certain affinity with the police. His admiration for them stems from his belief that they are trained to kill.[72] Their profession is a corrupting agent and the realization of this fills him with a spiteful pleasure. "The search bulletins posted on walls, the photos and descriptions of wanted criminals, the contents of the registers, the objects under seal, create an atmosphere of foul infamy and it gives me pleasure to know that these big strapping fellows are breathing it in and that it is corrupting them, that it is evilly corroding their minds."[73]

The criminal group as a whole is less enamoured of the police: They know that the real game here is dog eat dog and the only relationship is unending warfare. The stakes are the confession by or conviction of the criminal. The police try to achieve their ends by means of interrogation, which often includes violence.[74] But the criminal has a trump card – he can withhold his confession. The crucial point is that members of the criminal group believe that the police do not really care whether someone has actually committed a crime. Guilt is outside their interest – all they are after is a conviction to enter in their files. The prominence of stigma in determining their brand of guilt is portrayed by the following conversation between two police officers apprehending a suspect:

> "Let him go. Come on, Gaubert. After all, he hasn't committed a crime."
> "Him with that baby doll mug of his? He's capable of it, all right." (*The Screens*, pp. 59–60)

Looking capable of committing an offence is proof.

Another aspect of stigma emerges from the dialogue between the policeman and the flute-player in *The Screens*. The flute-player is accused of confusing the order of things, of infringing every decent rule and legal norm, when he played two flutes with his nostrils. The flute-player, in the best tradition of innovators, tried to explain to the judge that it took him two years to perfect the art of playing with his nostrils, but he did not realize that the mere conspicuousness, difference, strangeness and irregularity inherent in his innovation were the necessary evidence to prove his guilt. The policeman, in the best tradition of the righteous law-enforcer, deplores the thanklessness of the criminal; "We" – legitimate society, which he as a policeman represents – "give you everything: schools, hospitals and police-stations . . . We try to be humane to you, but the better we treat you scum of the earth, the worse you become" (*The Screens*, p. 58). This is reminiscent of the "give them hell" school of criminal justice and the well-known speeches by J. Edgar Hoover on the "vermin of the underworld" and the "sewer-rats spawned by prisons". The policeman takes it as a personal affront if the criminal fails to confess, or even worse, tries to escape. This, he feels, is a scheme, a plot against him: the criminals are trying to ruin his career. This is what comes of being decent to this scum. The politicians and policy-makers up there are full of rights for the criminals "and nothing but duties for us policemen. They even advise us to talk to you politely . . . you little louse", laments the gendarme. "They have really funny notions, the boys up there at the top, with their politeness: I'd like to see them in close contact with you, like us little blokes."[75]

The prison governors, the turnkeys and the guards and the rest of the echelon of the administration of justice, " . . . are not all fools", decides Genet condescendingly, "but they are purely indifferent to the game they play" (*The Balcony*, p. 19). They are neutral in this war between "our world" and "your world". They are like keepers of tombs totally disinterested in the identity of the corpses they guard. Racketeers, crooks, pimps, forgers, killers, are all the same to them, cell-fodder to fill the prison. All they ask is to leave them alone; and if you do they won't bother you. The judicial system more than any other branch of the administration of justice yields the branding tools of formalized stigma. However from the stigmatized side of the barricade, it appears that the judge needs the criminal much more than the criminal needs the judge. The phoney judge in *The Balcony* realizes that his whole existence depends on his being able to declare thieves to be thieves and treat them accordingly: "My being a Judge", he tells the prostitute-thief, "is an emanation of your being a thief." The judge illustrates the main theme of chapter one by declaring that stigma can divide the bad from the good by declaration. Stigmatizing is therefore one of the main functions of the judge: "If no line had to divide the Good from the Evil, what use would I be?" (*The Balcony*, p. 20).

In this phoney world, Genet believes that, being a thief, he gives an ethical anchor to the world. He does a wonderful service to the "legitimate" world in providing the criterion (a false one, of course) for dividing the black from the white. As the judge says to the thief: "I'm going to be judge of your acts! On me depends the weighing, the balance. The world is an apple; I cut it in two: the good, the bad. And you agree, thank you, you agree to be the bad" (*The Balcony*, p. 20).

Without criminals there are no judges, no punishment and no condemnation; yet to condemn is the essence of judging and justice. It is as if the criminals owe the judges their crime, so that by meting out just deserts, they can perform their function. Here again the criminal has all the trump cards. What if he does not wish to confess, does not choose to play the game of "your world" by committing the kind of crime that a "your-world" judge can condemn, if he refuses to take upon himself the projected guilt of the judge? How is the judge going to assert his righteousness? The judge in *The Blacks* is horrified at the prospect. If there is no corpse at all (that is, no crime), he exclaims in fright, "Why, that could kill us".[76] The judge reproachfully implores the criminal not to rock the boat, not to shatter the order of things. The show must go on, and if the criminal becomes somewhat sick of his role, the judge accuses him: "It's you who keeps stalling, you promised us a re-enactment of the crime so as to deserve your condemnation" (*The Blacks*, p. 25).

So the judges need criminals; they can be defaced, can have no identity, anyone at all would be enough to comply with the forms and spirit of justice; whether or not they have committed crimes matters least of all. If they come before us we shall decide their guilt for them; after all, the function of the judge is to declare guilt and innocence. Objective innocence does not exist and if we declare someone guilty, he is guilty or becomes guilty. This is the way judicial stigma operates. The following is the image of justice, portrayed by a judge in "your-world" in *The Blacks*:

> "Who's the culprit? You won't answer? I'm offering you one last chance. Now listen: it doesn't matter to us which of you committed the crime. We don't care whether it's X, Y, or Z. If a man's a man, a Negro's a Negro, and all we need is two arms, two legs to break, a neck to put into the noose, and our justice is satisfied. Come, be decent about it." (*The Blacks*, p. 109)

The dilemma here is expressed by the Qadi in *The Screens*; being branded by the judge reinforces the criminal's self-image. His identity has been clarified for him, which is literally essential for his coherent self-perception. Genet presents Said, the defendant, as actually pleading with the Qadi to convict him, otherwise "you'd be killing me",[77] his ego-identity is in danger of diffusion. But if the problems of the criminal are solved by the Qadi, who is out to solve his own problem, what criteria should be used for branding the stigma of conviction which he is actually obliged to do? God? Yes. "God knows all . . . but He is no longer here . . . God has lit out, skidaddled, scrammed. God has gone away" (*The Screens*, pp. 45–6). Morality is a nursery rhyme, a fairy-tale; both "your-world" and "our-world" are rife with larceny, false pretence, dishonesty and even murder.

How should a judge, a Qadi, decide whom to brand with stigma and whom not to brand? These problems are very rarely related to the material issue, or to the offence of which the defendant is accused. Genet and his Qadi may not have the inclination to look for those symbolic links between the personality of the stigmatized, his behaviour and the actual tag branded on him. What they did sense is the absence of any clear-cut scale of measuring rods to define the criminal or the deviant. They reject the conventional criteria of religion, morality and justice. The gist of the dilemma is summarized by the Qadi himself: "It is all right for you, Said, because you have me to tag you, to identify you for yourself. I see very well", he says, "what you gain by each new condemnation." Said, the defendant, receives a reinforcement of his ego identity with each new condemnation; but who is going to define the judge for the judge? "But what about me"? cries the Qadi. "To where does each new condemnation lead me?" (*The Screens*, p. 47). Apparently nowhere: without saintliness and sin, without right and wrong, without good and evil, there can be no criminals, and without criminals there are no judges, and the circle is complete.

Of the four major objectives of criminal justice: retribution, expiation, deterrence and reformation, Genet imputes to his judge only the first two. It is not surprising that he does not impute any utilitarian purposes to the judiciary. A sentence intended to reform an offender would obviously seem to him a contradiction in terms. Prevention or social defence against crime is purely a "your-world" affair. The primary purpose of judicial punishment is talionic retribution. The Roman Tables brand of *talio* seems too sophisticated for Genet. His Qadi interprets retribution with the crude symmetry of the Code of Hammurabi (*The Screens*, p. 44). Expiation as a purpose of punishment has been the perennial escort of retribution. From the point of view of the bench, expiation is achieved when the defendant submits to the judicial powers of the court; objective guilt is not enough; subjective recognition of guilt, submission, humility, and in our terms, willing acceptance of the stigma of guilt and conviction not only lower the retributive drive of the court but also amount to expiation. In *The Blacks*, Archibald urges his fellow defendants to squat, and humbly asks the judge if they may whimper. The judge then orders the defendants to tremble: "Tremble! Harder! Tremble! Come on, shake!"[78] This is the proper courtroom atmosphere for the judge to carry out his judicial duties. The defendant, by his confession of the crime, experiences an expiatory release of tension, a sensation of liberating fulfilment ensuring the acceptance of stigma. Our Lady of the Flowers actually has no control over the confession, which keeps surging in his chest, upwards and outwards:

> First, there came from his liver, right up against his teeth, the confession of the old man's murder. He didn't make the confession. But the confession was rising, rising. If he opens his mouth, he'll blurt it all out. He felt he was lost. Suddenly he gets dizzy. He sees himself on the pediment of a not very high temple. "I'm eighteen, I can be sentenced to death", he thinks quickly. If he loosens his fingers, he fails. He pulls himself together. No, he won't say anything. It would be magnificent to say it, it would be glorious. No, no, no! Lord, no! Ah! He's saved. The confession withdraws, withdraws without having gone over. "I killed the old man."[79]

This is the masterful portrayal of a modern Orestes driven to his destiny by the Erinyes. For inner identity, salvation and expiation lay in murder, and to be worthy of one's *moira*, a murder has to be apparent and confessed, so that one complies with the image everyone has cast on one. Our Lady of the Flowers has arrived; the criminal is somebody now, and is fulfilled. After the confession comes the relaxation from expiation. Our Lady falls asleep, spent, exhausted and content. As a direct corollary to Genet's conception of the courts as organs of retribution and expiation, he visualizes the criminal procedure as a festive ritual of a religious offering. Not the rite of an animal, but of a human, sacrifice – the Molloch of "your world" has to be pacified from time to time by an execution. There must be wide participation; the courtroom should be as packed as the arena of the public stoning, so that the expiation engulfs everyone present. After the human sacrifice, the men of religion proclaim the absolution of crimes (the scapegoat has carried them away with him) and everybody present prays, cleansed and purified.[80] The courtroom crowds certainly do come for the release of aggression. This, as we have seen, is one of the basic sources of stigma: a struggle goes on between the prosecution and the defence over the accused. There the process is more refined than in public hangings or stonings, but the crowds come for the same trophy – the defendant's head. "The public comes here (to the courtroom)", says Genet, "insofar as a word (the confession of the accused or the court's pronouncement of sentence) may result in a beheading and so that it may return, like Saint Denis, carrying its severed head in its hands."[81] The severed head carries away with it the combined aggression and projected guilt of righteous members of "your world", so that their righteousness is reinforced, until reaccumulated aggressiveness and frustration call for another head. The jury system seems vile to Genet because it makes judges – their job evil, by definition – out of decent men. The court psychiatrist is depicted as an amorphous diagnostician throwing around words such as: "Unbalanced . . . psychopathy . . . interrelation . . . splanchnic system . . . schizophrenia . . . unbalanced, unbalanced, unbalanced, unbalanced, unbalanced."[82] One term is repeated in his flow of verbosity: "unbalanced".

We demonstrated in chapter one that the adjustment-centred approach to mental health takes the modal, mean or median values of behaviour in a given group to denote the "ins" and to exclude the "outs". This statistical construct to measure adjustment is quite hopeless in real situations, because nobody seems to know what kinds of behaviour and personality traits should be included in the eclectic, multi-dimensional concept of adjustment, and which traits should be taken to denote the opposite, maladjustment. Even more amorphic than the term "adjustment" is the adjective "unbalanced"; it is as though the psychiatrist has a means to determine who is and who is not so. It comes down, therefore, to a conclusion which we have reached by deduction, and Genet by intuition, namely that this sort of psychiatric diagnosis is no more than a tool of social control, a stigma, to keep in line those who leave the herd or are conspicuous in any other way, not necessarily related to the crimes or deviations imputed to them.

As an appropriate summary of the stigmatizing function of the court, we have the following observation by Our Lady of the Flowers:

> The court smiled, that is, with the smile imparted to the face by the austere choice (already made) between the just and the unjust, the royal rigour of the brow that knows the dividing line – that has seen clearly and judged – and that condemns. (p. 285)

Genet's court of justice comes to the bench with a predetermined decision. It smiles benevolently at the innocent and glares darkly at the obvious depravity of the guilty. With his branding powers, the judge divides, but not the just from the unjust, because for this he has neither the ability nor the inclination; he makes a formal, extrinsic distinction between the acquitted and the condemned.

Genet's view of religion is set forth in *The Balcony*, a rather detailed tally sheet against "legitimate" society and its institutions. The play takes place in a brothel where illusion and reality are intermingled. The clients, who come to purchase temporary make-believe status and power, represent the main institutions of society. The fake bishop realizes that all his power stems from the deep symbolism of the cloth. He therefore worships this source of his power: "Mitre, bishop's bonnet, when my eyes close for the last time, it is you that I shall see behind my eyelids, you, my beautiful gilded hat, . . . you, my handsome ornaments, capes, laces."[83]

Apart from the mitre, lace, gold cloth and glass trinkets, there is only one function which is important (the others are irrelevant – "To hell with the functions!" (*The Balcony*, p. 7) – to forgive sins. The bishop is horrified at the idea that this function loses its *raison d'être* because in a world of evil (which Genet wholeheartedly believes our world is) you cannot commit sins. He realizes that "here there's no possibility of doing evil", and the whore teases him: "Reality frightens you, doesn't it?" Of course, it does. Without real sins, where "Good is only an illusion and Evil is a nothingness which arises on the ruins of Good", (*The Balcony*, p. 11) there is no need for mitres, for gold cloth or for bishops.

The sham general in *The Balcony* is overjoyed to hear his exploits described by the prostitute:

> "Splinters of shell had gashed the lemons. Now death was in action. She moved nimbly from one to the other, deepening a wound, dimming an eye, tearing off an arm, opening an artery, discolouring a face, cutting short a cry, a song. Death was ready to drop. Finally, exhausted, herself half-dead with fatigue, she grew drowsy and rested lightly on your shoulder, where she fell asleep." (*The Balcony*, p. 11)

War is waged in order to conquer; so the conquerors may win a war but die "or half-die . . . return crippled, armless, legless, broken and bent, balls torn off, noses eaten away, faces blasted" (*The Balcony*, p. 25). "And the vanquished – who are the vanquished? Conquer what? Or who? You've seen them dragging in the mud, living on peelings . . . conquer that!"[84] These are the lethal games played by politicians and generals.

The following is the image conceived by our thief–philosopher of the "respectable" employer–employee relationship. The domestic relations in madam's household are not exactly puritan, and as seen by Genet, Madam's most ardent desire is to be the prostitute kneeling at the feet of her lover, the thief.[85] The respectable Madame not only practises promiscuity, but is a whore; apparently Genet agrees with his criminal brethren that the false respectability in domestic relations is less palatable than a common whore, who has no illusions about her profession. Of crucial importance to our present context is that Genet imputes actual criminality to Madam's lover, while making it clear beforehand that he has been falsely accused. This shows the importance of stigma in Genet's eyes; like a typical professional, he knows that what one does is not as important as what one is reputed to have done. A professional criminal is horrified by a false accusation because he knows that he cannot defend himself; he would rather have a true charge, so that at least he knows what to expect. Genet, the professional criminal, knows that the actual results of true and slanderous accusations are very similar.

We have examined the images of society's most important institutions: the priest, the judge and the warrior as portrayed by the philosopher–thief. As for the respectable bourgeoisie as a whole, the

Madame at the end of *The Balcony* has a real (not illusory this time) message. "Dress up . . . judges, generals, bishops, chamberlains, rebels, . . . You must go home now, where everything – you can be sure – will be even falser than here."

The adjustment problems of the criminal would have to be solved, as we have mentioned in the previous chapters, within the areas of occupation, domestic relations and social images. Reverting back to crime, patronising prostitutes and developing a *ressentiment* rationalization towards society comprise the active phase of the solution. However, the criminal value-structure regarding these three adjustment areas is masterfully expounded in another play of Genet: *The Maids*. Clair and Solange, the criminal maids, try to murder their mistress, falsely accuse her lover of the crime and denounce him to the police. Meanwhile, Genet lets us know how the criminal regards legitimate occupation, domestic relations and "respectable society".

What are the various uses that "your world" finds for the criminals and outcasts? One can start from the aesthetic pleasure that "your world" derives from "slumming". They find poverty picturesque. The miseries of the beggars and their shabby rags remind them of the Goyas and Dorés adorning their own walls: "There's a perfect harmony between the tonalities of the sky and the slightly greenish shades of the rags", remarks one over-clad matron to her overweight escort. "We've seen them when they all are frozen", answers her escort with the air of a connoisseur, "they have to be seen in the right weather".[86] They take pictures of the *clochards* (*The Blacks*, p. 244).

The mechanisms of projection and transference make the criminal an appropriate receptacle for the primitive urges of society, which stem from its own aggressiveness: "I wanted to oppose society, but it had already condemned me, punishing not so much the actual thief as the indomitable enemy whose lonely spirit it feared . . . an anxiety – a wound from which flowed its own blood which it dared not shed itself" (*The Blacks*, p. 30). This release of pent-up aggression is the fuel which kindles the fires of stigma. The inner aggressiveness is generated by the various normative proscriptions, moral social and legal, which riddle man's life. The constant inner struggle and especially the desire to act against these morals and laws create guilt feelings which are eased by righteously punishing the criminal. The overflow of guilt is then absorbed by the criminal trail and punishment. The other outcasts carry the condemnation of "your world" by moving along its edges, out of its bounds and in its shadows (*The Blacks*, p. 126). This is why the grief and misery of the criminal and deviant are perpetuated by "your world" – so that they may continue to bear the cross of its condemnation. The dull, routine lives of the bourgeois are tinged with excitement as they vicariously identify with the daring exploits of the criminal (*The Blacks*, p. 126). But the criminal's is actually a self-condemnation because it stems from his complying with the judgement of "your world". Archibald, in *The Blacks*, even talks about deserving the reprobation of "your world", its judgement and subsequent condemnation (*The Blacks*, p. 39). This is the need for an "ego-identity" – fulfilment and salvation through stigma. We, the criminals, the deviants, the queers, the rejects, the blacks, regard ourselves in "our world" the way we have been, tainted and tagged. As Archibald continues gloomily: "We are what they wanted us to be. We shall therefore be it to the very end" (*The Blacks*, p. 39). The force of the stigma is portrayed by the judge who proclaims that as from a given date, God being dead, the colour of black ceases to be a sin, it becomes a crime" (*The Blacks*, p. 39).

One of "our world" who has been tainted and branded does not have to do anything to be a criminal; his stigma alone suffices to define him as such, both to "your world" and to "our world". Once stigmatized, the road back is hazy, uncertain and sometimes blocked. The blacks, the criminals and deviants must deface themselves; to discolour themselves by eradicating stigma, an impossible task anyway, is not enough. "Go join them", concludes the satanic Archibald, pointing to the audience, "if they'll have you, and if you succeed in winning their love, come back and let me know" (*The Blacks*, p. 39).

So arise, ex-cons of the world, and tell of the acceptance and love offered you by "your world" after you were released from prison; or, for that matter, tell of the success of the little bastard, Genet, how he regained the love of the peasant family in Le Morvan after he was proclaimed a thief.

Chapter six
The Creative Villains

"Je suis un autre." *Arthur Rimbaud*

The main thesis of the present volume is that in order to be innovative, one has to see the world differently than most people. By looking, perceiving and absorbing one's human and other surroundings differently, one is predisposed to reacting differently than others to one's environment. Hence, the likelihood of being labelled a deviant, with a feedback cycle towards further oddness and aberrance. One has to have talent and opportunity to be creative, but being an outsider also appears to enhance artistic innovativeness. Graham Greene wrote his wife that he suffered from an incurable antagonism to normal life. This antagonism was the raw material for his creativity.[1] As for our three protagonists, we have already seen that Gesualdo was a morbidly melancholic sado-masochist, who couldn't move his bowels without first being flogged by husky youths engaged by him especially for that purpose. He not only killed his wife and her lover in a fit of rage, but probably also his son, whom he suspected of being the offspring of adultery. Since then, he composed disturbing, chromatic music, sad and disheartening, yet brilliantly innovative, to texts which he had chosen for their depressed and mournful moods.

Concerning Caravaggio, we know that he spent his early days in Rome in the homosexual menagerie of Cardinal Del-Monte. Caravaggio wounded one Flavio Canonico, the captain of the guards at Castel San Angelo, with a sword. He was incarcerated because of a libel suit by the painter Baglione; he assaulted a waiter in Osteria del Moro, and was jailed for throwing stones at the police. Later that same year, he insulted a police corporal for asking to see his license to carry arms. He also injured a notary by hitting him on the head, killed one Ranuccio Tomassoni in the Campo Marzo and fled from Rome. On October 24, 1606, he was badly beaten in a brawl in Naples, leading to complications that caused his death in July, 1610. Police reports on these incidents point to a violently psychopathic personality; yet he was the most innovative Italian painter of the seventeenth century.

Jean Genet attests in his *Thief's Journal* that following his adoption by a viciously stigmatizing peasant family, "I became the traitor, the thief, the pederast, which they labelled me . . . Since I have been abandoned by my (original) family, I added to my exceptional miseries the love of boys, theft and further crimes. I thus counter-rejected a world which refused me."[2] Genet thence became the most celebrated mouthpiece of thieves, homosexuals and outcasts, performing that role with unsurpassed sensitivity and brilliance.

As for writers and poets, we find that many times foreigners are more sensitive to the subtleties of their acquired languages, and thus may achieve greater depth and grasp of the creative potential of language than native speakers. The prominent place of Irish novelists and poets in English literature is a prime example. Also, there is the fact that there was a relatively large number of Jews among writers, poets, as well as scientists, in Germany between the two world wars, and in the present-day United States. The innovative artist is also more often than not estranged from his native society. Kafka, one of the foremost *poéte maudit*, of the cursed writers of the last century, was not only estranged from his family; his brilliant account of his turning into a cockroach was apparently perceived by him as the stigmatizing subterranean wish of his father. He was certainly alienated from Bohemia, his birthplace. He also felt like an exile in this world, in which Mr. K, the victimized protagonist of *The Trial*, laments that "the lie has turned into the world order".

Rimbaud willingly left Europe, from which he felt estranged, particularly despising the search for success and fame in the hypocritical artistic cliques of Paris. He was the precursor of the "beat generation", ever seeking the unattainable by wondering endlessly "on the road"? à la Jack Kerouak. He moved to Malaysia, then Africa, looking for "infinity cashed from us by our soft brains". The poet has to "see" through the opaqueness of the worldly senses, to become a pariah, powerless on the outside; yet through his fear he is able to see the unseeable and know the unknowable. This is the apocalyptic vision of the artist sacrificing his animal comfort and spiritual well-being for a glimpse of eternity. *Time* magazine described Dylan Thomas, the Welsh *poéte maudit*, after his death as "a slob, a liar, a moocher, a thief, a two-fisted boozer-fighter, a puffy

Priapus, who regularly assaulted the wives of his best friends, an icy little hedonist who indifferently lived it up while his children went hungry". Yet he is acclaimed as the most dazzling English-language poet of the twentieth century.

Francis Bacon, a Genesque painter, was thrown out of the house at sixteen by his father, who discovered that young Francis wore his mother's underwear. This is echoed in his painting, "*Screaming Pope*" (a study from a portrait of Pope Innocent X by Velasquez), in which a terrifying transparency barks damnation and anathema emanating from the paternal authority of the pope. Bacon was violently manhandled, even tortured, by Peter Lacy, a sadistic bully. "Lacy," recounts Bacon, "hated my painting right from the beginning." He said, "You can leave your painting and come and live with me." And I said, "What does living with you mean?" And he said, "Well, you could live in a corner of my cottage on straw. You could sleep and shit there." He wanted to have me chained to the wall . . . And then he liked to have someone bugger me, and then bugger him right after . . . " Not surprisingly, Bacon's favourite theme was the crucifixion with mutilated bodies dripping blood from their gushing wounds. Francis Bacon was depicting a black passion with his own body perversely sacrificed on the cross of societal cruelty, horror and pain.

Deviance is instrumental in causing suffering and pain, which would be sublimated by the artist into authenticity and depth of expression. The relationship between suffering and creativity is curvilinear. Some pain can be conducive to creativity, but too much could hurl the artist under his Sisyphean stone, which would stifle, paralyse and ultimately crush him.

Of greater importance is the transgression which extrudes the artist from the commonplace of diachronicity into the authentic domain of synchronicity. Gesualdo and Sade transgressed against all norms and conventions, so that their deviance would distil their otherness onto a different plain of existence; their experience and hence creativity would thus be on parameters diverging from the central diachronic measures.

Caravaggio never wanted to be accepted by the established artists. The moment he felt the establishment's petrifying kiss of fat, he rebelled and got himself expelled from organizations and exiled from the cosy bosom of a cardinal's court and the *dolce-vita* of seventeenth-century Rome, regaining the freedom of the outsider. Such extraterritorial status enabled him to create according to his inner directives and not in conformity with the mandates of the power cliques or the tastes of the generalized other. Caravaggio chose as his model for Maria Magdalena a repenting whore, whereas the dead Mary, mother of God, was the body of a drowned prostitute fished out of the Tiber. Such freedom from the stifling here-and-now onto the authenticity of synchronicity brings to mind Vincent van Gogh, who shacked up with a whore from whom he contracted gonorrhoea, enraging his puritanical family, his mentor, and even his otherwise loyal brother Theo. His planned marriage with her would have led to his complete ostracism. Their separation allowed him to carry on his brinkmanship with isolation far enough to gain him insights, without leading to the abyss of complete estrangement from Theo, which would have severed his lifeline to creativity and even existence.

Wagner embarked on a radical method by which to assert his uniqueness: He observed the artistic realm of his time to determine the consensus in music, the canon in drama, the approved style in opera, and inverted them all in a gushing, throbbing avalanche of divergent originality. Wagner's deviant innovation may be likened, *mutatis mutandis*, to the oeuvres of Jean Genet, who asserted the accepted laws, rules and norms, only to infringe them both in his behaviour and by his art, staging in his plays variations on the theme of a black passion, brandishing a cross with the perverse trinity of theft, homosexuality and betrayal.

Marcel Duchamp, the prophet of surrealism, gained notoriety with the 1913 exhibition in New York of his mechanical *Nude Descending a Staircase*. Yet his fame rests on his zany *The Bride Stripped Bare by her Bachelors Even*. The "bachelors", fragmented zombies, try to impregnate the scaffolding of their two-dimensional bride by masturbating, in emulation of Egyptian cosmogony. Duchamp was a complete recluse, retreating to his Manhattan flat with no radio or telephone, playing chess with himself and smoking his pipe. Luis Buñuel, another innovative surrealist artist, oscillated in his work between hell and salvation, grace and damnation, with nothing in between. *Viridiana*, his Gnostic masterpiece, contrasts bourgeois hypocrisy with the blind belief in an arbitrary, apathetic and silent God. "In this world," says Buñuel, "there is no humanity, no mercy; there is only corruption, which reaches its apogee when fuelled by abject piety and good heartedness . . . If Jesus would have come again, he would have been crucified *da capo* by the church . . . The only way to exist is to seek God within man himself."[3] The Last Supper in the film *Viridiana* is staged by the thieving beggars who raided the ranch presided over by a blind Jesus, who is a Genesque thief, traitor and lecher. The drunken whore lifts her skirt, as if taking a picture of this last supper of murderous, raping rascals, while a Handel's *Messiah* booms in the background.

Vincent van Gogh's whore model attracted him probably subconsciously, because her prostitution was sure to scandalize his prudish family, thus assuring him the freedom of an unattached pariah. Likewise, Oscar Wilde's internal saboteur pushed him subconsciously to the disastrous lawsuit which catapulted him into the secluded dejection, yet authentic suffering, of Reading Gaol, which he could never have achieved consciously and voluntarily. Indeed, *De Profundis* and *The Ballad of Reading Gaol,* written in prison, are his most profound and authentic works.

The accounts, stories and legends of the egocentricities, weirdness and bizarre behaviour of creative artists are legion. We shall just add a few additional vignettes. Rembrandt, one of the greatest painters of all time, was an egotistic manipulator of everybody around him, especially in money matters, which he could never manage. When his *Night Watch* was rejected by its sponsors, his reputation declined and he could not earn a living. His suffering lent depth to his art, but that was approximately the time when he schemed and executed one of the vilest and most callous deeds imaginable. After the death of his beloved wife Saskia van Uylenburgh, Rembrandt hired Girtia Direx as a governess to his son and she became his mistress. Eventually he proposed to her. Later on he hired another governess for his son, Hendrickje Stoffels, who also became his mistress. Rembrandt rejected his older mistress and refused to marry her. Consequently, Direx sued him and won alimony. Rembrandt connived with her brother and bribed one of Direx's neighbours to testify as to her loose morals, and Direx was imprisoned for five years.

Samuel Beckett was a drunk, deeply depressed and wandered around Dublin and Paris. He confided to a friend that all he wanted to do "is sit on my arse and fart and think of Dante". He had a fierce love–hate relationship with his domineering mother, reflected in his play *Unnamable*, with the protagonist "looking for my mother to kill her . . . I should have thought of that a bit earlier, before being born." His emulation of James Joyce is ludicrously neurotic. His biographer tells us:

> To the dismay of some of his friends, Beckett began to imitate Joyce's mannerisms. He dangled his cigarette carelessly from limp-wristed hands. Although he was near-sighted, his eyes were not then seriously troublesome, but he held books and papers up close to his glasses in the same attitude of languid exhaustion that Joyce affected in order to cover his very real inability to see clearly.
>
> Beckett even wore pointed-toe patent leather shoes that were too small, because he wanted to wear the same shoe in the same size as Joyce, who was very proud of his small, neatly shod feet. Joyce had been vain about his feet since his youth, when poverty forced him to go about Dublin in a pair of white tennis shoes, the only footwear he owned. It is impossible to know if Joyce was even aware of Beckett's slavish gesture, for his eyes were so weak that he saw very little. What is intriguing about this imitative gesture is the sacrificial element involved in the picture of Beckett, suffering terribly from huge corns and terrible calluses, walking only with great pain. He must have pulled off his shoes in much the same was as his char-

acter, Estragon, pulls off his horrible misshapen boots in the first act of *Waiting for Godot*, with a sigh of infinite relief.[4]

Isaac Bashevitz Singer neglected his only son; yet when they met after a 25-year separation, he appointed his son as his Hebrew translator. When the son wrote a book of his own, however, Singer senior was enraged: "How dare you write books?" he hollered, "when you have to devote yourself to the translation of my books." Bashevitz Singer was an egocentric bully, who verged on autism; a miser who exploited everyone, including his family, to further his own interests. His son tells us that when he came to visit him in New York, he gave him a dollar pocket money. He invited him to lunch in a cafeteria; the son, who came from the austere and famished Israel of the fifties, wanted to but did not dare to order meat, due to stories about his father's stinginess. He took two bowls of rice and some bread. His father remarked that his son looked too fat. The son returned one of the rice bowls and the bread.

We do not claim that a work of art should be interpreted according to the personality or character of the artist. A work of art is a self-contained structure, the examination of which should be carried out by itself, from itself, and through the relationship of its parts to its whole. We do hold, however, that the deviant, non-attached and esoteric creator is in a better position to observe the art object or model from a hitherto unnoticed angle, and hence is more likely to describe it in an innovative manner.

Our claim is that an artist's innovative perception, and subsequent creativity, must be linked with his deviant values and behaviour. One cannot be authentic without actually experiencing the objects and events one describes. That was the credo of Caravaggio and van Gogh, and their works provide a *post facto* illustration of this premise. An artist who writes from imagination may be likened to a theoretical, armchair physicist, whereas a writer who examines the sites, mingles with subjects and states the joys and sorrows of the protagonists is a practical physicist who chases particles in a high powered accelerator. When we examine, for instance, the biography of Lawrence Durrell, one of the most stunning writers of modern times, with his epoch-making "*Alexandria Quartet*", bustling with decadent sex, surrealist scenes and stormy emotions, we may discover certain facts. He treated his wives and lovers callously and brutally. He was rabidly anti-Semitic, leaving Paris because it was "dominated by Jewish intellectuals". He drove a *Luftwaffe* staff car formerly owned by Herman Göring.[5] He neglected his daughters Penelope and Sappho; the latter committed suicide, probably after having been violated by her father.

The innovator has to rebel against the commonplace, familiar and conventional. Vincent van Gogh not only saw himself a rebel against all bourgeois conventions, but declared to his otherwise loyal brother Theo that in an ideological war, he and his brother would be on opposing sides.[6] Indeed, Vincent's rebellious aim was a new aesthetic cognition, independent of bourgeois conventions. The goal of the authentic artist is to rebel against historicist conventions and reach the synchronic viability of the authentic domain. It is important to stress that what is linked to innovation is not the immorality of the artist or his being a "bad guy", but his "otherness", or rather his being an "outsider".

Therefore we do not accept any correlation, positive or negative, between art and morality, be it Judaeo-Christian righteousness, the Kantean Categorical Imperative or the Greek equation of aesthetics and goodness as reformulated by Ruskin. We hold with Pater that art is an end in itself. Its authenticity makes for its viability, by "raising" it from diachronicity unto sinchronicity. Also, its durability is related to its effective linkage of artist and audience, through the artistic medium. Van Gogh shrieked his ardent quest for dialogue with transcendence, with nature, with other life forms and human beings. He tried at first to reach the dejected miners of Borinage through religion. He was brutally rejected by both the miners and the church hierarchy. He also tried to reach an amorous dialogue with women, failing miserably. Finally, he tried to achieve a dialogue with the only person he thought would understand his innovations, Paul Gauguin. He painted Gauguin's chair in florid colours and vivid exotic shapes reminiscent of Paul's Peruvian background, and his penchant for faraway lands and cultures. Van Gogh depicted a lighted candle symbolizing the Promethean fire that Gauguin was destined to bring to the commune of painters to be established in Arles and the enlightenment of new vistas of art to Vincent himself. Vincent painted his own chair as an austere straw and rough wood seat with his pipe and tobacco pouch on it.[7] His failure to reach a meaningful dialogue with Gauguin was seemingly the trigger to Vincent's loss of sanity and eventual suicide.

As authentic creativity is a continuous process, involving a constant search for new ways of expression; resting on laurels is tantamount to stagnation. However, *in extremo*, a constant pursuit of innovation may turn into a cult of newness which accepts anything, pseudo-art included, provided it is novel. "We have learned so well how to absorb novelty", says Richard Hofstadter, "that receptivity itself has turned into a kind of tradition – the tradition of the new. Yesterday's avant-garde experiment is today's chic and tomorrow's cliché."[8] Many phoney artefacts or performances intended to shock, overwhelm or simply fool audiences may thus pose as art. Such fake innovators are very likely to be accepted by some of the public, because they are very sensitive to power and fad fluctuations in dominant cliques. They make sure through flattery or catering to vested interests, that they are favoured by the current reigning powers, pace-setters and *arbiteri elegantiari*. This process may be described mytho-empirically as the transformation of the creative Sisyphus into the tortured Prometheus. Mythological transformations are very common and we have studied extensively elsewhere the transformation of Koré, Demeter's "good" daughter, into "horrible" Persephone.[9] The process of transformation in the present context is that the creative Sisyphus commits *hübris*, raising the jealousy of the Olympian gods, the mythical projection of separant men. The gods then punish Prometheus in the same way the jealous and competitive power elites in groups stigmatize the unruly and rebellious creative innovators. The rock-burden of Sisyphus is thus symbolically transformed into the rock to which Prometheus is chained. It is also symbolic in that the regeneration of Prometheus's liver and his subsequent torture by the vulture is cyclic, analogous to the cyclic trials of Sisyphus with his stone. It might be interesting to mention here that the makers of Persian carpets deliberately introduce flaws in their work in order not to commit the *hübris* of perfection, and thereby incur the wrath of the jealous gods.

The plight of the creative Prometheans is liable to be pathetic, when they do not understand the dynamics of the relationships between innovators and power structures. They may complain that their innovation benefited the group and humanity at large, so why have they been punished? Haven't the Promethean innovators brought light to humanity? Of course they have! But in the process they have "rocked the boat", they have hurt the vested interests of, for instance, gas companies, which are bound to be hurt by Edison's electric light bulb. Above all, however, the creative innovators have raised the jealousy of the Olympians, the mythical, separant projections of power elites. These are much more concerned with maintaining their power than with artistic excellence, scientific progress or the welfare of humanity. The creative Promethean outsiders demand, with typical *naïvité*, that they be accepted by a public led and controlled by the power elites against whom they rebel and the vested interests of which they harm. The Promethean's misfortune is thus exacerbated, because he is asking for the impossible. His difference and otherness fill the *vulgus* with apprehension and anxiety. Finally, his creativity makes him seem powerful, yet socially and materially he remains powerless. Hence, he is a powerless power symbol and, as we have shown in *The Mark of Cain*,[10] this combination makes for a perfect scapegoat.

In existentialism, authenticity is a moral principle, inauthenticity an immoral one. Inauthenticity consists of hypocrisy, pretence; deceiving oneself and others. Hypocrisy, involving double or multiple moral standards, stems from the Greek *hypokrites*, an actor, a role player. Another possible etymological source is *hypot krinein*, to pass judgment. Judging others, the kabbalist "stern judgment", and bourgeois righteous indignation, are sources, etymologically at least, of hypocrisy. Hence, one of the characteristics of Camus' judge-penitent's fall into authenticity is his refusal to judge others. Inauthenticity is a basic attribute of demiurgal social structures, which can function only by power manipulation and deception of those normatively subject to them. These are mostly politicians and other yielders of power in social institutions, ranging from churches to the *arbiteri elegantiari* of artistic cliques. They possess finely tuned social antennae, to detect any change in the balance of power, fads and prevalent tastes of the reigning elites in their membership groups, in order to manipulate them to their advantage. They jump onto all safe bandwagons and wear the current uniforms of the age: the crew cut in the fifties, long hair and pot parties in the sixties, careerism and capitalism in the seventies, still paying exorbitant prices for tickets to a Bob Dylan concert of Woodstock songs with other balding, pot-bellied ex-protesters who park their Cadillacs far from the reunion site. In the eighties and nineties, they were "yuppies", later the high-tech "start-ups", and if they have made it, they will have modest *Veuve Cliquot* champagne and Beluga caviar around the swimming pool with their "friends", who happen to be the right combination of government, legislative, judicial and mass communication's people, popular artists and, of course, the *ad hoc* manipulants whom they have to manipulate or to impress. They exude a love of humanity with the depth of the smile on a toothpaste commercial; their actual compassion for their fellow humans is that of a piranha. Camus describes bourgeois society within the context of piranha morality, thus:

> Haven't you noticed that our society is organized for this kind of liquidation? You have heard, of course, of those tiny fish in the rivers of Brazil that attack the unwary swimmer by the thousands and with swift little nibbles clean him up in a few minutes, leaving only an immaculate skeleton? Well, that's what their organization is. "Do you want a good, clean life? Like everybody else?" You say yes, of course. How can one say no? "O.K. You'll be cleaned up. Here's a job, a family, and organized leisure activities." And the little teeth attack the flesh, right down to the bone. But I am unjust. I shouldn't say their organization. It is ours, after all: it's a question of which will clean up the other.[11]

Not all deviants can be creative innovators; but the original artist must have a divergent *Weltanschauung*, so that he may perceive things differently, and depict them in his artistic medium in an innovative manner.

This deviance would rate a defensive and repressive reaction from the membership groups of the innovative artist, since his actions "rock the boat" and disrupt the model values and median manner of behaviour.

As we have shown throughout the present work, myths are projections onto mythology of human experiences. We therefore conclude our explorations of creativity and revelation within the mytho-empirical framework of our theoretical model.

Our personality theory, which served as a basis for our model, was constructed along a continuum between the Sisyphean and Tantalic predispositions. We could therefore envisage both revelatory and creative personalities at the extremes of this continuum. The Sisyphean tries to project on his burden-stone his creative involvement with the object, in order to emerge from his inauthentic drudgery. If this creative innovation is too extreme, like van Gogh's revolution of painting, Artaud's innovative view of aesthetics and Caravaggio's original style of painting, they commit the *hübris* of rocking the societal order, by leaving the boundaries of "proper" conduct of the ruling cliques. Societal reaction is therefore furiously repressive by stigma. The creative Sisyphus, who then becomes a Prometheus, is sanctioned by his father Zeus, representing the normative system. Prometheus is then painfully bound to the rock and he engages in his creativity in cyclic alternations of creation and misery, parallel to the cyclic trials of Sisyphus. On the other extreme we might have a Jordano Bruno or any other Tantalic virtuoso, whose revelation makes him soar Icarus-like too high, to be exposed to the scorching rays of the sun, causing him to fall and drown in the sea. Tantalus here is extreme in his revelatory aspirations and becomes an Icarus, who did not heed the warnings of his father Daedalus, again representing the normative system, not to fly too high or too low. Icarus thus committed the *hübris* forbidden by societal norms, as expressed by the mandate of his father and his innovation was duly punished.

This brings us back to our initial thesis in our present work: in order to innovate, the artist has to be deviant. If and when society is not ready yet to absorb the innovations, which are liable to harm reigning interests, it curbs the innovation by imposing sanctions on the deviant creator. This is the ingenious "evolutionary leash" of society: since the deviant behaviour is punishable, society defends itself by disciplining the non-normative behaviour of the artist, since it cannot castigate his innovation. Yet the result achieved is a crushed Icarus who can no longer innovate.

Chapter seven
Genius and Madness

"Genius and madness have a common ground where they border and indeed overlap." *Arthur Schopenhauer*

"A man prefers to become mad in the socially accepted sense, rather than forfeit a certain superiour idea of human honour." *Antonin Artaud*

Since our present work was conceived as an expansion on the theme of the efforts of the Camusean Sisyphus to find a creative *modus vivendi* with his stone, we ask in the present chapter whether the mad Sisyphus can still be creative, and how he can regain or lose his sanity.

We would like to present the link between stigma, creativity and madness, as related both to classical theories of morbidity, to our own work on predisposition to crime and madness, as well as the more contemporary theories relating to the link between social control and the stigmatizing of the insane. As such, this chapter serves as an introduction to our two concluding chapters (eight and nine), on van Gogh and Artaud. These two giants serve to illustrate in bold relief the relationship between creativity and insanity, on the one hand, and insanity and stigma on the other.

Artaud has written an extensive analysis of the case of van Gogh[1] but he actually projected on van Gogh his grappling with his own madness and stigma. We shall therefore relate ourselves to Artaud's description of van Gogh, but as illuminating the situation of Artaud himself.

The gist of our argument is that predisposition to morbidity is a combined biological potential and skewed familial interaction, especially with the mother or her surrogate at early orality. This predisposition is exacerbated at the social level in the case of creative innovators by social stigma. By presenting the model as a combination of both predisposing factors and dynamic initiation into morbidity, which has been elaborated *in extenso* in chapter one, we are presenting a new, synthetic approach. We combine the classic treatment of schizophrenia, in which what we have called predisposing factors are the only factors considered, with a relative disregard of the interactional factors. On the other hand, we do not accept the extreme "anti-psychiatry"[2] which totally disregards the predisposing factors and claims that madness can be induced by societal reaction to behaviour. However, in the present chapter, we concentrate on the dynamic processes of initiation into madness, while taking into account that the predisposing factors are a necessary component of our aetiological model.

The highlights of van Gogh's biography as relevant to our context are as follows: Vincent van Gogh was born in 1853 to an industrious, talented, plain mother and a minister of the Dutch Reformed Church. In appearance, he resembled his plain mother. "He was medium in height and stocky in build; his eyes were blue and he was adorned with red hair and freckles that did not vanish with his youth".[3]

The young Vincent was melancholy, depressive and unhappy from his very early years. He wrote: "My youth was gloomy, cold and sterile."[4] His depressive disposition is very apparent from his letters to his brother Theo.[5]

A significant factor in van Gogh's life is that he was named after the family's first child who had died at birth, only a year before his own. Vincent grew up in an atmosphere of mourning. His whole childhood was shadowed by the death of his brother whose grave he was obliged to visit each week. He ever sought feminine warmth and acceptance. These quests, however, were inevitably disastrous, because he asked for an intensity of love such as the women could not possible give, since he tended to become involved with cold women, like Ursula and Kee, who actually belonged to others to begin with, and refused to give him the warmth, love and attention he so desperately needed. This is consistent with the mechanism of "the least interest principle"[6] which posits that the more one runs after a woman, the less likely one is to win her love, especially if one asks of her more than she can possibly give to begin with. Ultimately, however, van Gogh managed to establish more or less stable relationships with two whores, Sien and Margot. They were the dregs of society, the rejects, the downtrodden, the unloved. He could easily identify with them and give them the love which he himself had never had.

Freud[7] suggested that both morbidity and deviance should be viewed etiologically, as a combination of predisposing factors and social interactional dynamics. He meant that a person who has a predisposition for morbidity may have a high probability of being recognized as schizophrenic by his relevant others. The whole theory of stigma and labelling is in fact related to this premise. Indeed, in our study of schizophrenics, we have demonstrated the role of scapegoating and stigma in the genesis of the initial stages of morbidity,[8] whereas the role of stigma in deepening the morbid cycles of mental illness is well documented.[9]

The sociological approach to the genesis of mental illness, with its stress on the importance of the breakdown of human communication as a predisposition to mental aberration, has highlighted the importance of stigma in the formation of the self-concept, roles and images of the mentally ill. Moreover, some scholars find a close similarity between the core mechanisms of social deviance and mental illness. Scheff,[10] for instance, regards social deviance as the main dynamic underlying mental illness, stating:

> The culture of the group provides a vocabulary of terms for categorizing many more violations; crime, perversion, drunkenness and bad manners are familiar examples. Each of the terms is derived from the type of behaviour involved. After exhausting these categories, however, there is always a residue of the most diverse kinds of violations for which the culture provides no explicit label.

Consequently, the mechanisms of stigma in social deviance apply, *mutatis mutandis*, to mental illness. The role of stigma in accelerating and deepening mental illness is similar to its role in forming the deviant career. This has been pointed out by Scheff,[11] thus:

> In a crisis, when the deviance of an individual becomes a public issue, the traditional stereotype of insanity becomes the guiding imagery for action, both for those reacting to the deviant and, at times, for the deviant himself. When societal agents and persons around the deviant react to him uniformly in terms of the traditional stereotypes of insanity, his amorphous and unstructured rule-breaking tends to crystallize in conformity to those expectations, thus becoming similar to the behaviour of other deviants classified as mentally ill, and stable over time. The process . . . is completed when the traditional imagery becomes a part of the deviant's orientation for guiding his own behaviour.

Stigmatic factors had an important function in the genesis of morbidity in the case of van Gogh, as described by Artaud.[12] These, no doubt, also had a major function in the genesis of Artaud's own illness, as he himself has described.

The diagnosis of van Gogh's illness operated on many levels. On the biomedical level, he was found to be suffering from epileptic seizures. His condition was thought to be hereditary, because his father suffered from "Ictus Apoplectique", and many members of his mother's family were also epileptic. His sister Wil was psychotic, apparently schizophrenic. His brother Theo had severe attacks of anxiety and depression, and committed suicide after Vincent's death. Vincent's younger brother, Car, a mental patient at the time of his death, is also believed to have committed suicide. According to one doctor,[13] van Gogh's madness was therefore biologically predetermined. These formidable predispositions are indeed macabre, but we do not necessarily need biological determinism to explain van Gogh's predisposition to mental aberrations. The authoritarian father, and even more so compulsive mother, could provide predisposition enough for his mental condition. However, if the stigma of madness, when internalized, is a potent triggering mechanism, causing the tendency to morbidity to sprout into actual disease, then the fact that all the members of his family suffered from severe mental conditions made the young van Gogh very receptive to the idea that madness was his inevitable fate. Madness seemed to be his lot in life, ordained by his *moira*, which he could not escape.

Another group of doctors[14] claimed that van Gogh was a constitutional psychopath. This diagnosis was based on the fact that he left his parents' home at the age of 16, and thereafter became a vagabond. His places of abode were: four years in The Hague, two years in London, ten months in Paris, ten months in London as a vagabond minister, three months in Dordrecht as an assistant librarian, fourteen months in Amsterdam as a student in a religious seminary, four months in Brussels in a school for missionaries, twenty-two months in a village in Belgium as a resident pastor, six months in Brussels studying painting, eight months' rest at his father's home, twenty-two months in The Hague again, two months wandering around Holland as a vagabond, two years in a mental institution in Asile Nuenen, two months in Paris, fifteen months in Arles, a year in a mental institution in Saint Remy, and finally two months in Auvers-Sur-Oise, where he committed suicide. Doctors who adhere to this view maintain that he lacked an awareness of material needs. He was led by contradictory and convoluted mental structures. He had a negative self-image and a high level of aspiration. He was very sensitive and inventive, with a well-developed imagination, but was lonely and dejected. This diagnosis of van Gogh as a psychopath is patently and overtly stigmatic. We have shown elsewhere that the diagnosis of psychopathy is amorphic and unclear, and capable of so many interpretations that labelling someone with the tag of psychopath cannot but be stigmatic, because in content it hardly meant anything.[15]

Another diagnosis of van Gogh's condition, in the existentialist tradition, was made by Minkowski[16] and centred on the breakdown of van Gogh's ontological equilibrium.

As for Artaud, until about 1936 he was considered one of the leading exponents of the Theatre of Surrealism, known as the Theatre of Cruelty. After 1936, however, he was hospitalized in a mental institution, where he remained for nine years. When he was discharged he wrote forceful indictments of the psychiatric system, and his lengthy work on van Gogh is actually an expression of the injustice, cruelty and perversity of the psychiatric system, which labelled outstanding creators, such as van Gogh and himself, with a tag of madness to justify their incarceration. His condemnation shows van Gogh, and for that matter Artaud himself, as the crucified scapegoats of society. Outwardly the mental institution protects and cures "the mad", but in the case of van Gogh, and by implication in his own, it was simply a means of keeping them out of sight, and ultimately, of annihilating them.

It was society, through its psychiatrists and mental institutions, that created the delirium, the chronic madness, and the specifications of abnormality. "Mental treatment" is in fact a web of deceit, of guilt, of suspicion and injustice, organized into a system well oiled to achieve its goal. Society, says Artaud, invented psychiatry in order to fight the rebellious creator who has a deeper, yet different, insight than the pacesetters in the power structure. Psychiatry is simply an instrument for subjugating people with original ideas, who endanger its vested interests and the supremacy of those in power.[17] Van Gogh was not mad, but his ideas and paintings threatened the accepted academic institutions and dominant tastes ordained by the leading *arbiteri elegantiari*. They threatened the whole accepted notion of art, and therefore they became a danger to the entire conformist social structure and cultural system. The whole of nature rocked from the moment it was ingested by van Gogh's sharp and rebellious gaze. So he was ostracized and labelled abnormal and strange, until he was forced to commit himself to a mental institution. Society stifled him, narrowing his living and creative space, but he stood firm, and so they used the ultimate weapon – he was labelled a madman, a nonentity to be shut up in a place worse than a prison. At least a prisoner is still a human being, but an inmate of a metal institution is nothing. Once this has been accomplished – and the person has become a nothing – he ceases to be a danger to society and its power structures.

Man does not see with his flesh-and-blood eyes, declared van Gogh, and he painted what his inner being perceived his environment to be. Van Gogh's art was so disruptive, that he was ostracized out of fear. He became the proverbial scapegoat for society's own inner pits of horror and anxiety, and he had therefore to bear the consequences. Yet the more he was hunted, the more his art and his artistic *Weltanschauung* crystallized. His expression became more stylized in his own specific way, and he developed a shield against the stigmatizing effects of society. This, says Artaud, was unacceptable to his human environment. Finally, the agencies of society flushed their trump card – van Gogh would be committed to a mental hospital, where he would be totally defenceless. Their triumph was now complete. Moreover, the artistic truths which were so dangerous to the stigmatizing agencies could now safely be ignored, because a madman is a nonentity, and whatever he says or does is totally insignificant.

Artaud conceded that the behaviour of van Gogh was unusual, but claimed that it was based on logical needs. For example, van Gogh wanted to paint in the fields at night. But how could he paint in the dark? He solved the problem by sticking candles into his hat, and then he went out, equipped for painting at night. This behaviour, argues Artaud, was perfectly instrumental for achieving his logical aim. In another incident his uncle accused him of being mad because he put his hands in the flame of the candles on the table at his home. But van Gogh did this in order to prove that it was his ardent wish to marry his uncle's daughter. He wanted to show that the suffering of the body is nothing compared to the determination of the spirit. Indeed, when he put his hands in the fire, he did not utter a sound despite of the pain. Is this not, says Artaud, heroic behaviour, a spiritual triumph?

Van Gogh committed suicide when his psychiatrist, Dr. Gachet, convinced him that he should give up painting for his own sake. But it was precisely this creative activity that was his whole *raison d'être*. If he could not paint any more, he could not *be* any more.

Artaud stated that the same process was imposed upon him. He tried to create, to express himself. But the psychiatrists saw in him, as they saw in van Gogh, a strange genius, and therefore a menace to their own mediocrity. This is no doubt an expression of Artaud's paranoia, but then paranoia itself is a psychiatric label which Artaud did not want to, and could not, accept. Most of the time, he had no inclination to commit suicide. But after each apparently therapeutic, but inwardly aggressive, session with a psychiatrist, he declared that he was ready to hang himself.

Van Gogh's creative energies were a Sisyphean synthetic outcome of his fight with stigma and madness. However, when this creative outlet was blocked by a violent incident with Paul Gauguin, his creativity stopped and madness erupted, taking over his whole personality.

Van Gogh had developed a very high regard and admiration for Paul Gauguin. He felt that both Gauguin and he had effected a revolution in painting, as of course they had. He had dreams of inaugurating a new artistic school and offered the leadership of the revolution to Gauguin, who tried to persuade Gauguin to come to Arles where he was then living.

The intensity of expectations may be gleaned from the following excerpts from a letter to his brother Theo:

> If Gauguin comes, there is his bed ready in a minute . . . the prettier room upstairs, which I shall try to make as much as possible like the boudoir of a really artistic woman. Then there will be my own bedroom, which I want extremely simple, but with large square furniture, the bed, chairs and table all in white . . . The room for Gauguin, if he comes, will have white walls with a decoration of great yellow sunflowers . . . crammed into this tiny boudoir with its pretty bed and everything else smart.[18]

After much persuasion, Gauguin did indeed agree to come to Arles in the latter part of 1888, but his visit proved a disaster. Van Gogh's disappointment with Gauguin's rejection of him was so intense that he broke down, and a psychotic incident took place in which, according to Gauguin, he threatened him with an open razor. Then, on Christmas night, the notorious episode occurred when van Gogh cut off his ear and gave it to a prostitute in a local brothel as a token of friendship. For van Gogh, however, it was the episode with Gauguin that was by far the worse. Apparently his disenchantment with Gauguin and their violent quarrels, added to van Gogh's greater sensitivity, caused him to accept the other's judgement as to the low quality of his creation, and as a result he could not paint any more. He could no longer grapple with his predisposition to madness. He was also unable to continue to utilize the stigma branded upon him by his surroundings as fuel for creativity. For van Gogh, creativity was his means of interacting dialectically with his predisposition to morbidity, producing his magnificent paintings. To stop creating meant to lose all his defences against morbidity. When he could not create any more, he not only became mad, but also stopped being, and the only way out for him was suicide.

In the same way, the psychiatrists petrified the creativity of Artaud. In his case they claimed that his madness annihilated his creativity, but Artaud maintained that the contrary was true, that by labelling him mad, by exposing him to the various shocks he experienced at mental institutions, they destroyed his ability to create, and hence destroyed his life. We claim, therefore, that what Gauguin did to trigger the madness, and hence the destruction, of van Gogh, the psychiatrists and their electric shocks did in the case of Artaud. Both had utilized their predisposition to madness as dialectical raw material for creativity, which was their only way to adjust to being outsiders, creative innovators, and therefore, by definition, deviants. Their creativity was also their sole means of defence against the tagging and labelling by their surroundings. When this dialectical interaction with their predisposition to madness and stigma was blocked, producing creatively became impossible, and they succumbed to the emptiness (*le vide*), the nothingness, the non-being of madness and of death.

To sum up, the creative innovator is bound to see his surroundings differently from the accepted way. This is inherent in his authentic creativity. By perceiving and envisaging things differently, a van Gogh or Artaud can create their art with a different technique, as well as a different content, from the accepted forms of creation in their particular fields. Social stigma against the creative innovators, is sure to follow and the creative innovators may indeed become deviants by a self fulfilling prophecy. Nevertheless, both van Gogh and Artaud were able to carry on their innovative creativity while interacting dialectically both with their predisposition to madness and the social stigmas branded upon them.

Moreover, these predispositions, along with the social stigma, became fuel for their creativity.[19] However, creativity became impossible – for van Gogh because of severe pressures, both internal and external, culminating in his violent fight with Gauguin; and for Artaud, due to his incarceration in mental hospitals and exposure to brutal methods of psychiatric treatment. Thereafter, the dialectical interaction of both van Gogh and Artaud with their predispositions to madness and stigma became impossible. The precarious system in balance broke down, and both madness and stigma took over the whole personality, effectively extinguishing creativity.

Predisposition to morbidity, as well as stigma, can be contained, manageable and even functional for the creative innovator, as long as he is able to make use of it for his creativity. When this dialectical interaction becomes impossible, then stigma and madness become the harbingers of non-being and death.

Indeed every creative act is abnormal, insofar as it pushes the artist out of his modal routines. Since we accept Sullivan's stance that madness is a matter of the degree of the skewedness of a person's interaction with his objective and human surroundings, the intensity of such interaction, inherent in creativity, may catapult the artist out of normatively sanctioned behaviour, predisposing him to being branded deviant and/or mad. Seneca was one of the first to proclaim that there is no great genius without great madness. In order to be innovatively creative, one has to forgo the mental defence mechanisms which make for normatively contained behaviour. Yet the relationship between such renunciation is not linear, but curvilinear. Some forfeiture of the strictures of normative defences can facilitate creativity, but too much may lead to anarchy and madness. The core predisposition to madness with a fractured ego-boundary would make for a frantic individual seeking to "mend" his blemished self by means, *inter alia*, of creativity.

The mytho-empirical support for this premise comes from Lurianic kabbala, which contends that a blemished, wholly other (God) has to be "mended" by dialogic interaction. This revelatory mechanism, which in Buberian terms is the dialogic "mending" of the other and the "universal other", is the essence of our conception of creativity. The I and the Thou become an ontological whole by the creative interaction. Both van Gogh and Artaud desperately tried to communicate their creative efforts. When they felt their artistic medium and audience escape them, they resorted to an insane act of attention-seeking: van Gogh by cutting off his ear, and Artaud by emitting rhythmic shrieks in a theatre hall packed with stunned celebrities.

If the deviant and criminal delineates the boundaries of normativeness for the "law abiding citizen" through a definition, by contrast the creative innovator proclaimed insane marks the limits of historical ontology *vis-à-vis* transcendence and the possibilities of the creative dialogue between the artist and his audience. Indeed Dali, who made a career out of his paranoia, intimated: "Standing altogether apart from the influence of the sensory phenomena with which hallucination may be considered more or less connected, the paranoiac activity always employs materials admitting of control and recognition."[20] Van Gogh, with rare insight and clarity, wrote Theo that his fits of madness were: "hours when the veil of time and immutability seemed to be raised for a moment",[21] and also: "There are moments when I am shaken by enthusiasm or lunacy as a visionary gift like a Greek oracle."[22] The revolutionary painter proves to be a superb verbal master in describing his insanity as a lifting of ontological veils towards new horizons of perception and being.

Chapter eight
St. Vincent – Absolute Authenticity

"I do not want the beauty to come from the material but from within myself."
Letter 195 from Vincent to Theo

When I first met Vincent van Gogh, I felt that he would either go mad or surpass us both; I did not realize at the time that he would do both.
Camille Pissarro

The sources for our deliberations on the life of Vincent – his tribulations, misery and art – are his letters to Theo. Vincent was gifted at letter writing, an art in itself. The letters reveal not only the complete financial dependence of Vincent on Theo, but the partnership of the two. In his letters, Vincent describes in detail not only the paintings he contemplated, but also asked Theo for advice as to the manner, method and colours of their execution; Theo was Vincent's alter ego. Vincent's letter writing helped him to verbalize his artistic goals, and hence structure the mythogenes to be subsequently ingrained in the artistic medium.

Vincent was socialized into the Dutch Reformed ethic of hard work and an unwavering adherence to one's task. His artistic skills were mostly self-taught. His stupendous output was carried out in the ten years between his twenty-seventh year and his death at 37. He was egalitarian, modest and self-effacing, honest to the point of *naïvité*, lonely, romantic and moody. He had a Gnostic attraction to darkness, yet was aware of its underlying luminosity.[1] He was also a desperately creative Sisyphus in the Camusean mould, ultimately crushed by his stone-burden.

Vincent was influenced in his art by Millet, Delacroix, Rubens and Rembrandt. One may also discern in his paintings older Flemish impressions from Bosch and Breughel, as well as strong Japanese influence; many of his blossoming twigs emulate Hiroshige. He also followed the Japanese practice of linking art to the seasons[2] and to related agricultural activities.

Like Caravaggio, Vincent learned how to illuminate his objects, models and portraits from within. Indeed, the portrait of his mother[3] radiates internal light, emanating from her forehead and cheeks. Love and grace flow from her blue eyes, the contours of which express a tinge of concern. However, Vincent's Gnostic dualism emanated from the dark, the sombre and grim. *Field with Ploughman*[4] was painted in Saint Remy, where short periods of hectic painting alternated with bouts of schizophrenia. This is also where he painted *Starry Night*, with its anxiety-laden whirls in the sky, each vibrating with Munch-like shrieks around wobbly trees under a lifeless moon hovering aimlessly in the sky.[5] While in Auvers, he painted the nightmarishly leaden sky hanging over a field of wheat, jittering like a dervish in a St. Vitus' dance, attacked by a squadron of fighter crows.[6] Still, Vincent's Gnosticism was "monarchic", insofar as he believed that by faith one can overcome evil. Vincent was a master colourist, and towards the end of his life in Auvers-sur-Oise, he became a virtuoso in the expression and composition of colours. The canvases depicting a young peasant woman with a straw hat[7] and a young man with cornflower[8] are masterpieces of colour composition, with one tint leading the other into a symphony of dancing shades, Vincent serving as both the choreographer and conductor.

Vincent believed in the unity of life and art. It was a sublimation of his earlier religious phase, in which he loved nature as a creation of God. But when he became a painter, his art linked his self to the trees, fields and flowers he painted. He regarded art as sacred and himself as its martyr. Indeed, his painful and suffering face appears as Lazarus resurrected by Christ.[9] The Arles canvases exude a pagan worship of the sun and the seasonal cycles of growth and decline. Vincent wrote to Theo: "Lately everything has a certain air which makes one long to dash it off on paper. All nature is an indescribably beautiful black and white show."[10] Indeed, for the deeply religious Vincent, all nature is a tremendous revelation, to be depicted by charcoal and paint. Vincent's mythogenes, ingrained in his paintings, strike us with a force similar to the energy mustered by him at the time of painting. Hence, his canvases are the synchronic bridge linking us to him outside time and space. The structured longing for nature ingrained in his mythogenes is the vehicle which links Vincent to his artistic medium, and to us. The canvas thus becomes the medium with which the artist achieves a dialogue with his audience.

Vincent believed the function of his art was to "express a sincere known sentiment".[11] This is in line with our conception of art as authentic communication. With the lonely, socially awkward and loveless Vincent, such seeking of communication, understanding and meaningful dialogue was paramount. This was also the reason for Vincent's courting of Paul Gauguin – the only one, he believed, who could understand his art. When this quest for dialogue failed, as we shall see later *in extenso*, the results were disastrous: Vincent lost his sanity and ultimately, his life.

Vincent painted orchards bewitched by destructive spirits, which haunt the trees, the clouds, meadows and flowers, making them burst at their seams.[12] In order to reach eternity, which eluded him in his bouts of religious mania with the miners at Borinage, and in his futile attempts to reach divine grace in his one-sided love affairs, he embraced the delicate, fragile cherry, apple and apricot blossoms, and structured synchronic mythogenes with them. He then flowed with their transience into the crevices and furrows of wide and jittery brush strokes, and through them beyond the Venetian blinds of time onto eternity.[13] Still, the demiurgical anguish, fright and consternation loom over the blooming orchards and flowering fields, in the form of low, black, nightmarish clouds containing stifled shrieks.[14] Once the synchronic mythogenes have been structured into the artistic medium, the canvas gets a life of its own, becoming the means of linking the artist with his audience in a meaningful dialogue transcending temporal barriers. In the process, it bridges history with transcendence, yet the glimpses of eternity in history could be meagre and erratic, a mere reflection in the dark, murky waters of the Rhône.[15] A sower sheds his grains onto the opaque, hostile, black, asphalt-like terrain, which never lets the seeds sprout.[16] White butterflies hover over a disintegrating field. The contrast between the fragile butterflies and the shattered field gives a sense of imminent disaster.[17]

However, all these dark moods, and the images, of burgeoning life and vigorous growth, bursting from his sunflower paintings, are evidence of the authentic spirituality of his revelatory mythogenes structured in synchronicity, and then ingrained within the historic, artistic medium.

Vincent's art, being authentic, links our two modes of existence. The synchronic revelations structured into a timeless mythogene, visible after embedding in canvas, become a time machine, conveying to us a century later the clarity, ingenuity and force of Vincent's prophetic vision. In Arles, Vincent invented his personal technique and style, by which he would be known. He discovered the way in which to depict the light and colours emanating from transcendence, infusing them in the space–time of a given artistic medium. Hence, he found a way to link our two modes of existence – the synchronic and diachronic – by means of his authentic art. His unique canvases "elevate" his mythogenes from time and space onto the synchronic present; and when embedded in the artistic medium, they can link anyone who beholds and is attuned to it to the same ontological synchronic level on which it has existed since being painted.

Of special importance is Vincent's preoccupation with the cycles of the growth and decline of flora, and their miraculous resurrection after wilting. Tilling, sowing, sprouting, growth, flowering, fruiting and reaping constitute the bulk of his work. Such attuning to the cycles of nature made Vincent feel in greater communion with the God of the changing seasons than the stern God of the Dutch Reformed Church. He aggressively transferred his models of nature onto his canvases with staccato speed, as if aiming to overpower, possess and dominate them; indeed, he conceived his paintings in martial terms, denoting his artistic excursions as "striking the hot iron [and] pressing home the attack".[18] This, in our terms, would classify Vincent as a separant, aiming to incorporate within himself the painted objects. Since this aim is ontologically impossible, the obsessive Vincent was ever trying to conquer the object, structure it in mythogenes and subjugate it by permanently infusing the canvas with those mythogenes.

Once Vincent discovered that the world is dualistic, in a Gnostic good versus evil dichotomy, he painted the demonic, the sinister and macabre, side by side with the cycles of growth, life and resurrection. His cypresses menace the helpless figures beneath them,[19] while skies, clouds and stars descend nightmarishly over a tortured earth,[20] and the earth trembles, just about to burst in a cataclysmic earthquake.[21]

* * *

Vincent Willem was born March 30, 1853.[22] His father Theodorus, a pastor of the Dutch Reformed Church, strongly disapproved of the lifestyle and behaviour of the fiery, single-minded, and often fanatic, Vincent. The alienation between father and son is quite apparent in Vincent's portrait of his father (p. 9). *Per contra*, his mother he loved. Vincent painted the rather plain looking Anna Carbentus with idealized affection, her face exuding glowing warmth (p. 8). She was the one who protected him, or rather over-protected him, taking his side against the rest of the family, who protested his scandalous behaviour. He most probably had a "black hole" personality, double-fixated by an overprotecting mother and a rejecting, or distantly indifferent, father. It might well explain his frenzied search for love, which mainly had the effect of chasing away his prospective lovers; or perhaps it might explain his agitated religious extremism, preached to the Borinage miners, who needed better food and shelter for their families and medicines for their collapsing lungs, more than sermons by a wild-eyed, fanatical lay preacher. Ultimately van Gogh's effort to fill the "black hole" yawning in his personality was his total concentration of agitated energies in frenzied painting.

Vincent began an apprenticeship selling pictures at the Hague branch of Goupil & Co, which sold paintings by well known and established artists, and was partly owned by Vincent's uncle, also Vincent ("Cent"). At twenty, he was transferred to the London branch of Goupil. He loved London and fell in love with his landlady's daughter Ursula, without confessing the fact to her. When he finally did, she rejected him, as all women whom he courted would. His rejection led to deep depression, and his uncle decided to send him to the Paris branch of the company. Contrary to expectations, gay Paris further depressed Vincent, who meanwhile underwent a religious conversion: God is less resistant to love than women, or for that matter, men. He lost interest in selling paintings, neglected his work and was fired. He returned to England as a teacher in a rundown boarding school but held the job only for a month. At about the age of 24, he took a job as a bookseller in Dodrecht, spending most of his time translating the Bible from Dutch into French, German and English. After a few months, he had to leave this job too. Vincent then decided that his vocation was to be a man of God. He began to study Greek and Latin so he could pass the entrance examinations to divinity school, but lost patience with the convoluted Greek verbs and gave up. He decided that to bring the love of God to the poor, and try to ease their misery, one does not need Latin and Greek, only to learn to comfort the downtrodden "at the free course in the great university of misery" (p. 13). Hence, he went to the most wretched coal-mining area in Belgium, the Borinage, as a probationary non-ordained lay preacher. He gave up his comfortable lodgings and rented a rundown hut in the miners' quarters, where he slept on the floor to better empathize with the miners' misery. He gave away his good clothes and dressed in rags like the miners. He also didn't wash the coal dust from his face so that he looked like a miner.

As might have been expected, the missionary society in Brussels dismissed Vincent because of his "excessive zeal". He remained down and out in the Borinage, in abject poverty, wandering about, staying *incommunicado* with his family for almost a year, finally surfacing with a scathing letter against the church: "I must tell you," he wrote Theo, "that with evangelists it is the same as with artists. There is an old academic school, often detestable, tyrannical, the accumulation of horrors, men who wear a cuirass, a steel armour of prejudice and conventions" (p. 154). Always the rebel, ever authentic, fanatic in his love of women, men and God, rejected by women, misunderstood by those he tried to help, regarded as a failure by his family, he decided to become a painter.

Folie a Deux

Altman's idea, in his movie *Vincent and Theo,* about the relationship between the two brothers is far from true. It has a saccharine tinge of the earlier biographies of the brothers, whereas none portray the conflictual relationship between the two that can be deduced from their correspondence. In letter 378, reacting to Theo's "high and mighty" opinion that he could not sell any pictures in the next few years, Vincent said that the two brothers should separate. Letter 379 is especially vitriolic. Vincent starts with the assertion that he as artist and Theo as art dealer are on the opposite sides of a barricade. "My sneers are bullets", writes Vincent, "not aimed at you, who are my brother, but in general at the party to which you belong, once and for all. Nor do I consider your sneers aimed expressly at me, but you fire at the barricade and think to gain merit by it, and I happen to be there . . . " He concludes this letter with an insult and a curse: "If you are no artist in painting, try to be an artist as a dealer . . . do a great deal or drop dead." Some brother! In letter 315, Vincent laments: "I do not quite understand it and think it is going a little too far – when you as well as Father feel ashamed just to walk with me." Whether it is "objectively" true or not is irrelevant. If Vincent defines the attitude of his father and Theo as rejecting, to invoke W. I. Thomas' dictum, it will be rejecting in its consequences. It could also have been a self-fulfilling prophecy. After the death of their father, he wrote in letter 408 that "it is not pleasant to them [his mother and sisters] if I came too often; nor is it pleasant for me to go there very often . . . I think those at home [are] very, very far from sincere . . . as I foresee that the character of the three sisters (all three of them) will not improve with time, but on the contrary, will get worse and at any rate just now it is utterly unsympathetic to me." In fact, Vincent was estranged from his family. Earlier, on Christmas Day, 1881, he was thrown out of his father's house following a violent scene in which he declared he would never go to church again (letter 166). Vincent also complained to Theo (letter 201) that he was stigmatized by his family: "I know quite well," he wrote, "that in our family very ugly things have been said about me repeatedly, although I do not know the source from which they originated." He then went on to describe with deep insight how stigma evolved against him: starting with some gossip, which was then exaggerated out of all proportion.

Even with Theo he had an ambivalent dialectic, ranging from total dependence to sheer hatred. Theo evidently did not understand Vincent's art. He just felt obliged to look after him, so that he would not go under. Since we hold that the essence of art is communication, and nobody in

Vincent's family or among his very few acquaintances understood his artistic message, he fell prey, as we shall see later, to Paul Gauguin, who could have given him valuable feedback about the quality of his art, since they had similar conceptions of colour and style. But Gauguin chose not to, thereby contributing to Vincent's early death.

The power of money and its saving grace was ingrained in Vincent by his low church Protestant upbringing. Weber's thesis on the Protestant Ethic and the spirit of capitalism is apparent in Vincent's attitude towards money. For him, it was clearly a tool of salvation, since without it he would not be able to buy canvases and paint. Art was Vincent's redemption. Without Theo's allowance, he was damned. When Vincent used to live with the prostitute Christine and her child, Theo threatened to sever his relationship with him, to which Vincent reacted thus:

> At present money is what the right of the strongest used to be. To contradict a person is fatal, and if one does, the reaction is not that the other party is made to reflect, but that one gets a blow with the fist. Today is to say, in the form of, "I will not buy from him again", or, "I will not help him again."
>
> This being so, I risk my head when I contradict you, but, Theo, I don't know how I could do otherwise; if my head must be cut off, here is my neck. You know the circumstances and know that my life or death depends on your help. But I am between two fires. If I reply to your letter: Yes, Theo, you are right, I will give up Christine, then first I tell a lie in agreeing with you and second, I commit myself to doing a vile thing. If I contradict you and you act like T. and M., it will cost me my head, so to speak.
>
> Well, for heaven's sake, off with my head, if that's the way it has to be. The other thing is even worse.[23]

By the Protestant Ethic, to ask for money rather than to earn it is shameful and sinful, and it was painful for Vincent to do so. Many times his pitiful begging reminds one of Oriental beggars in Old Jerusalem, or the homeless in New York. In letter 456 Vincent wrote:

> Dear Theo,
> At the moment all my money is gone, absolutely gone. I write you once again. If you can send anything, even if it's only 5 fr, do so. There are still ten days left in the month, and how am I to get through them? For I have absolutely *nothing* left. Even for the baker's, *nothing*.

According to the Protestant idea of predetermination, the losers have it coming to them. At least a tinge of this attitude towards Vincent is apparent in his family. Vincent felt that Theo was ashamed of him, the black sheep of the family, ill clad, ill mannered and unkempt. He also felt that he did not want him nearby in Paris, and sent money so Vincent would be out of the sight of Theo's censorious bourgeois milieu. In letter 386a Vincent wrote:

> Your position – isn't this true? – does not admit of our associating with each other intimately, frequently, cordially. Your position – to mention only one thing by way of example – would not admit of my going to live at your house in Paris, let's say, either with the intention of studying or for financial reasons, however necessary and useful it might be, and which might become more and more so, if circumstances permitted. For against my person, my manners, clothes, words, you, like so many others, seem to think it necessary to raise so many objections – weighty enough and at the same time obviously without redress – that they have caused our personal, brotherly, intercourse to wither and die off gradually in the course of the years. To this must be added my past, and that at Goupil & Co.'s, you are quite the plush gentleman, and I am a black sheep and an ill-natured fellow . . .
>
> Ergo conclusion – I acknowledge being under an obligation to you with the greatest pleasure. Only – lacking relations with you, with Tersteeg, or with whomever I knew in the past –I want *something else* by way of compensation.
>
> For – personally I have to think of my future – I want to get on. If a hussy won't have me, it's all right with me; I can hardly take it ill of her – but nothing is more certain than that I shall try to find compensation elsewhere. And the same is true of other relations. I shall not obtrude myself upon you, neither shall I *force* you to be affectionate toward me – but – as a friend – let alone as a brother – you are too cool for my taste. Now as to money, old fellow; I am not speaking of that. But personally you aren't for the slightest use to me, nor am I to you. And it is possible, and it ought to be, that we should mean more to each other personally.

We don't know whether Theo agreed to Vincent's analysis of their relationship. Yet if Vincent defined for himself the attitude of his brother towards him – this would be the basis of his behaviour towards Theo. Vincent had his dignity and artistic principles in relation to money, even if he was painfully short of it. Thus, when he suspected that a friend was behind the commission of a painting – who wanted to make him indirectly a present of the money – he refused it right away.[24]

Vincent's desperate demands for money have a tinge of emotional blackmail. In letter 202, he wrote his brother:

> But, brother, it has been a hard fortnight for me. When I wrote you about the middle of May, I had only 3 or 3.50 guilders left after I had paid the baker; and I have had hardly anything to eat but dry black bread with some coffee, and Sien too. Because we had bought some things for the baby, and she had been to Leyden, etc.
>
> Now I have to pay the house rent on the first of June, and I have nothing, literally nothing. I hope you will send me something.
>
> A week ago I felt very faint from continuous sleeplessness. Now that I have had some luck with a few drawings and the order for C. M. is almost finished, I have new courage and am a little calmer.

> But, brother, do write to me soon and deliver me from the landlord, for you know he won't be put off.

Even if we are aghast at Vincent's extortionist tone, there is no doubt that his quandary was real. Painting was the only activity that gave meaning to his existence. In all other occupations he had tried his hand at, he failed abysmally. His amorous endeavours were invariably disastrous. His family relationships, except the ambivalent one with Theo, were all but severed. Yet this sole meaningful occupation was dependent on money he did not have, for buying canvases and paints.

Vincent's inability to repay Theo caused him excruciating pain. In the Dutch Reformed Church, not to pay one's debts is a sure way to damnation. He could not predict that one day his pictures would sell and that he would be able to more than repay his debts. That he was right did not help him at the time. Self-doubt and despair led to depression. Theo apparently didn't believe in the commercial value of Vincent's paintings, and was angered by Vincent's incessant demands for money, and lost his patience with him.

Vincent regarded the money he received from Theo as a business transaction. In letter 390, he wrote:

> Know this once and for all. When I ask you for money, I do not ask it for *nothing*, the work that I make with it is at your disposal; and if I am in arrears *now*, I am on the right road even to getting ahead with it. [. . .]
>
> And most seriously, I repeat, Can't you find a way to help me with 20 francs, for instance, to cover those last days? What I mind most is the time I should lose otherwise. Good-bye.

There never was a deeper abyss of misunderstanding between two brothers, who have been romantically described as spiritual Siamese twins. Vincent, being sure intuitively that "he was the Beethoven of painters", knew with an inner certainty that proved to be a clairvoyance, that one day "they will fetch more than the price of their canvas and paint". His error was anchored on his customary self-deprecation; his work eventually fetched the highest prices in art history. *Per contra*, Theo never believed in the commercial value of Vincent's paintings, regarding the monthly allowances he sent his brother as charity, ordained by fraternal duty. Vincent's guilt at sponging his brother was assuaged by sending all his paintings and drawings, which he thence considered Theo's property. Vincent regarded Theo as his partner in an economic enterprise, which was sure to bear fruit.

In letter 399 Vincent wrote:

> I repeat, let us paint as much as we can and be productive, *and, with all our faults and qualities, be ourselves*; I say *us*, because the money from you, which I know costs

> you trouble enough to get for me, gives you the right, if there is some good in my work, to consider half of it your own creation.

Theo, the hard-headed art dealer, never shared Vincent's dreams of success and glory, dismissing his brother's utopian visions of creating an artists' commune in Arles, with Paul Gauguin as its ordained Messiah. He just wanted his screwball brother to be immersed as deeply as possible in his bizarre artistic endeavours, so that he did not have free time to brew up mischief for himself and his family.

The money Theo sent was transformed in Vincent's mind alchemically to artistic energy. Theo surely saw in this absurd view as further proof of his poor brother's derangement, since to his Reformed Dutch *Weltauschauung*, money was sacred and pictures were merchandize. When the divergent attitudes of the brothers towards art and money caused strain that threatened to become a permanent rift, Vincent wrote (letter 652):

> Well, the truth is, we can only make our pictures speak. But yet, my dear brother, there is this that I have always told you, and I repeat it once more, with all the earnestness that can be expressed by the effort of a mind diligently fixed on trying to do as good [work] as possible – I tell you again that I shall always consider you to be something more than a simple dealer in Corots, that through my mediation, you have your part in the actual production of some canvases, which will retain their worth even in the catastrophe . . .
>
> Well, my own work, I am risking my life for it, and my reason has half foundered because of it – that's all right – but you are not among the dealers in men, as far as I know, and you can still choose your side, I think, acting with humanity, but *que veux-tu?*

Since we have only a few letters from Theo to Vincent, we have to infer Theo's attitude from Vincent's letters. This, of course, is problematic and biased. However, Vincent's atrocious demands for more money, even when Theo let his brother know that his financial situation was bad and creditors were harassing him, cannot be accounted for by the egocentric hard-headedness of Vincent. He regarded Theo and himself as joint apostles announcing to the world an aesthetic revolution. Hence, *La Revolution comme á la Revolution*: everything should be sacrificed to the cause; all one's nervous energy, skills and worldly possessions should be made available to the sublime goal. Letter 443 is an outrageous document, if taken out of the context of the lofty ideals assigned by Vincent to both himself and Theo:

> Now just tell me, always supposing that you want to be a financier – and I have nothing against it, it is even a thing that I highly approve of; but are you quite satisfied with your own argument when at the beginning of the year you say, to my

> disappointment, "I have so much to pay. You must try to manage till the end of the month."
>
> Just listen, this is what I have to say against it, and just think it over whether I am right or not, at least if there is truth in my argument. Am I less than your creditors? – Who must wait, *they or I???*

If Theo and he were defending the "besieged city" of their artistic innovation, a creditor or two could surely be warded off to save the castle besieged by the enemies of their aesthetic revolution.

Vincent's early oral fixation on pantheistic unity joined him with his brother and his drawings, watercolours and oils into one vibrant entity. Hence, asking Theo for money is not begging, just a transfer of the means of creativity from one pocket to another. Vincent suffered from the dilemma of the outsider. On the one hand, he rejected authority, the artistic establishment and the pompous bourgeoisie. Yet on the other, he expected this very same artistic establishment to praise and buy his work. He was asking the impossible. Also, since he regarded Theo as responsible for sales in their symbiotic relationship, he demanded aggressively that Theo do his share, since he more than fulfilled his part. He did not accept Theo's excuses that the pictures did not sell. In his omnipresent delusions, he expected Theo to do the impossible, as he deemed himself to be doing: creating even in the face of insurmountable hardship. If we do not accept the thesis that Vincent regarded Theo and himself as Siamese twins engaged in creative innovation, then Vincent's demand that Theo ward off his creditors in order to send him money would seem preposterous. But if two people are engaged in a single task, with each contributing his specialized skills to it, one can demand that the other do his share. If the paintings did not sell, that was Theo's fault. Vincent's autistic, egocentric and doctrinaire *Weltanschauung* did not allow for the possibility (which was in fact the case) that Theo did not accept this division of labour. Neither did Vincent agree with Theo's claim that he could not give him more money. He projected on his brother his own grappling with insurmountable hardships, writing him imperatively: "what one *must* have *can* be found" (letter 384).

Vincent asked Theo to borrow money and help him pay his long overdue colour bill. It did not occur to him that the demand was outrageous, since he incorporated Theo into his early-oral autistic self. In this pantheistic unity, Theo surely would put himself in financial hardship so that the common goal of bringing to the world a new artistic vision did not suffer (letter 389). He conceded that Theo had been hard up too, but "your life has never been so hard as mine for the last ten years . . . and I protest against my always being neglected". This is a combination of a Dutch Reformed belief in just deserts and resentment against being the black sheep of the family. Above all, however, Vincent really believed that when you give money to artists, you are yourself doing an artist's work and that "I only want my pictures to be of such a quality that you will not be too dissatisfied with *your* work" (letter 550). We have here a total transference and juxtaposition of roles: Theo paying Vincent money and promoting his pictures makes him an artist on equal ground with his brother. Theo is actually championing his own paintings. This kind of transmutation is either sheer hallucination or transmigration *in vivo*, or both.

* * *

Vincent had a "black hole" personality, as we have mentioned. This is apparent from his rejection by his father, on the one hand, making for later- and post-oral fixations,[25] and on the other hand by an emotionally absent mother, linked to an early oral fixation. The non-coordinated personality (faulty *ity*) is apparent throughout Vincent's life. Vincent borrowed a verse from Michelet to describe his prevalent mood: "But there remains the void in the heart that nothing will fill." Vincent tried to heal the void in his personality with God, but failed. His frantic efforts to flood his "black hole" with love for women was also an abysmal fiasco. Only art brought grace into the "black hole". When he could paint no more, for reasons we shall later describe, he killed himself.

Theo recognized the abyss in his brother's personality: an almost Gnostic bimodality, with uncoordinated alternations. "It is as if two people dwell within him", Theo wrote his sister, "one of them marvellously talented, refined and tender, the other selfish and hard-hearted! They appear alternately, and in consequence he can be heard expressing one opinion one time and quite a different one the next – always with arguments for and against."[26] Vincent himself felt the rift within his personality. In letter 212 to Theo, he wrote: "I then felt an inexpressible melancholy inside . . . The emptiness, the unutterable misery within me . . . it is like a large, deep wound." He understood that the most effective way to fill the abyss within his soul was with creativity.

While replenishing the inner abyss with authentic creativity gives meaning to an otherwise meaningless void, it does not coordinate the two modalities of the disjointed personality. Hence, Vincent went through life a man of extremes: violent likes and dislikes, all or nothing, total acceptance or total rejection. This immoderation led to the *hübris* of perfectionism, and whenever a coveted goal was not achieved – which quite often was the case – tantrums, depressions, exhaustion and despair would ensue. Also, the lack of coordination between his inner participant *ani* and the separant interactive *atzmi* made for a constant struggle between his inner cognition and outer perceptions. Hence, if he felt he had painted a particularly good picture which did not sell and was not appreciated by the critics and art dealers, then the entire society allowing this unfair and self-defeating state of affairs was immoral, unjust and non-viable. *Per contra*, in moods of despair and uncertainty he would tend to accept the pejorative judgement of some relevant others, and deem himself worthless, a failure and hence damned by the Dutch Reform doctrines he kept internalized even in his later years.

As an ardent Gnostic, Vincent professed the reality and reign of the demiurgos. His way of fighting the evil archons, both in spatio-temporality and within himself, was through the saving grace of art. Vincent's *Weltanschauung* was also essentially existentialist. He believed in man's pilgrimage on earth and his being a stranger there (Psalm 119:19). He did, however, develop this ideas along the lines of Heidegger's *Geworfenheit zum Tod mit Angst und Sorge*, and man's ability to attain joy within suffering, bringing to mind the Camusean Sisyphus, who was happy, even in the midst of his tribulations. He believed with Kierkegaard and Rabbi Nachmann of Bratzlav that to come to grips with pain, to struggle with suffering, lifts one to a higher level of awareness, and may effect a revelation lending depth to the artistic medium.

Vincent aimed to be a martyr, sacrificing himself first to the suffering miners of the Borinage, then to his unrequited love for women, and finally to his art. Humiliation and abject want do not degrade, but rather lift up from the gutters to the salvation by art. Vincent was the foremost martyred saint of creativity. He beatified art and brought the Logos, the holy word, trembling within the wide, thick brush strokes and struggling out through the serpentine tree roots onto synchronic eternity.

The ornate chair of Paul Gauguin and the ascetic chair of Vincent[27] conduct a dialogue by means of the eloquent mythogenes Vincent embedded in them. There was no dialogue between Vincent and Gauguin, since the latter never intended to have one, only an I–it exploitation of Theo through his brother Vincent, to promote his own paintings. Vincent did intend to have an I–thou dialogue with Gauguin; therefore, his openness made him an existentialist winner and Gauguin the manipulator, an inauthentic loser. The social stature of the interlocutors is irrelevant for dialogue. Vincent had his closest rapport with Sien the whore. She understood him, catered to his whims and was very sensitive to his erotic character (letter 202). She was his companion in squalour. In a moving passage, Vincent writes to Theo (letter 201): "I ask but one single thing: to let me love and care for my poor, weak, ill-used wife as well as my poverty permits without their (his family) trying to separate, worry or hurt us." At the back of his mind was the love affair between Jesus and Mary Magdalene, in whose footsteps he deemed himself to walk, and whose martyrdom he saw himself emulating.[28] Ultimately, his martyrdom was to his creativity, which became his religion, as well as his link both to history and transcendence.

Vincent infers the need for modesty and for avoiding spiritual *hübris* from God's theophany to Elijah, "in a thin voice of silence". He was convinced that once an artist becomes greedy, he loses his powers of creativity. Hence authentic creativity must be a goal in itself, without ulterior motives, such as the quest for money and fame. The aim of art is dialogue. Since Vincent's longing for a dialogue with someone through his painting was paramount, he ever tried to convince Theo, the only person with whom he had a continuous correspondence, to become a painter, so the two of them could reach a true dialogue. His estrangement from his family was complete. He never had real rapport with his fellow painters. In fact, he was utterly lonely with his brother, an art dealer and, therefore, "on the other side of the barricade". Hence, he kept hammering on the theme that filial pairs of painters have left their indelible mark on the history of painting from time immemorial: the Van Eykes, Jules and Emile Breton, and many others. Thus, he created in Theo a *virtual* partner in a dialogue which could never materialize, in the same way as his delusive, one-sided infatuation with Kee Voss, which continued long after he was assured of its hopelessness. Likewise, his quixotic dream of creating an artists' commune headed by Gauguin was a *fata morgana*. Still, his longings by themselves were sufficient to structure mythogenes in the artistic media. He also tried to identify totally with the models he painted – be they elements of nature or human – and thus achieved maximum authenticity in his art, and through it a dialogue with his audience.

Vincent complained to Theo that an art dealer related to their family (Tersteeg) declared his canvases unsalable and without charm.29 He said he could not help it if his paintings did not sell, expressing the hope "that the time will come when people realize that they are worth more than the cost of the paints". Well, poetic justice has arrived: Vincent's paintings today are priceless; they sell for scores of millions of dollars, and it is not a buyer's market, since almost no one sells a van Gogh even at these prices.

The complementary dogma to that of worldly success as a sign of grace in Calvinism is the fear of failure, the disgrace of having been damned by the wish of God, through the worldly verification of defeat. Later, Vincent extricated himself from the Calvinist idea of predestination and adopted the existentialist stance that one should find meaning in the process of creativity itself, without ulterior motives. Still, he felt guilty about spending Theo's money without any hope of repaying it (letter 617).

Hence, his most strenuous efforts went into selling his work, so he could repay Theo. But as we know, his efforts were to no avail. What kept him going was the realization that he had to keep struggling uphill. Even if in doubt as to the ability to perform, one must ever try, since the process of creativity is the meaning of art.

The Lust for Dialogue

The desire to create structured the revelation of the mythogenes, which in turn effected the *fiat lux*, the miraculous luminosity, of his art. Vincent believed that in himself he was worth nothing; only his relationships with the objects and people he painted gave meaning to his existence, and to theirs. This is in line with the Buberian philosophy that the "I" or the "thou", or for that matter the "it", are but inchoate entities. Only the I–thou and the I–it are entire ontological existentials. These relationships are effected by art, if authentic. Hence, creative authenticity is the key to entering the spirituality of nature, the means to feeling unified with the whole of Creation.

Indeed, Vincent's art was his sole means of expressing love and his need to be loved by people, nature and God, whoever kept rejecting him. He conducted a dialogue with his tools – his brushes, paints and crayons. He attributed a soul to his crayons. It reminds one of the dialogue Buber carried out with his walking stick and the spiritual rapport he achieved through it with a tree.[30] The animistic link Vincent felt with nature explains the dancing and whirling trees, and stars infused with the painter's own jittery soul and trembling psyche.

In his work, Vincent demonstrated how one element of nature can be related to another in one pulsating whole. He unified his consciousness with matter through the mythogenes he embedded in his drawings and canvases. Art and life are thus a single entity; Vincent adopted the ideals of Puvis de Chavannes, according to which art should serve as a unifying agent of man and nature. For Vincent, however, art was more: he intended to use it to reach through the "universal thou" – the Buberian God in nature and man. This was the existential God created through the artistic dialogue of man and nature, to supersede the stern God of the Dutch Reformed Church. Vincent was always attuned to nature and tried to ingrain himself into it by means of his penetrating brush strokes. Such infusion into the unseen layers of nature was Vincent's manner of reaching the divine inner essence of the trees, meadows and human figures. He reprimanded painters who paint from pictures and memory, as well as the critics who never bothered to immerse themselves in nature.

Vincent's desire for dialogue with God and other human beings was incessant and total. He thus suffered from what we denoted elsewhere as "the least interest principle",[31] which operates in most dyadic human interaction. If one desperately wishes to sell, the buyer shies away. If one wishes to be popular with one's membership group, making frantic efforts to gain acceptance, more often than not the result will be rejection. Finally, if one tries to force one's point of view on another by vociferous attempts at persuasion, one is liable to be cold-shouldered and scorned. Vincent suffered all these hurts. The only realm accepting his total involvement was his art. He knew that the love of art is the sublimation of the love of man.

But he knew that for him it was not a matter of choice, since the love of art was the sole emotional outlet open to him. Still, his most ardent wish was to achieve a dialogue with a kindred soul through his work, since he felt that he could achieve a wonderful harmony, a rapport of grace, with nature through his paintings and wanted to transmit this rapport to another human being. He was a sharer; he wished another to partake of the ecstasy, the joy, the meaningfulness which art brought him. This was why he was so vulnerable to the likes of Gauguin, who could have had an authentic dialogue with him, but chose instead to take advantage of and manipulate him. The lack of dialogue may be linked to an "I–it" petrification and the acceptance of the condemning labels of the generalized other, à la Sartre's "hell is the other". This may lead to a sense of failure and suicidal melancholy, which indeed is what would eventually happen to Vincent.

Vincent learned from the Japanese the quality in painting of "soul" (letter B10), the means by which the artist articulates his aesthetic criteria, embedding them in the artistic product. In our conceptualization, this "soul" is the mythogene structured by the artist into the artistic medium. Hence, the mythogene is the vehicle of dialogue between the artist, the artistic medium and the audience. If art is authentic, the mythogene is synchronic, and lifts the artist, the artistic medium, and its viewers, onto eternity. However, the dialogic link is, perforce, maieutic. Thus, Vincent structured his mythogenes through his unique bio-psycho-social configuration: his genetic potential, his stormy "black hole" personality, and his upbringing in the Dutch Reformed Church. The author has experienced the maieutic impact of Vincent's work; he was completely mesmerized by his paintings in the Vincent van Gogh Rijksmuseum in Amsterdam. The author's bio-psycho-social configuration could not be farther removed from Vincent's: his bio-genetic potential is Slavic, his personality related to a depressive mother and to a father who was a stubborn, ascetic, idealistic pioneer. His socialization was in a Jewish, Zionist, socialist environment in Mandatory Palestine and later Israel. However, the synchronic mythogenes within Vincent's paintings gripped him with such force that he remained transfixed by them, entirely entranced within them, irresistibly drawn to them for endless hours, until forcibly dragged away from the museum by a travelling companion. This is the most complete possible dialogue over time, place, personalities and cultures through the authentic art of an offbeat genius.

Vincent regarded his models as maieutic catalysers between his consciousness and his paintings. Hence, his models were of paramount importance to him. He chose them very carefully – they had to be central to his person, ideas and beliefs. One such model was Dr. Gachet, the enlightened therapist from the asylum at Auvers-sur-Oise. A precursor of Harry Stack Sullivan, Ronald Laing and Michel Foucault, Dr. Gachet became a friend to Vincent, who wrote (in letters W22; L638) to his sister:

> I have found a true friend in Gachet, rather like a brother, so great is the physical and even mental resemblance between us. He himself is a nervous, eccentric man. He has given numerous proofs of friendship to the artists of the new school, and has been of service to them whenever it was in his liking for orgiastic language. He described the artist himself a sort of intoxicated giant, better equipped to move mountains than to toy with bric-à-brac, a seething brain irresistibly pouring forth its lava into all the gorges of Art, a terrible and half-mad genius, frequently sublime, sometimes grotesque, at all times very nearly sick.

Vincent's portraits of Dr. Gachet[32] indeed reflect his deep affinity, understanding and admiration for the doctor, who also radiates reciprocity towards the painter. His painting *Old Man in Sorrow* is an attempt to reach a dialogue with an old depressive[33] catatonically oblivious to his surroundings. Vincent's portrayal of the old man's utter despair and dejection cannot be described in words. The dialogue in misery of the old melancholic and Vincent is transmitted to us with unparalleled force. In the *Raising of Lazarus*, Vincent utilized the technique perfected by Caravaggio, in which model and painter coincide. St. Lazarus has Vincent's face,[34] so that the dialogue, indeed the identification of the mythogene in the artistic medium, effect a perfect match. With *Lazarus*, Vincent suffered a diachronic death, but in it, he is resurrected into synchronicity to live with us forever.

Vincent believed that art would bring him close to nature and to "something on high – inconceivable, awfully unnameable – for it is impossible to find a name for that which is higher than nature".[35] Painting from nature, unlike the academic artists who paint from memory, books and other media, Vincent carried on a dialogue with the trees, flowers and fields he mythogenically ingrained in his canvases. In letter 228:

> I see that Nature has spoken to me, has told me something that I have written down in shorthand. My shorthand may contain words that are indecipherable – but some of what the forest or shore or figure said still remains.

But he also reached God with his art – the deity he so ardently courted while preaching in Borinage, but who painfully evaded him. It seems that Vincent structured his unrequited longing for God and the transcendental into mythogenes he embedded into his paintings. In this he followed the Hassidic Jewish notion of "worship in the concrete", the beatification of art and artefacts by embedding into them sparks of Divinity strewn in the mires of history and "lifted up" by the creator of the most mundane objects. With each brush stroke, Vincent ingrained his longing for God into mythogenes, and thence into his canvases.

Vincent was engaged in his staccato creativity while renouncing, in a Kierkergaardean manner, any goals within history. Hence, his creativity became a pure process. As long as he could renounce ulterior motives, he was immune from despair. Only when he was dragged into temporal ambitions and utopias, like the artists' commune in Arles, did he court disaster. His anchoring on the process of art led him to mount the fleeting moment within synchronicity. He thus discovered through his art the means to reveal, in the Heideggerean sense, the flow of eternity within history, and the link between the two.

Vincent wrote Theo (letter 529): "Fortunately for me, I do not hanker for victory any more, and all that I seek in painting is a way to make life bearable." This is the process of art pure and simple – the creative endeavours of a Camusean Sisyphus, which extricate him from the drudgeries of routines, the vicissitudes of subsistence and the vileness of mediocrity. His interest was in art itself and not its temporal rewards. Hence, he had a latent horror of success, although he wanted to sell his paintings to cover his debts and expenses, but nothing more. This was the Jonah syndrome of a subconscious wish to avoid recognition – he committed suicide just about when his chips started to turn up, with a gradual yet steady public interest in his work.

First and foremost, Vincent was a lover, an existentialist lover loving the other on the other's terms. Once he fell in love with his prostitute model, Sien, he tried to blot out his own ego and be concerned empathetically with her passions, desires and grief. He was genuinely delighted when his companion, who gave him gonorrhoea, gave birth to a child who was not his. He cried with joy at his perceived happiness for Sien delivering a baby. This is the epitome of existentialist identification with the emotions of the other, while blotting out one's own ego *vis-à-vis* the other. His love of the outcast prostitute was total, while rejecting the reprimands, rejection and ostracism of his family and colleagues. It was nobody's business to alert Don Quixote that Dolcinea was a two-bit whore, if for him she was the queen of his dreams. Vincent's one-sided love affairs were quite Kierkegaardean, since he all but renounced reciprocity; his love must be absolute and invulnerable. To all his approaches and supplications, another lover, Kee Voss, reacted with an adamant refusal. She sent back his letters, unopened, but he remained undaunted. He wrote Theo (letter 154): "Life has become very dear, and I am very glad that I love. My life and my love are one. Her [Kee Voss] 'No, never-never-never' I regard as a block of ice which I press to my heart to thaw." This is an infatuation with love as a goal in itself. As in his art, nothing less than the absolute is acceptable to Vincent. And an absolute love would be tarnished by acceptance. Rejected, Vincent could use Kee's "no, never-never" as a cross of ice to re-enact the passion of another reject crying *Eli, Eli lama sabakhtany*. For Vincent, the cross is tangible, ever present. Love, even if unrequited, gives life a meaning that in our terms would structure mythogenes of both longing and experience to be embedded in art. Vincent's art, rejected no less than his love, became a labour of grace flowing from the lover–artist – sublimated into mythogenes embedded in the artistic medium and resurrected in all those attuned to his timeless wavelength.

Altman's movie ingeniously depicts Vincent cutting his tongue and inserting it while dripping blood in the gaping mouth of Gauguin, who cringes with fear and disgust. Yet for Vincent it was the ultimate in the meeting of body and soul. The very same shattered emotions structured by a Munch into his *Le Cri*, the howls of an Ivan Illich embedded by Tolstoy in the *Death of Ivan Illitch,* and Gesualdo's tortured anguish framed in his madrigals also reach us, since they have been catapulted into authentic mythogenes and thence onto timeless synchronicity, where a maieutic dialogue between artist and audience could, and should, occur.

Vincent's renunciation of the fulfilment of his quests, longings and loves, so that they could be structured in his art, is his major spiritual sacrifice, aside from the sacrifice of his health. He thus became the first saint of modern art, a role denied him when he aimed to martyr himself for the Borinage miners. Likewise, Vincent the artist–saint bridged the abyss between nature and the Authentic Domain through art; he mediated through the mythogenes embedded in his paintings between his own quests and ours, so that the rich, ecstatic convolutions of his martyred soul pump grace into all who open up to his genius. We may even suspect that with his autistic solitude, he even created a virtual viewer to whom he wrote and with whom he could carry on a viable dialogue. Thus Vincent wrote Theo (letter 379):

> And in my opinion it cannot be helped that we are in different camps opposed to each other. And whether we like it or not, you must go on, it must go on. But as we are brothers, let us avoid killing each other, for instance (in the figurative sense). But we cannot help each other as much as two people who are standing side by side in the same camp. No, if we should come near each other, we should be within each other's range. My sneers are bullets, not aimed at you who are my brother, but in general at the party to which you belong once and for all. Nor do I consider *your* sneers aimed expressly at me, but you fire at the barricade and think to gain merit by it, and I happen to be there.

What a dichotomy! The money-conscious Theo, Vincent's link to the outside world, is worlds apart from him, yet is the first audience of Vincent's art, the soul brother to whom Vincent sent sketches of every drawing, watercolour and painting, before they were actually executed.

* * *

Vincent immersed himself, perfecting the technique of embedding his mythogenes of longing and experience with staccato speed onto his canvases, and returning home to his monastic abode, would fall on his bed exhausted. He needed nobody and nothing beside his art. But then *hübris* crept in. He sought a dialogue not through synchronic eternity in the Authentic Domain, but within diachronic history, right here and now! His target was Paul Gauguin, not a mediocrity, not a Salieri to Vincent's Mozart. Gauguin was a talented artist in his own right, but personally the two could not have been more different. Their divergence is epitomized by the two chairs we have already mentioned. Paul's armchair is of lacquered, multi-coloured wood; Vincent's of roughly hewn logs, coarse, grained and unpainted. Paul's chair has lordly arms. Vincent's is a lowly peasant's, tough and ascetic. The back of Paul's chair is arched for comfort and expansive hedonism. Vincent's chair is structured for suffering, Paul's for sophistication, poetry and the light of knowledge and leadership. Vincent's is a chair of the provincial, luckless and lustreless labourer: a hard-up artisan whose only pleasure in an otherwise miserable existence is an occasional tobacco pipe. And with this person Vincent sought a dialogue, not through the maieutic authenticity of his art, but within the drudgery of every-day life, exacerbated by financial problems and his own temperamental eccentricities.

Vincent sought in Paul the bosom friend he never had. Theo was his only lifeline, but Theo did not really understand Vincent or his art. Paul would penetrate both his convoluted, tortured soul, and his art, so similar to his own. He also longed for feedback from fellow painters as to the extrinsic value of his work. His art gave meaning to his life, but did it give similar meaning to the lives of others? He needed, so to speak, an Archimedean point, provided by another professional painter. He remembered with pride that once a painter entered his studio by chance and looked at a drawing on an easel, and spontaneously uttered, "This is vigorously drawn and seriously studied" (letter 277). This kind of support and, if need be, critical yet always candid feedback, was what Vincent hoped to receive from Paul Gauguin.

He also felt a deep affinity with Gauguin because of his tribulations, comparing them to his own. He enumerated the similarities between himself and Gauguin: their unseen sensitivities and their misunderstood, poetic qualities. His expectations from their encounter soared higher each day, until their heights were altogether out of touch of reality. Symbolically, the two chairs remained empty: the potentiality for dialogue remained unfulfilled. Vincent's openness to a meeting of souls with Gauguin was true to his character, his expectation from the encounter utopian. Yet Vincent's quest for dialogue, and his expectations of it, were not shared by Gauguin. Vincent wrote to Paul about the plans for the artists' commune in Arles with him, Gauguin, its poet-leader. As such, he would need comforts and status symbols.

Gauguin's plans were simpler – Theo, the simpleton's brother, of the renowned Goupil & Co. art dealers, would sell his pictures. He would ask Theo to pay his debts, and in exchange he would spend some time with his weird brother. Having been a stock exchange dealer, he knew how to strike a hard bargain. One day he promised to come to Arles, the next he announced that he unfortunately couldn't come, the third day, with the subtlety of an elephant in a china shop, that he could come only if some pressing, financial problems were solved.

As for Vincent, everything was in suspended animation until Paul came. He decorated Paul's room to his liking, and borrowed money to put in new drawers, and to fix the bed, because Gauguin had a bad back. With the "Second Coming", when Paul the artistic saviour came, Vincent aimed to decorate the walls of the studio with sunflowers – the expression of the van Gogh mythogene of resurrection.

The commune of artists headed by Gauguin would be monastic, with art as its religion. In letter 332, Vincent wrote Theo that the master to emulate would be Millet, the painter of rural nature, a Puritan and a great believer in God – what the Puritans were of old, such would be the painters of today. He also assumed the role of the Good Samaritan, helping Gauguin out of his quandary, like Corot, who helped the downtrodden and dejected Daumier. In letter 544 Vincent wrote to Gauguin:

> I think that if, from now on, you begin to feel like the head of the studio, which we shall try to turn into a refuge for many – little by little, as our strenuous work furnishes us with the means to complete the thing – I think that then you will feel more or less comforted after the present miseries of poverty and illness, taking into consideration that probably we shall be giving our lives for a generation of painters that will last a long while.
>
> The part of the country where I live has already seen the cult of Venus – in a Greece essentially artistic – and after that the poets and artists of the Renaissance. Where such things could flourish, impressionism will too.
>
> I have expressly made a decoration for the room you will be staying in, a poet's garden (among the sketches Bernard has there is a first rough draft of it, later simplified). The ordinary public garden contains plants and shrubs that make one dream of landscapes in which one likes to imagine the presence of Botticelli, Giotto, Petrarch, Dante and Boccaccio. In the decoration I have tried to disentangle the essential from what constitutes the immutable character of the country.

The artists' colony would also be a therapeutic community. "Ah, my dear friend", wrote Vincent (letter 573a to Gauguin), "to make of the art of painting what the music of Berlioz and Wagner already is – an art of consolation for broken hearts." The Arles centre for art therapy would cure souls and console hearts, with Gauguin as its grand master and Vincent its jack of all trades, from mixer of paint to caterer to the slightest whim of the absolute *arbiter elegantium*. But above all, they would paint together. It would break their respective solitudes, forge their friendship and continuous dialogue, and revolutionize the world's conception of art for generations to come.

Gauguin shared nothing of Vincent's visions. All he intended was to spend two months with the crazy Vincent in Arles, as the price of the cool-headed Theo paying off his debts and selling his paintings.[36] This was the betrayal of Christ by Judas for some pieces of lucre; it was also the martyrdom and passion of modern art's foremost saint. Gauguin's betrayal led not only to the dispersal of the vision of the artists' utopia, but also to the insanity and suicide of art's purest idealist and most self-less prophet.

Gauguin tried later to play down his role in Vincent's destruction, but his apologies are *post facto* excuses. The truth is to be gleaned from Vincent's letters; unlike Gauguin, Vincent was incapable of lying, and stated plainly that Paul was the trigger of his loss of sanity. Vincent expected Gauguin to give him feedback as to the value of his work, and considered him the only man who could do so. But not only did Gauguin not provide such supporting evaluation, he actually downgraded Vincent's work. In so doing, he not only shattered Vincent's self-respect, but also the meaning of his life. Gauguin left Arles on Christmas Eve without telling Vincent, and it was then that Art's Prophet was anointed by the blood from his ear and the oblation of his sanity to the higher revelation of the dialogue between art, life and the Authentic Domain in transcendence. The present author's mentor, Martin Buber, once told his students that in Hebrew violence (*alimut*) and silence (*elem*) stem from the same root. Hence, when there is no possibility for dialogue, when the routes for a meeting of minds are blocked, the almost sole alternative is violence. This struck many of Buber's students at the time as a most insightful revelation. It certainly applied to the relationship between Vincent and Paul. The first opened up completely, unequivocally and without reservation, expecting a Buberian I–thou dialogue. The other had a manipulative I–it attitude from the outset. Hence, no dialogue could have ensued and the resulting violence demeaned, blemished and martyred the innocent Vincent.

Technique and Authenticity

Vincent realized from the outset that to be a painter of worth he had to master its technique, what he called "*La cuisine de l'art*" – the kitchen of art. Indeed, in a remarkably short period, he mastered a vast technical knowledge of paints, oils, charcoals, watercolours and canvases. Still, he knew that technique is secondary to the artist's inner spirit. As he wrote to Theo (letter 195): "I do not want the beauty to come from the material, but from within myself." Eventually, he did develop his very unique technical method, which made his paintings tremble, virtually burst at the junctions of the wide, thick brush strokes, imbued with the circular tornadoes storming out of his soul and onto the canvas. However, his main technical inspiration came from Japanese painting, drawings and prints. Vincent had the walls of his studio decorated with prints of Japan's Ukiyoe school of painting, among them woodcuts of such celebrated masters as Hokusai, Hiroshige and Utamaro.

The main Japanese technique he borrowed was the juxtaposition of large areas of unmixed colour. He also adopted the Japanese use of steep diagonals and sudden shifts in perspective (p. 292). His reliance on Japanese technique was so great that in letter 510, he told his brother: "My whole work is founded on the Japanese." In letter 221, he stressed the paramount importance of outline, which he also adopted from the Japanese. However, Japanese technique was only one major, formative, influence on Vincent. There were many others: He had great admiration for Rembrandt, as well as some of the other Dutch and Flemish painters, among them Frans Hals, de Vos, Ruisdael and Vermeer. As for Rubens, he liked his technique, but criticized his "lack of soul". In letter 444 he told Theo:

> Rubens is extraordinary in painting ordinary beautiful women. But he is not dramatic in the expression.
>
> Compare him, for instance, to that head by Rembrandt in the Lacaze Collection; to the man's figure in *The Jewish Bride* – you will understand what I mean, as for instance, that his eight pompous figures of fellows performing a feat of strength with a heavy wooden cross in *The Elevation of the Cross* seem absurd to me from the standpoint of modern analysis of human passions and feelings. That Rubens' expressions, especially of the men (the real portraits always excepted), are superficial, hollow, pompous, yet – altogether conventional, like those of Jules Romains and even worse fellows of the decadence.

Pissaro's work he cherished as pioneering impressionism. Delacroix he considered the greatest colourist of them all. Also Delacroix, like himself, had taken his models from nature and *in situ*. Vincent also acknowledged as his masters Daumier, Doré, Corot, Daubigny, Breton and Troyon, but his alter ego was Millet, whom he emulated in many of his rural scenes. Like Millet, he considered painting a form of prayer, a supplication to a God unknown. For Vincent, Millet had unsurpassable genius (letter 241). Millet depicted the archetypal peasant, which served as a model for Vincent in all his agricultural themes. The fact that he followed in the giant footsteps of Millet lent Vincent a vigour, serenity and confidence, knowing he was on the right artistic track.

He knew at the outset, from the very moment he decided to be a painter, that draughtsmanship is paramount. In letter 176, he wrote about his drawing practice and exercises: "I am very glad that I find my drawing is improving. It gives me courage. Drawing is the principal thing, whatever they [the generalized other] may say, and it is the most difficult too." In letter 221, Vincent criticized young painters who start painting watercolours and even oils without mastering drawing first. He was determined not to touch watercolours or oil before he became a competent draughtsman. His guide in the technique of drawing, like in many other things, was Delacroix, who advocated the *Gestalt* technique of draughtsmanship.

Vincent also solved the controversy raging at the time between the followers of Ingres, advocating the primacy of the line in painting, and those of Delacroix, anchoring on colour: he invented the technique of drawing with colour by a brush directly on the canvas, an innovation of his own (letter 308).

Apart from the contrasting planes of intense coloration and thick contours he adopted from the Japanese masters, Vincent also incorporated techniques of the Renaissance, Baroque and Mannerist masters. We see in his art traces of the *chiaroscuro* employed by Giotto, whom Vincent very much admired, and the ingenious method of Caravaggio in illuminating without revealing the source of light, so that the viewer sees the painting as if shining from within. Yet Vincent did not just collect these techniques in a haphazard manner; he integrated them into a style of his own. The physical proportions of his human figures are somewhat arbitrary, yet the way he painted his figures, for instance, made them seem lively and fresh. He painted his models the way he perceived and felt them in his inner self. As a colourist, aside from Delacroix, he learned from Manet and Courbet, whose work was "a wedding between form and colour" (letter 519). He was also influenced by Gauguin's palette, but his colours writhed, whereas Gauguin's colour technique was more static. Above all, he loved yellow, which he used more and more in his unique style; the hot yellow of the sun, the warm yellow of sunflowers, the golden yellow of wheat-fields. He smeared paint directly from the tube onto the canvas. He chose a palette of colours for each painting, in agreement with nature and his model (letter 429). He always regarded nature as his guide and inspiration. Although he might have struggled with nature on his choice of palette, he always came back to it, since "one can never study nature too much or too hard".

Still, colour expresses something in itself; it has autonomy of expression. Vincent had a Greek conviction as to the relationship between aesthetics and truth; he felt that a really beautiful combination of colours is also correct and true (letter 429). His use of thick layers of paint allowed him to endow a canvas with three dimensionality. Colours change in nature according to the time of day and the season. Hence, the exactness of the colours is not important; their composition, though, should harmonize with nature. Therefore, nature should be painted directly from observation, be it a landscape, flowers or a human figure. The model must always be before the artist's eyes. In this way, the painter effects a dialogue with nature, and the model, if authentic, emerges ecstatically onto synchronicity, thence enabling a dialogue with a viewer. In letter 442 to Theo, Vincent expresses his credo that in painting the human figure, one must start with the soul and then go on to the body and clothing. This, to our mind, is the essence of authentic art: an I–thou Buberian dialogue with the spiritual essence of the model, which carries this linkage onto the Authentic Domain in transcendence, for anyone who chooses to "open up" to the artist's creation and partake with him in a timeless dialogue. When Vincent writes of creating paintings with soul (letter 230), he had in mind precisely this process of embedding into his canvases mythogenes of longing and experience, which could pass eventually to his viewers in a synchronic meeting of souls.

After he lost his absolute belief in God, art as an end in itself was probably the sole firm, normative conviction on which he anchored his life. In letter 448, he wrote his brother: "More and more I believe that *l'art pour l'art*, to work for work's sake, *l'energie pour l'energie* – is after all the principle of all great artists." Hence, one has to work as authentically as one can and to treat the rest - sales, societal and critical acceptance – as beyond one's powers. In chapter 2, we have mentioned that quite likely, there exists a curvilinear relationship between innovation and societal acclaim. Some innovation has a good chance of being accepted in the artist's lifetime. But revolutionary innovation, like Vincent's, is likely to be acclaimed, if at all, after the artist's death. The creative process is continuous, never ending, always changing, in a Heraclitean *panta rei* flux, with the authentic artist ever looking for new methods and ways of expression, without ever being completely satisfied or resting on his laurels; which would be tantamount to creative stagnation. Vincent, like a Camusean Sisyphus, never rested; he always reached frantically for different methods of seeing his subjects, structuring them into mythogenes to be incorporated into his canvases.

He was also able to innovate in the technical realm, since the strict rules and procedures of various academies left no inhibiting imprint on him. It brings to mind Einstein's answer as to the secrets of his innovation: being a sickly child, he often did not go to school, and thus avoided becoming either intellectually maimed or emotionally petrified by the authoritarian and ossified Prussian school system. With Vincent, the expressive energy was so explosive that it more than made up for any technical weaknesses in his work. In letter 195, he wrote:

> Thank God I have my work; but instead of earning money by it, I need money to be able to work, so that is the difficulty. When in a year – or I don't know how long – I shall be able to draw that Geest or any other street as I see it, with those figures of old women, workmen, girls, the Tersteeg's, etc., will be very kind. But then they will hear me thunder, "Go to hell"; and I shall say, "You deserted me when I was in trouble, friend, *I don't know you*, go away, you're standing in my light."
>
> Dear me, why should I be afraid, what do I care about Tersteeg's "unsalable" or "without charm"? Whenever I feel depressed, I look at *The Diggers* by Millet and *Le Blanc des Pauvres* by De Groux, and then Tersteeg becomes so small, so insignificant, and all that drivel of his becomes so foolish, that my spirits rise, and I light my pipe and start drawing again. But if ever a "civilized" person should cross my path at such a moment, he might hear things which would sober him.

These are Vincents's own inner struggles, his psychomachic storms structured into mythogenes and embedded into paintings. These explosive yet convulsive energies have marked the whole Arles period, his most productive. Vincent's technique was first of all to write to Theo and describe in detail what he intended to draw or paint. By articulating his artistic intentions, he actually formed the mythogenes, which would be subsequently ingrained in the canvas. He thereby emulated the primary act of the Creation, which commenced with the Logos – the word – and the word emanated and ordained the *fiat lux*. The mythogene is, therefore, the verbal conceptual medium, the vehicle that carries the dialogue between the artist and the artistic medium. This process, if authentic, raises the work of art onto synchronicity, lending it timelessness.

Even though Vincent's religious faith wavered after his brief Borinage period, his mental framework remained religious, and his art was geared to reach out to transcendence. Indeed, the deep religious sentiments of Millet were one of the reasons for Vincent's identification with him. In a sense, deep down, he remained a preacher even when painting, since he proclaimed in his art his infatuation with nature, his love of humanity and his re-affirmation of whomever moves the cosmos. He also saw himself as God's emissary in history, with the duty to convey to Him through his art the abject misery of man, amidst the gorgeous extravagance of nature and the dire need for meaning in an otherwise absurd existence.

Being thrown onto his death in the Heideggerean sense, with worry and anxiety, or as Kierkegaard put it, fear and trembling, Vincent was anxious and painfully intense all his life. This explosive intensity drove away women, alienated his friends and was bad for business, reflected in non-existent sales (except for some disguised charity). In his work, however, this vibrant intensity made for spectacular originality and uniqueness. His awareness of his *Geworfenheit zum Tod* induced him to set an order of priorities to his finite years, with work, creativity and art at the top of the list.

He gave a reason for his creativity, characteristic of the view of the Calvinistic theology of predetermination, saying that man must "repay" God and the universe for the privilege of having been born. Hence, Vincent felt an obligation to adorn the earth which hosted him, with his art works. Also, in the spirit of Protestant theodicy, Vincent found a functional reason for his suffering. Pain would be sublimated into creativity lending it greater depth and scope.

The relationship between pain and art was not clear to Vincent, but he did feel intuitively that they are related. He was convinced that his tribulations had a purpose, deepening his experiences and structuring them, as per our concept, into mythogenes. Discovering his vocation in painting, he felt compelled to work frantically to be saved, according to the Protestant Ethic he had internalized. He approved of Carlyle's maxim:

"Blessed is the one who has found his work." When he worked he felt alive, but on days he could not work or succeed in painting the way he wanted to, he felt damned.

Since the process of creativity is all there is, our creative efforts must be our best. After our work is complete, we must be satisfied with the artistic details, to the last brush stroke. One should not be a Mrs. Lot, full of regret and self-pity, casting a last look over one's shoulder. One should also not look into the future; only the present is meaningful. Vincent felt intuitively what we claim mytho-empirically, that authentic creativity "lifts" us onto synchronicity, unto the continuous present. This is also the Camusean Sisyphus for whom Vincent is the prototype.

This is the uphill struggle of Sisyphus in a never-ending road, since when the stone rolls down he has to lift it and roll it up again, *da capo*. Indeed, when Vincent finished painting a canvas, he was rarely satisfied (letter 607). Hence, he would start painting a new canvas almost every day, cherishing the process of creativity, but knowing that when it was complete, he would lose interest in it and start a new painting all over again. Since the process of painting is an end in itself, he was obsessively meticulous, working out every detail to perfection. Thus, in order to get at the true character of a certain corner of a garden, to glean "the fundamental truth of it; that's three times now that I've painted the same spot" (letter 541). True to the archetype, the moment he felt he had grasped the way to render a certain tree, figure or furrow, the revelation started to recede from him (p. 292). But ultimately it did not: Vincent's inner conflicts were registered by his genius in every crevice of a wheat-field, in every bursting synapsis between heavy brush strokes for all of us to see and admire. When he was working, Vincent was never depressed. The revelation the religiously oriented Vincent experienced while painting brings to mind Catharina di Sienna's dictum that the road to heaven is also heaven. Authentic creativity as a process in itself can carry one to salvation.

Vincent was an innovative rebel and well aware of it. In letter 337 to Theo he advocated a *radical* renewal of all approaches, methods, styles, execution and sales of works of art. Nothing short of a continuous, total revolution. This complete rebellion against all artistic institutions, art-dealers and critics led to conflict on all fronts: with fellow artists, art salesmen and family. Yet Vincent never gave in. In letter 408, he asserted his decision to go his own way, against all odds. Since he never had any artistic feedback from a constructive critic, he had periods of self-doubt and occasionally a wish to be accepted by the artistic establishment, without giving up any of his revolutionary principles. He obviously was asking, as we have mentioned, for the impossible. Ultimately, he developed what we call "an active melancholy". Such melancholy is very similar to what we have denoted elsewhere as *desperation*, and is a major component of authenticity.

*   *   *

If each moment should be lived as if it might be the last, then its intensity and authenticity are important, irrespective of any attendant's joy or pain. An authentic event is related least of all with the generalized other's evaluation of whether it is a success or failure. Jacques Brel stopped performing his commercially successful songs because he felt that he did not express himself through them creatively any more. The process in itself should also be rewarding; a Kierkegaard, a Camus, a Brel reject the bourgeois notion that the interests of the present should be sacrificed in bondage, drudgery and petrification for the glory, comforts, security, power and money to come. There is no dull creativity or authentic tediousness. Joy may be experienced by the strenuous, even painful, dialectical involvement with one's surroundings to produce a work of art or a creative scientific or industrial result.

The existentialist anathema is inauthentic slumber in bondage to the "they-selves", whereas creative rebellion, even if accompanied by pain and suffering, is an existential triumph. Gauguin in Tahiti, dying of syphilis and forgotten by almost everybody, and painting pictures without knowing whether at all they were going to be sold, was an existential success. *Per contra*, Gauguin in Paris, with a lucrative business, applauded by his bourgeois associates and painting every Sunday afternoon by the banks of the Seine, was an existential failure. Joy and pain are interchangeable so long as the experience is intensively authentic.

*   *   *

It certainly didn't help Vincent to hear constantly from his "well wisher" that he could not draw, that his paintings lacked charm, and wouldn't sell. But then, what did he expect? Moving around in dirty clothes, unkempt hair, quite often reeking of absinthe, short tempered with a fanatical glint in his eyes, offering weird paintings that nobody bought. And yet he was sure of his intrinsic value, and that the day would come when the whole world would recognize his greatness, which indeed it did. His grievances against the artistic establishment, and especially Theo's own company, Goupil, were the same as artists from time immemorial against art patrons, critics, collectors and merchants: "*L'excellent leur échappe toujours*" – they never recognize excellence.

Goupil & Co. ignored Millet, Daumier and the young Corot (letter 380 to Theo). A rather Christian statement in the spirit of "the meek shall inherit the earth" was made by Delacroix in his diary:[37]

> One must hope that the great men who were despised or persecuted in their own lifetimes will one day be granted the reward that was denied them on earth when they enter into a sphere where they enjoy a happiness of which we have no conception, part of which is the happiness of looking down to witness the fairness and justice with which Posterity remembers them.

Vincent recognized intuitively what we denoted as the "evolutionary leash", society's defence mechanism against too much innovation, which has the potential of damaging its fragile infrastructure. Hence, he felt that society was not yet ready for his starkly divergent mode of artistic expression. He suggested to Theo (in letter 312) not to press sales too hard, but wait till society was readier for his work. Vincent's credo, however, was still to immerse himself in the process of creativity, to make sure it was sincere, true to nature and authentic. Such fidelity would serve as a force field against stigmatizing critics, and pompous art merchants.

Vincent also knew the scourge of self-important mediocrities, who snubbed him and denigrated his work. When finally, in January 1890, six of his paintings were accepted by the Seventh Belgian Exhibition, a certain Henry de Graux, a Belgian illustrator of religious books, withdrew his pictures from the exhibition, declaring that he did not wish his work to be exhibited together with "the revolting pot of sunflowers by Monsieur Vincent".[38] It was Kuhn who enunciated the theory that a revolutionary outside a currently accepted paradigm could not be recognized by the reigning powers within the paradigm. But Vincent was sure the generations to come would open up, admire and love his artistic, brilliant innovation and excellence. How right he was!

Vincent also had the "Jonah Syndrome", which we have denoted elsewhere as a fear of success. He probably had a subterranean dread of being accepted by the *vulgus*, because of the "kiss of fat" which writers and artists experience after they are publicly recognized, stifling their creativity. In letter 524 he wrote to Theo:

> What touches me most deeply in Zola's *L'Oeuvre* is the figure of Bongrand – Jundt. What he says is so true. "You think, you poor souls, that when an artist has established his talent and his reputation, he is safe. On the contrary, henceforth he is denied producing anything which is not perfect. His reputation itself forces him to take more pains over his work, as the chances of selling grow fewer. At the least sign of weakness, the whole jealous pack will fall on him and destroy that very reputation and the faith that the changeable and treacherous public has temporarily had in him."
>
> Even stronger than this is what Carlyle says: "You know the glow-worms in Brazil

> that shine so that in the evening ladies stick them into their hair with pins; well, fame is a fine thing, but to the artist it is what the hairpin is to the insects. You want to succeed and shine, but do you know what it is you desire?"
>
> So I have a horror of success, I am afraid of "the morning after the night before" of an impressionist success, even these difficult days will later seem to us "the good old times!"

This could explain his subconscious "internal saboteur", which prevented him from cultivating cordial relationships with art dealers, and caused him to be curt and short tempered with prospective buyers. In letter 527 to his brother, Vincent wrote, "It is to be feared that as soon as the painting is appreciated the painters will go soft". Never had a creative Sisyphus to carry a heavier burden on his aching, exhausted shoulders.

"Madmen" like Bosch, Nietzsche, Nerval, van Gogh and Artaud test the limits of our endurance, and thus activate the "evolutionary leash" on the boundaries of the viability of the deviant and mad innovator; they thus expand the range of the survival of the species, even if these "deviants" perish in the process. However, the "mad" innovators do more than that: We have mentioned that they widen the experience of spiritual ontology, by transcending the boundaries of known awareness through "peak experiences".[39] Madness enhances the forbidden passage between object and subject. Norman Brown put it thus:

> It is not schizophrenia but normality that is split-minded; in schizophrenia, the false boundaries are disintegrating. Schizophrenics are suffering from the truth . . . the ego being no longer distinct from the object; the subject no longer distinct from the object; the self and the world were fused in an inseparable total complex.

The escape from history onto transcendence can also be triggered by madness, Describing the paradoxical ontology of many, Nietsche put it thus: "Nature entraps the genius in a prison and stimulates his wish to break free to the utmost."[40]

Mauve, a fellow artist who taught Vincent to paint, and of course Tersteeg, ostracized him, because he lived with a prostitute. In letter 192 to Theo, Vincent defended his liaison with Sien:

> Last winter I met a pregnant woman, deserted by the man whose child she carried. A pregnant woman who had to walk the streets in winter, had to earn her bread, you understand how.
>
> I took this woman for a model, and have worked with her all winter. I could not pay her the full wages of a model, but that did not prevent my paying her rent, and, thank God, so far I have been able to protect her and her child from hunger and cold by sharing my own bread with her. When I met this woman, she attracted my attention because she looked ill. I made her take baths and as much nourishing food as I could afford, and she has become much stronger. I went with her to Leyden,

> to the maternity hospital where she will be confined. (No wonder she was ill, the child was not in the right position, and she had to have an operation – the child had to be turned with forceps. However, there is a good chance of her pulling through. She will be confined till June.)
>
> What I did was so simple and natural that I thought I could keep it to myself. Posing was very difficult for her, but she has learned; I have made progress in my drawing because I had a good model. The woman is now attached to me like a tame dove. For my part, I can only marry once, and how can I do better than marry her? It is the only way to help her; otherwise misery would force her back into her old ways, which end in a precipice. She has no money, but she helps me earn money in my profession.

Vincent's inability to acknowledge the other's point of view made him think that his art and personal lives should be separate, not knowing, or preferring to ignore, the stigmatizing mind of the bourgeois who would rush to smear the art of a person because he "has a vicious character". But the idea of marrying a prostitute was the epitome of depravity. In the nineteenth century, the cities of Europe had scores of thousands of prostitutes, and hundreds of thousands of people had venereal disease. But the whole topic of sex was taboo, as Freud eventually would discover. Vincent couldn't, or wouldn't, understand that the hypocritical bourgeois painters, or for that matter, his own family, could not but reject his noble sentiments towards Sien and cast him out. In Nuenen, the local priest forbade anyone to model for him. Since Vincent was being ostracized, he in turn spurned persecutors, real and imagined. He complained to his brother (letter 302) that in moments of despair he would have liked to be made of iron and not have flesh and blood. These are also the moments when depression set in. When such dark clouds engulfed him, he started blaming himself for having succumbed to the pressures of his family and deserting Sien, instead of following the directives of his heart and marrying her.

Many times his depression alternated with a mania, and then he started to be paranoiac, accusing the only person who helped him, or for that matter, the only person with whom he was at all in contact, Theo, of all sorts of imaginary wrongs. The attacks of depression *cum* paranoia became more and more frequent and severe. He also declared to Dr. Gachet, the psychiatrist of the Auver-sur-Oise institute, to be sicker than he. In his celebrated portrait of the physician, he appeared to him just as ill and confused "as you or me, with the heartbroken expression of our time". He asked Theo (letter 648) how the doctor could help him, since "when one blind man leads another, don't they both fall into the ditch?" He also launched himself on a binge of self-destruction. He drank vast quantities of corroding absinthe, and often subsisted on coffee, barely eating while working at a furious pace. In the last year-and-a-half of his life, from his mental breakdown to his suicide, he painted 300 oils and made hundreds of drawings. Frantic creativity was Vincent's mode of defending himself against insanity and stigmatization. His work engulfed him in a cocoon of authenticity, which also served as a barrier against depression and mental breakdown. Only when he felt he could not work any longer did he shoot himself.

His art also brought him to God; like Christ, he felt the more he was despised by human beings, the nearer he was to the kingdom of God. Still, his painting towards the end was jittery, indicating that Vincent was ever on the verge of an abyss. The brinkmanship of his staccato painting barely kept him in a precarious mental balance. However, the mythogenes of mental breakdown were apparent in many of his later paintings. The courtyard of the hospital at Arles[41] looks as if it was shattered by an earthquake. The clumps of grass look like scimitars, just ready to fly into the viewers' eyes.[42] The *Starry Night* at Saint Remy undulates in a demonic dance, whirling within a devastating tornado.[43] Still, working on the verge of madness enabled Vincent to reach new heights of revelatory insight, and deeper internal anxieties and pain were sublimated into unique art. The perfectionist authenticity carved the inimitable mythogenes from within Vincent's tortured psyche, which were then honed into the philosopher's stone ingrained in his canvases, displaying like never before the *coincidentia oppositorum* between motion and equilibrium, chaos and order, and aesthetics out of madness.

In the end, he projected the torrents of hell within his crucified soul. He even swallowed paint, emulating present-day "body art". His last canvas, *Wheat Field with Crows,*[44] has heaven black, low and threatening to drown the world with torrents of pitch. The earth is soaked with blood, the crows won't let anyone escape their dire fate. There is no need for a reaper.

Chapter nine
Antonin Artaud – Outside of Time

"The Big Bang made God deaf." *Anonymous*

Antonin Artaud is the last of the geniuses whom we will consider as an anchor for our thesis of the link between insanity, deviance and innovation. He was a poet, painter, filmmaker, playwright, theatre director and theoretician, and was one of the founders of the surrealist movement. His essays *The Theatre of Cruelty* and *The Theatre and its Double* had a strong impact on French theatre. He was born in 1896 and died in 1948. He was in and out of mental institutions for the last ten years of his life. A 1937 portrait of him shows a young, glowing face, with the proud beauty of a god. A 1947 photograph is that of an old man, with a wrinkled, twisted face, his mouth gaping and eyes opaque, a result of electric shocks and psychiatric drugs, whose side effects were worse than the symptoms of his disease. His identification with Vincent van Gogh was one of brotherhood in art and misery. His essay on van Gogh was one of his most sensitive and profound works, and like him, he committed suicide.

Basically, Artaud's thesis is that society defends itself from great innovators by labelling them mad. In *The Theatre and its Double,* he expressed his dualistic, rather Gnostic, belief that the theatre reflects life, yet must liberate itself by expressing the primary instincts of sex and cruelty, engage in fetishistic rituals, replete with tribal masks and primitive background music. As such, it was to have a layer of therapeutic psychodrama. Artaud lavishly used onomatopoeia and gibberish, but required the actors to concentrate on what they were saying and make their replicas with maximum force. His ideas influenced such giants as Roger Blin, Jean-

Louis Barraux, Julien Beck and Samuel Becket, and through them European and world drama. Like his idol Vincent van Gogh, he opted for maximum authenticity, and for rejection of the generalized and certain petrifying others. Both endured the ostracism and misunderstanding suffered by the creative innovator, believing that what was important lay in the process of art, and not in its material and social rewards. However, since we consider art a communicative process, if only with a single kindred soul, at the end of his life Artaud had ceased to be an artist. Vincent van Gogh in all probability had not sold, as we have seen, a single painting during his lifetime. Yet he never ceased to seek dialogue through his art with someone who would understand it. *Per contra*, Artaud invited all the who's who of Paris culture to a theatre hall and howled at them with blood curdling shrieks. With this non-communicative event, he labelled himself a mad, pitiful has-been.

Artaud revealed himself to be an existentialist phenomenologist by trying to cope with the essence of the self, and to reach the core of the "pure self" by phenomenological reduction. Like his alter ego van Gogh, he saw himself as the suffering Christ, despised by the demiurgical "others", the *Wiedergeists*, the double-dealing hypocrites. Artaud wrote:

> But there is someone that has always loved me for my goodness within me, not only in my body but also in my soul. This is somebody called Jesus Christ, because the priests have always the greatest tenderness for my devotion and my piety. I did not realize this in the beginning but it is some years now that I know that all the mass prayers on earth have been based on my piety.[1]

When van Gogh depicted himself in one of his paintings as St. Lazarus (and the Saviour), nobody saw it. But when Artaud claimed that masses were being held in churches all over the world for his soul, he was quite well (or rather notoriously) known, in Paris, and the statement guaranteed him the tag of insanity.

Deploring the existential loneliness of man, Artaud wrote:

> My solitude is without a name and without any identity. It exasperates by the horror which has haunted me that in reality I have always been by myself. I know now that I have always been a stranger to this earth. (p. 213)

Man is a tantalic being who cannot be saved from his fate: he is destined never to achieve what he longs for. Moreover, while the fox has his lair and the bird its nest, man has no place to escape from his misery (p. 187). Yet again, like van Gogh, Artaud never ceased to seek, indeed crave dialogue. He was always attuned to the other, any other, who might open a window to his soul. He never aimed at a superficial rapport with the exterior of the other; only a dialogue with his inner self would satisfy him. Such Buberian "I–thou" dialogues were rare indeed. Most of the time he was frustrated and retreated into his lonely corner, or became immersed in a catatonic stupor. Artaud understood that the theatre is a means for structuring mythogenes which lend meaning to the lives of both performer and spectator, just as the paintings of van Gogh mythogenically link the artist and his audience over time and space, revealing to both important insights. Artaud was a participant retreatist, who courted annihilation within history. He held a lifelong interest in *Unio Mystica*. He studied the doctrines of Ruysbroeck, San Juan de la Cruz and Jacob Boehme. While van Gogh committed suicide when he could no longer contain the ever-widening horizons of his being, for Artaud suicide was an alternative to seeking union with the all-embracing unity in entirely unknown circumstances, the ultimate adventure in face of the unfathomable. He believed, as he wrote to his friend Riviere, that in order to grasp the meaning of being, one must annihilate one's cognition, perceptions, and nervous energy (p. 38).

Artaud was certainly eccentric, deviant, bizarre, and what is commonly known as "mad"; yet, we wish to ascertain what effect all this had on him, and to what insights and creative domains it brought him. Admittedly, being mad revealed to him the meaning of the world. Hence, insanity for him delineated the limits of understanding; yet, for the stigmatizing others, such reaching out towards the normative boundaries of comprehension constituted madness, since the agencies of social control take deviant and antisocial behaviour as the main indications of insanity (p. 187). Artaud's writings are as explosive as van Gogh's paintings. Yet, the work of van Gogh was structured and communicative, whereas Artaud opted for intellectual anarchy, which in the last analysis cannot be communicative, and therefore does not amount to art. Artaud's experience of insanity was very similar to van Gogh's, and both regarded psychiatry and mental asylums as tools of social control, not of therapy. In his essay *Le Suicidé de la Société*,[2] he projected his own experiences and longings – as well as his structured mythogenes – onto van Gogh and his art, so that the mythogenes were Artaud's, while at the same time relating to van Gogh and to their common *Weltauschauung*. Like Vincent, he saw himself as a martyr for his art; he abhorred its lack of appreciation by the coarse *vulgus* and its artistic institutions. He called van Gogh the organist of an enclosed storm.[3] This poetic metaphor is apt and forceful, but describes Artaud himself and his non-communication more than it does the expressive torrent of Vincent's work. He was also convinced that his suffering was sublimated into art as a theurgic means to transcendence. In his surrealistic, poetic style, he denoted van Gogh's paintings as "old sins, which have not yet been absolved".[4] Their absolution would seemingly be effected by their *extasis* from history into the synchronic authentic domain in transcendence. Artaud projected onto van Gogh his own experiences of stigma, ostracism and the stifling of his excellence during the nine years of his incarceration in mental institutions.

This brings to mind the ostracizers in the Agora of Athens, who voted to expel Aristides from the *polis,* being fed up with hearing all the time how righteous and talented he was. Hence, both van Gogh and Artaud "preferred" to become mad rather than forfeit their superior conception of human dignity (p. 157). They did not want to conform to the slavish rules of the asylum, so they could be declared "cured" and be released. They preferred to stay inside the institutions rather then feign acceptance of their draconian, petrifying, humiliating regimes. The danger posed by "madmen" like van Gogh and Artaud to the mediocrities of the *vulgus* and "total institutions" was their greater lucidity, their ability to see farther, to feel deeper than the average man (p. 177).

Artaud wrote that since van Gogh's creations were like an artistic atomic bomb, uncontainable by the power elites, their way of defending themselves was to declare Vincent mad (p. 14). This is in line with the anti-psychiatric claim that the stigma of madness is a means of social control. Like van Gogh, Artaud's love affairs were total, absolute and hence impossible. He also regarded art as a goal in itself, not as a means to material gain. Art is communication through an epistemic wall, which only the creative energy of a Vincent can affect (p. 40).

Another painter with whom Artaud identified was the Florentine Paolo Uccello (1397–1475), a marginal figure in Renaissance art. He was actually more Gothic than Renaissance, and his personality was split between intellectualism and artistic creativity.[5] He was a genius alienated from the main current of the art of his time, which was dominated by Brunelleschi, Masaccio and Donatello. So much so, that Alberti did not include him in his directory of artists, *De Pictura*. Precisely this alienation attracted Artaud, who considered Ucello one of his alter egos, and called him Paul des Oiseaux (Birds) – *uccello* in Italian is a bird. Artaud had birds in his soul that longed to be liberated. Like Uccello, he had a psychosomatic, rather Gnostic, dualism in his personality, the "black hole" characteristic of our other subjects. He actually recognized in himself two entities: one dominated by the Gnostic demiurgos, and therefore suspended in an unbearable temporality, and the other in the mystical realm of the spirit, envisaged by such Christian mystics as Jacob Böehme, Ruysbroeck and San Juan de la Cruz. Artaud saw himself vacillating between these dualities, always at the intersection of phenomena, not within them. Hence, he is mostly marginal to both dualities, and alienated from human groups and institutions, like his two role models. Yet his suffering, caused by the ostracism of the generalized others and by the clashes with stigmatizing and depriving groups, was sublimated into a profound creativity.

The relationship between pain and creativity is, as we have pointed out, not linear but curvilinear. Some suffering may be enriching, but too much may break the artist, as it did both van Gogh and Artaud. Not only does the bourgeoisie reject "mad" outsiders; society itself, aided by its controlling agents, fights the "insane" innovators, who expand man's limits of awareness and widen their own and others' normative being and conception of aesthetics. The bourgeoisie begrudges creative individuals for being creative, which its own members are not. Hence, it ever pushes them into line and if they do not comply, they pay dearly, with their well-being, freedom and sometimes with their very lives. Such agencies of social control are the crows in van Gogh's last painting, pumping dark lead into the clouds and blood into the earth. Artaud's main concern was his crusade against the psychiatric establishment and its institutions. He realized that madness is culture-bound. He demanded to know what the justification was for declaring Vincent insane and committing him to a mental institution.[6]

A society engaged in the kind of atrocities described in Orwell's *Nineteen Eighty-four* should be regarded as an instrument of organized crime.[7] Hence, Artaud "preferred" to remain "sick" and not forfeit his superior lucidity; yet the psychiatric institution and its repressive "treatment" exerted its toll. Artaud entered the mental hospital looking like a radiant young man; after nine years looked like a wrinkled old man with hollow cheeks, a toothless mouth and blank, opaque eyes. He was the authentic anti-psychiatric writer who experienced the atrocities of the mental asylum on his own flesh, while Foucault, Laing and Szasz merely wrote about them. Psychiatrists are the Orwellian "thought police" curbing rebellious creativity (p. 32). In order to hide their impotence, psychiatrists invent ridiculous terminology, which explains nothing and only serves to further stigmatize, segregate and alienate their patients (p. 15). Thus, hospitals for the insane perpetuate their inmates' afflictions, with the side effects of the treatments being much worse than the illnesses. Psychiatrists undermine their patients' ingenuity; their demand that their charges renounce their individuality is the basis of their creative innovation and the most frequent cause of their suicidal despair (p. 37). Artaud realized what more and more researchers have since confirmed: that mental illness is a conceptual sickness,[8] generated by the "poisoned tongues" of psychiatrists.

If one is desperately honest in one's quest to examine one's ontological boundaries, madness can be instrumental. Insanity can widen and deepen our consciousness, yet many times the mad pay the price of their inner enlightenment with religious and quasi-religious condemnation. The church, the rabbinate and the ulema do not intend to relinquish their monopoly on revelation. Also, psychiatrists wish to show their adeptness at "curing" the insane, even if their brains are "burnt" in the process. The only way to fight insanity is to remain authentic and refuse to relinquish one's insights.

Artaud goes a step farther than the Cartesian "I think, therefore I am" by postulating: "I am inside my body" (pp. 7, 30). He thus expresses one of the most mind-boggling paradoxes of human existence: Why has my body been chosen to be the channel of cosmic awareness? And why does every human being feel the same way? How can this paradox be solved? Artaud was most susceptible to solipsism, since his eccentricity and deviance set him apart, and the psychiatric drugs and electric shocks reduced his already meagre ability and desire to communicate.

The solipsism of Artaud was reinforced by his body-centred *Weltanschauung,* his belief that the human body, or rather his body, was the only ontological reality (p. 7). His inability and lack of desire to solve, at least for himself, the paradox of solipsism led him to anoint himself Bishop of Rodez; later he held the megalomaniacal view that he was the centre of the universe and that all Creation and its creatures were just his marionettes.

His most ambitious goal was to reunite man and woman by somatic alchemy into a self-sufficient hermaphrodite.[9] Thence, the solipsistic Artaud would not need to pursue the pain-yielding love of another person or the conflict-ridden sex between male and female; he would be a self-satisfying ouroboros. As for transcendence, Artaud professed an improvement on the dialectical concept of the Christian trinity and the *coincidentia oppositorum* of alchemy. His unity was completed by the annihilation of multiplicity and the big-crunch like compression of all Creation into the potential of timeless, spaceless singularity (pp. 69–105). Artaud was certainly an existentialist in his conception of life, of being thrown unto death with anxiety. This anxiety was both somatic and spiritual.

He did, however, carry out a phenomenological reduction of both life and death, and psychoanalyzed himself out of his fear of them. He followed his alter ego, Paolo Uccello, Paul of the Birds, in what he imagined the master had done: He traced all the paths of his thoughts within his body. Thence, he lived towards his death without pain, with a slow disintegration parallel to the entropy of his body (p. 31). The manner he chose of rebelling against death was creativity. Like van Gogh's painting, Artaud's writing was an affront to death. Art and life were synonymous.

Authentic art was not for entertainment, but for giving meaning to the life of the artist, and through him, to others who would open up to his creativity. Above all, art is not an ego-trip for applause and recognition, but a means for dialogue, for fusion with other human beings, for feeling their body and soul, for permitting them to breath and tremble in unison with the artist (p. 190). One also lifts oneself by authentic art into synchronicity, to partake of the authentic domain, where all authentic art is stored forever, for exposure to kindred souls attuned to the artist. Madness, for Artaud, was a means to widen and deepen the limits of consciousness, until it soared to the authentic domain in transcendence (p. 186).

"There is no other issue for pure thought than death" (p. 38), said Artaud, thus revealing his existentialistic outlook: He was a companion of Heidegger, who saw being as a *Geworfenheit zum Tod mit Angst und Sorge;* and of Camus, who regarded the dilemma of whether or not to commit suicide as the most important issue in philosophy. He was not afraid of death, since love and its sublimation into creativity confront and thwart the apprehension of death (p. 38).

Artaud's most interesting innovation is mytho-empirical, surrealistic and ideational; it is related to Uccello, whose fresco of Noah's Ark depicts a refuge for the mad, the deviant, the pariah, a *stultifera navis* in the synchronic authentic domain outside history. This Noah's Ark contains the authentic reservoir of mythogenes of creativity stored in synchronicity, waiting for the "right conditions and opportunities" to return to history and fructify its wastelands. Mytho-empirically, this Noah's Ark is a structured limbo between the hell of history and a timeless paradise. The raven belongs to the powers of demiurgal evil. When released, it did not come back. The dove came back with an olive branch, a creative, mythogenic symbol of an I–thou dialogue within history. A Midrash points out that Noah, before coming out of the ark, forced the hand of God, squeezing out of Him a promise that he would not be molested when emerging from the ark to resettle within history. Hence, the creative innovators, shunned and persecuted in their lifetimes, can bequeath their creations to history only when the artistic power cliques and establishments do not interfere.

The process of raising authentic creativity into the authentic domain within the mytho-empirical Noah's Ark commences with the mythogenes of longing and experience, which "lift" the work of art into timeless synchronicity. This is the artistic mythologization of reality, lending metaphysical significance to history. This is very much like the Hasidic "worship in the concrete", which sanctifies profane reality. Artaud understood that life gains meaning only through *coincidentia oppsitorum* by means of art. The philosopher's stone of alchemy is the artistic achievement which transforms the commonplace into an artistic triumph. Indeed, Artaud himself longs to partake of the transcendental Noah's Ark by means of a *denudation epidermique* and emergence from his ego boundary, which is known clinically as one of the manifestations of autistic schizophrenia.

The ontology of Noah's Ark does not need verbal communication. It is the mytho-empirical projection of pantheistic early orality, or rather the metaphysical womb of the structured authentic domain. It stores the seeds of art and culture for redissemination in the atrophied, degenerate or corrupt cultures, wiped out as dysfunctional by the pitiless decree of evolution. Artaud existed in the spiritual ark, away from and beyond his historical body. He escaped the drudgery of daily life and exchanged it for the moratorium of madness, i.e. the total cessation of normal progression in one's life. His Noah's Ark was a place of deliverance from infernal history. Artaud remained in Noah's Ark until his suicide.

Noah's Ark was believed by some church fathers, notably Origen, Tertulian and Augustine, to be a permanent haven, designated by divine wisdom to save humanity from periodic disasters, which could not have been prevented by the good God. This rather Manichean and Gnostic approach may have influenced Uccello, who depicts Noah's Ark as filled – contrary to Scripture – mostly with sick, mutilated and dejected humans, led by an authoritarian, majestic figure standing as if at the helm of a ship, who was, in all probability, the image of Augustine.[10] Noah's Ark, as a cosmic place of refuge, encapsulated outside of time, was adopted and elaborated upon by Artaud, replete with a psychotic identification with Uccello. Uccello, the bird, was transported into synchronicity, outside reality. He became a Noah saved from temporality.[11]

Artaud was not alone in Noah's Ark, but flanked by the luminaries of the Italian Baroque: Donatello and Brunelleschi (p. 26). These creative innovators, together with countless others (since the capacity of a timeless and spaceless capsule is infinite), cruise eternally outside history, seeking the proper recipients for the endless varieties of creative mythogenes stored in the authentic domain of Noah's Ark. The landing of the mythogenic dove in a historical time and place depends on background factors hospitable to the seedling mythogenes, enabling them to take root in their new host. Of special importance was Uccello's portrayal of Noah's Ark as a haven for deviants, contrary to the Darwinian conception of the evolutionary selection of the fittest. This is in line with the hypothesis hinted at by Artaud, and fully developed in the present volume, as to the link between deviance and creative innovation. If indeed the outcasts, the pariahs, have a greater chance of seeing things differently, both materially and aesthetically, and hence to innovate, the admittance of the socially divergent into Noah's Ark is evolutionarily functional from the standpoint of creativity. Hence, the historical *stultifera navis,* the total institutional solution for the incarceration and, indeed, elimination of deviants, madmen and sinners of medieval communities, was mytho-empirically transformed into Noah's Ark, the ahistorical refuge of the mythogenic structures of the creative innovators.

Madness for Artaud was a means of extricating himself from history and into synchronicity, the atemporal refuge of Noah's Ark. There, with the mythogenic innovations of nonconformist, stigmatized and inspired madmen, he would be stored in cultural limbo, outside history, until the olive branch in the beak of the dove signified that it was time for his innovations to land back in history, where they would be welcome, and not ignored or rejected as before. Noah's Ark is the mytho-empirical place of storage of the great innovations in art and science, which were liable to "rock the boat", and to upset the cultural system in their time.

Notes

Introduction Mytho-Empiricism

1 S. G. Shoham and G. Rahav, *The Mark of Cain* (St. Lucia: University of Queensland Press, 1970).
2 Frederick Robert Tennant, *The Sources of the Doctrines of the Fall and Original Sin* (New York: Shocken Press, 1968), p. 140.
3 Karl Abraham, "Formation of the Character on the Genital Level of Libido Development", *Selected Papers of Karl Abraham* MD (London: Hogarth Press, 1927): 407.
4 S. G. Shoham, *Valhala, Calvary and Auschwitz* (Cincinnati: Bauman & Cody Academic Publishing Inc., 1995), p. 25.
5 C. Lévi-Strauss, *Le Cru et le Cuit* (Paris: Plon, 1964), p. 9.
6 Jean Piaget, *Structuralism*, trans. Chaninah Maschler (London: Routledge and Kegan Paul, 1971), p. 5.
7 Albert Camus, preface to *The Myth of Sisyphus*, trans. Justin O'Brien (New York: Vintage, 1961).
8 Albert Camus, *The Rebel*, trans. Anthony Bower (Harmondsworth: Penguin, 1962), p. 241.
9 *Ibid.*, p. 219.
10 Rudolph Binion, *Frau Lou: Nietzsche's Wayward Disciple* (Princeton: Princeton University Press, 1968), p. 83.
11 J. P. Sartre, *The Prisoner* (New York: The Noonday Press,1957), p. 19.
12 Stefan Zweig, *Die Welt von Gestern: Erinnerungen eines Europaers* (Frankfurt am Main: S. Fischer, 1962).
13 Bettina Knapp, *Antonin Artaud: Man of Vision* (New York: Avon, 1971).
14 Lev N. Tolstoy, *What is Art* (Oxford: Oxford University Press, 1930).
15 S. G. Shoham *et al.*, *Violence* (Aldershot: Dartmouth Publications, 1995).
16 Peter Alekseevich Kropotkin, *The Conquest of Bread* (New York: New Press, 1926), p. 103.
17 Shoham and Rahav, *The Mark of Cain.*
18 Svend Ranulf, *The Jealousy of the Gods and the Criminal Law of Athens* (London: Williams Norgate, 1933).
19 Robert Graves, *Greek Myths* (Harmondsworth: Penguin Books, 1955).
20 Albert Salomon, "The Messianic Bohemians" in George B. De Huszar (ed.), *The Intellectuals* (Glencoe, Illinois: The Free Press, 1960): 20–1.

Chapter one The Personality and its Disruption

1 S. G. Shoham, *The Myth of Tantalus* (St. Lucia: University of Queensland Press, 1980); *Salvation Through the Gutters* (New York: Hemisphere Publications, 1980); S. G. Shoham, *Rebellion, Creativity and Revelation* (New Brunswick, New Jersey: Rutgers University Press, 1986).
2 Shoham, *Salvation Through the Gutters,* chap. 1.
3 F. Leboyer, "Birth Without Violence", in A. Macfarlane (ed.), *The Psychology of Childbirth* (London: Wildhood House, 1975).
4 Shoham, *Salvation Through the Gutters*, part 1.
5 Shoham, *The Myth of Tantalus*, chap. 1.
6 Shoham, *Salvation Through the Gutters*, pp. 141–2.
7 Shoham, *The Myth of Tantalus*, chap. 8.
8 Y. A. Cohen, *The Transition from Childhood to Adolescence* (Chicago: Aldine, 1964), p. 105.
9 Midrash Sifre Deuteronomy, 32.
10 Euripides, "Iphigenia in Aulis", in *The Complete Greek Drama*, vol. 2 (New York: Random House, 1938), p. 323.
11 *Ibid.*, p.334.
12 Albert Camus, *Myth of Sisyphus* (New York: Vintage Books, 1961), 3ff.
13 Shoham, *Salvation*, chaps 4, 8, 13.
14 Robert Graves, *The Greek Myths*, vol. 2 (Penguin Books, 1955), p. 26.
15 Shoham, *Salvation Through the Gutters,* part 1.
16 E. G. Schachtel, *Metamorphosis* (London: Routledge & Kegan Paul, 1963), p. 60.
17 J. Bowlby, *Attachment* (Harmondsworth: Penguin Books, 1972), chap. 11.
18 This is the stand adhered to, *inter alia*, by Sullivan. See R. Munroe, *Schools of Psychanalytic Thought* (New York: Holt, 1955), p. 360.
19 W. R. D. Fairbairn, *Psychoanalytic Studies of the Personality* (London: Routledge & Kegan Paul, 1966), chap. 11.
20 J. Piaget and B. Infelder, *The Psychology of the Child* (New York: Basic Books, 1969), 25ff.
21 Fairbairn, *Psychoanalytic Studies of the Personality*, chap. 1.
22 Sigmund Freud, *Mourning and Melancholia,* Standard Edition, vol. 14 (London: Hogarth Press, 1917).
23 C. R. Shaw and H. D. McKay, *Juvenile Delinquency and Urban Areas* (Chicago: Chicago University Press, 1942); E. H. Sutherland and D. R. Cressey, *Principles of Criminology*, 8th edn (Philiadephia: Lippincott, 1970).
24 M. E. Griffin, A. M. Johnson and E. M. Littin, "The Transmission of Superego Defects", in L. E. F. Vogel and N. W. Bell (eds), *The Family* (New York: Basic Books, 1972).
25 F. Lidz and S. Fleck, "Schizophrenia, Human Integration and the Role of the Family", in D. D. Jackson (ed.), *Etiology of Schizophrenia* (New York: Basic Books, 1972).
26 F. Mullahy, "Sullivan's Theory of Schizophrenia", *International Journal of Psychiatry* 6 (1967): 492.

27 S. G. Shoham, "The Tantalus Ratio", *The Journal of Genetic Psychology* 126 (1974): 44–119.
28 S. Rosenzweig, "The Experimental Measurements of Types of Reaction to Frustration", in H. A. Murray (ed.), *Exploration in Personality* (Oxford: Oxford University Press, 1962): 585–99.
29 G. Bateson *et al.*, "Towards a Theory of Schizophrenia", *Behavioural Science* 1 (1956): 64–152.
30 P. Watzlawick, "A Review of the Double Bind Theory", *Family Process* 2 (1963): 132–53.
31 M. Bowen, "A Family Concept of Schizophrenia", in D. D. Jackson (ed.), *Etiology of Schizophrenia* (New York: Basic Books, 1972): 346–72.
32 Shoham, *supra* note 2, *Salavation Through the Gutters.*
33 H. M. Cleckley, *The Mask of Sanity* (St. Louis: Mosby, 1964).
34 J. Zubin and B. Spring, "Vulnerability: A New View of Schizophrenia", *Journal of Abnormal Psychology* 86 (1977): 103.
35 *Ibid.*
36 H. S. Sullivan, *Psychoanalysis and Interpersonal Psychiatry* (New York: Science House, 1970).
37 M. E. P. Seligman, *Helplessness: On Depression, Development and Death* (San Francisco: Freeman, 1975).
38 E. H. Sutherland and D. R. Cressey, *Principles of Criminology* (Philadelphia: Lippincott, 1970).

Chapter two *Hübris*, Suppression and Stigma

1 Svend Ranulf, *The Jealousy of the Gods and the Criminal Law of Athens* (London: Williams Norgate, 1933).
2 Gaston Bachelard, "The Fetish of Newness", in C. Harrison and P. Wood (eds), *Art in Theory, 1900–1990* (Oxford: Basil Blackwell, 1992), p. 379.
3 *Ibid.*, p. 563.
4 *Ibid.*, p. 565.
5 Pages 54–9 have been written with Amit Pinchewski.
6 Maurice Merleau-Ponty, *Phenomenologie de la Perception* (Paris: Gallimard, 1963), p. 143.
7 Søren Kierkegaard, *Fear and Trembling* (New York: Doubleday Anchor, 1954).
8 Albert Camus, *The Rebel* (New York: Vintage Books, 1959), p. 266.
9 Albert Camus, *The Myth of Sisyphus* (New York: Vintage Books, 1975).
10 Erving Goffman, *Presentation of Self in Everyday Life* (Harmondsworth: Penguin Books, 1971).
11 S. H. Bergman, *Dialogic Philosophy from Kierkegaard to Buber* (Jerusalem: Bialik Institute, 1974), p. 261. In Hebrew.
12 Søren Kierkegaard, *Either/Or* (Princeton University Press, 1987), p. 90.
13 Bergman, *Dialogic Philosophy*, p. 264.
14 Neil Postman, *The Disappearance of Childhood* (New York: Dell, 1982), p. 30.

15 Martin Buber, *I & Thou* (Edinburgh: T&T Clark, 1970), p. 103.
16 J. Dubuffet, "Crude Art Preferred to Cultured Art", in *Art in Theory*, p. 595.
17 Alfred Rosenberg, "Der Mythus des 20 Yahrhunderts", in *ibid.*, p. 394.
18 Adolf Hitler, "Speech Inaugurating the 'Great Exhibition of German Art'", in *ibid.*, p. 423.
19 *Ibid.*
20 Vladimir Ilych Lenin, "On Proletarian Culture", in *Art in Theory*, p. 383.
21 "Red Group Manifesto", in *ibid.*, p. 388.
22 Alexander Rodchenko, "'Slogans' and 'Organizational Programme' of the Workshop for the Study of Painting in State Art Colleges", in *ibid.*, p. 315.
23 *Times Literary Supplement,* January 26, 1991, p. 3.
24 J. L. Simmons and H. Chambers, "Public Stereotypes of Deviants", *Social Problems* 13 (1965): 111.
25 S. G. Shoham and G. Rahiv, *The Mark of Cain* (St. Lucia, University of Queensland Press, 1982).
26 J. Nunnally, *Popular Conceptions of Mental Health* (New York: Holt, Rinehart & Winston, 1961), p. 233.
27 T. J. Scheff, "Negotiating Reality: Notes on Power in the Assessment of Responsibility", *Social Problems* 16 (1968): 3–17.
28 T. J. Scheff, *Being Mentally Ill* (Chicago: Aldine, 1966), pp. 33–4.
29 Nunnally, *Popular Conceptions of Mental Health*, p. 233.
30 T. J. Scheff, *Being Mentally Ill,* p. 82.
31 M. K. Temerlin, "Suggestion Effects in Psychiatric Diagnosis", *Journal of Nervous and Mental Disease* 147 (1968): 349–58.
32 D. L. Rosenhan, "On Being Sane in Insane Places", *Science* 179 (1973): 250–8.
33 W. R. Gove, "Societal Reaction, an Explanation of Mental Illness: An Evaluation", *American Sociological Review* 35 (1970): 874–84.
34 S. G. Shoham, *The Promethean Therapy* (Hebrew) (Kiriat Bialik: Ach Publishing Co., 1998).
35 Documentary film on compulsory incarceration as screened on channel one of the Israeli television, Autumn 2000.
36 W. Wickleburgh and D. W. Porritt, "Transforming Theory into Legislation", in E. Bates and P. R. Wilson (eds), *Focusing on Madness* (Brisbane: University of Queensland, 1978).
37 N. N. Kittrie, *The Right to be Different* (Baltimore: Johns Hopkins University Press, 1971).
38 S. Bloch and P. Reddaway, *Psychiatric Terror: How Soviet Psychiatry is Used to Suppress Dissent* (New York: Basic Books, 1977).
39 *Ibid.*
40 *Times Literary Supplement,* January 26, 1991, p. 3.
41 A. Janik and S. Toulmin, *Wittgenstein's Vienna* (New York: Simon and Schuster, 1973), pp. 61–2.

Chapter three Don Carlo Gesualdo – A Murdered Love

1 Glenn Watkins, *Gesualdo: The Man and his Music* (Oxford: Oxford University Press, 1973), p. 4.
2 Denis Arnold, *Gesualdo* (London: BBC Publications, 1984), p. 7.
3 Alfred Einstein, *The Italian Madrigal*, vol. II (Princeton: Princeton University Press, 1971), pp. 668–717.
4 Arnold, *Gesualdo*, pp. 14–15.
5 Watkins, *Gesualdo,* p. 260.
6 Henry Miller, *Sexus* (New York: Grove Press, 1965), pp. 181–2.
7 Norman Mailer, *An American Dream* (New York: Dial, 1964), p. 45.
8 Jean Genet, *Our Lady of the Flowers* (London: Panther Books, 1968), p. 14.
9 Mario Praz, *The Romantic Agony* (New York: Meridian Books, 1956), pp. 205–6.
10 Oscar Wilde, *De Profundis* (London: Methuen, 1911).
11 Frank Harris, *Oscar Wilde, his Life and Confessions* (London: Panther Books, 1965), p. 22.
12 S. G. Shoham and G. Rahav, *The Mark of Cain* (St. Lucia: University of Queensland Press, 1982), chap. 10.
13 Watkins, *Gesualdo*, p. 83.
14 *Ibid.*, p. 84.
15 Einstein, *The Italian Madrigal*, p. 715.
16 Naxos Flier for Gesualdo's Complete Sacred Music for Five Voices (Music CD).
17 Arnold, *Gesualdo*, p. 55.
18 Edmond Rostand, "The Last Night of Don Juan", in Oscar Mandel (ed.), *The Theatre of Don Juan* (Lincoln: University of Nebraska Press, 1963), p. 601.
19 Watkins, *Gesualdo*, p. 27.
20 *Ibid.*, p. 27–8.
21 Arnold, *Gesualdo*, p. 36.
22 *Ibid.*, p. 32.
23 *Ibid.*, p. 35.
24 *Ibid.*, p. 33.
25 Carlo Gesualdo, *Madrigaux Livre VI.*
26 *Don Juan* (Paris: Oblique, Edition Borderie, 1978).
27 Mandel (ed.), *The Theatre of Don Juan,* pp. 25–31.
28 "Don Juan and Faust" in Mandel (ed.), *The Theatre of Don Juan*, p. 322.
29 Tirso de Molina, "El Burladorado Seville y Convidada de Piedra Obras", in Mandel (ed.), *The Theatre of Don Juan,* p. *90.*
30 Gustav Flaubert, "Une Nuit de Don Juan", in Mandel (ed.), *The Theatre of Don Juan*, p. *540.*
31 Tirso de Molina cited in Mandel (ed.), *The Theatre of Don Juan,* p. 96.
32 E. T. A. Hoffmann, "Don Juan" in Mandel (ed.), *The Theatre of Don Juan,* p. 323.
33 Zorilla, "Don Juan" in Mandel (ed.), *The Theatre of Don Juan,* p. 524.
34 *Ibid.*, p. 537.

35 Moliere, "Don Juan or the Libertine" in Mandel (ed.), *The Theatre of Don Juan*, p. 154.
36 Einstein, *The Italian Madrigal*, p. 709.
37 S. G. Shoham, *The Violence of Silence* (New Brunswick: Transaction Books, 1983).
38 J. P. Sartre, *No Exit* (New York: Vintage Books, 1955).
39 J. Money and A. A. Ehrkard, *Man and Woman, Boy and Girl* (Baltimore: Johns Hopkins University Press, 1972), p. 12.
40 Cited in Rudolph Binion, *Frau Lou* (Princeton: Princeton University Press, 1968), p. 23.
41 Watkins, *Gesualdo*, p. 109.
42 Einstein, *Gesualdo*, p. 709.

Chapter four Caravaggio – The Violent Enlightenment

1 Walter Friedlander, *Caravaggio Studies* (Princeton: Princeton University Press, 1955), p. 23.
2 Howard Hibbard, *Caravaggio* (London: Thames and Hudson, 1983), p. 1.
3 Hibbard, *Caravaggio*, p. 8.
4 Friedländer, *Caravaggio Studies*, p. 119.
5 Hibbard, *Caravaggio*, p. 147.
6 Friedlander, *Caravaggio Studies*, p. 117.
7 *Ibid.*, p. 9.
8 Hibbard, *Caravaggio*, pp. 130–1.
9 *Ibid.*, p. 264.

Chapter five Jean Genet – A Criminal Manifesto

1 Jean Genet, *The Thief's Journal* (New York: Grove Press, 1960).
2 J. P. Sartre, *Saint Genet, Actor and Martyr* (London: Faber and Faber, 1967).
3 Jean Genet, *Death Watch* (London: Faber and Faber, 1961).
4 Jean Genet, *The Blacks* (New York: Grove Press, 1960).
5 A. Szogyi, *The New York Times Book Review*, December 1969.
6 Sartre, *Saint Genet, Actor and Martyr*, chap. 1.
7 Genet, *The Thief's Journal*, pp. 21, 167.
8 Sartre, *Saint Genet, Actor and Martyr*, p. 15.
9 Genet, *The Thief's Journal*, p. 176.
10 *Ibid.*, p. 87.
11 C. Wilson, *The Outsider* (London: Victor Gollancz, 1958).
12 Jean Genet, *L'Enfant Criminal* (Paris: Morihien Paul, 1949).
13 Genet, *The Thief's Journal*, p. 101.
14 *Ibid.*, p. 81.
15 *Ibid.*, p. 86.
16 Daniel Glaser, "Criminality Theories and Behavioural Images", *American Journal of Sociology* 61 (1956): 433–44.

17 Genet, *The Thief's Journal*, p. 84.
18 *Ibid.*, p. 91.
19 H. C. Lea, *A History of the Inquistion of Spain* (New York: Macmillan, 1906).
20 Genet, *The Thief's Journal*, p. 109. Page numbers in the paranthesis in the text are from the relevant Genet books discussed.
21 E. Erikson, "The Problem of Ego Idenity", *Journal of the American Psychiatric Assoication* 4 (1956): 121–56.
22 K. Lewin, *Field Theory in Social Science* (New York: Harper, 1951).
23 Genet, *The Thief's Journal*, p. 101.
24 Jean Genet, *The Screens* (London: Faber and Faber, 1953), p. 77.
25 Jean Genet, *Our Lady of the Flowers* (London: Faber and Faber, 1960).
26 Genet, *The Thief's Journal*, p. 58.
27 T. Reik, *The Compulsion to Confess* (New York: Books for Libraries Press, 1945).
28 Genet, *Our Lady of the Flowers*, p. 25.
29 Genet, *The Thief's Journal*, p. 25.
30 Genet, *Death Watch*, p. 10.
31 *Ibid.*, p. 35.
32 Genet, *Our Lady of the Flowers*, p. 82.
33 Genet, *The Thief's Journal*, p. 212.
34 E. Sutherland and D. Cressey, *Principles of Criminology* (Philadelphia: Lippincott, 1970).
35 Genet, *The Thief's Journal*, p. 226.
36 *Ibid.*, p. 14.
37 Genet, *Our Lady of the Flowers*, p. 244.
38 Glaser, "Criminality Theories and Behavioural Images", pp. 433–4.
39 R. A. Cloward and L. B. Ohlin, *Delinquency and Opportunity* (New York: The Free Press, 1961).
40 Sutherland and Cressey, *Principles of Criminology*, p. 125.
41 Genet, *The Thief's Journal*, p. 125.
42 Genet, *Our Lady of the Flowers*, p. 83.
43 Genet, *Death Watch*.
44 Genet, *The Thief's Journal*, p. 29.
45 Genet, *Our Lady of the Flowers*, p. 300.
46 Genet, *The Thief's Journal*, p. 243.
47 Genet, *Our Lady of the Flowers*, p. 214.
48 *Ibid.*, p. 211.
49 Genet, *The Screens*, p. 33.
50 Genet, *The Blacks*, p. 52.
51 Genet, *The Screens*, pp. 18–20.
52 Genet, *Death Watch*, p. 40.
53 Genet, *The Screens*, p. 39.
54 *Ibid.*, p. 40.
55 Genet, *Death Watch*, p. 23.

56 Genet, *The Thief's Journal*, p. 211.
57 Genet, *The Screens*, p. 38.
58 Genet, *Death Watch*, p. 20.
59 Genet, *The Thief's Journal*, p. 246.
60 Genet, *Death Watch*, p. 23.
61 Genet, *The Thief's Journal*, p. 243.
62 Genet, *The Blacks*.
63 *Ibid.*, p. 85.
64 Genet, *The Thief's Journal*, p. 107.
65 *Ibid.*, p. 107.
66 Genet, *Our Lady of the Flowers*.
67 *Ibid.*, p. 120.
68 Genet, *The Thief's Journal*, p. 51.
69 Genet, *The Screens*, p. 85.
70 Genet, *The Blacks*, p. 12.
71 Genet, *The Screens*, p. 123.
72 Genet, *Our Lady of the Flowers*.
73 *Ibid.*
74 Genet, *The Screens*, p. 42.
75 Jean Genet, *The Balcony* (London: Faber and Faber, 1963), p. 19.
76 Genet, *The Blacks*, p. 99.
77 Genet, *The Screens*, p. 46.
78 Genet, *The Blacks*, p. 97.
79 Genet, *Our Lady of the Flowers*, p. 165.
80 *Ibid.*
81 Genet, *The Blacks*, p. 101.
82 Genet, *Our Lady of the Flowers*, p. 269.
83 Genet, *The Balcony*, p. 189.
84 Genet, *The Screens*, p. 105.
85 *Ibid.*
86 Genet, *The Blacks*, p. 165.

Chapter six The Creative Villains

1 Letter from Graham Greene to Viviane Greene in Norman Sherry, *The Life of Graham Greene* (New York: Viking Press, 1966).
2 Jean Genet, *The Thief's Journal* (New York: Grove Press, 1964), pp. 92, 186.
3 Ze'ev Rav-Nof, *Great Creators and Their Films* (Jerusalem: Keter, 1982), p. 42.
4 Deirdre Beckett, *A Biography* (New York: Harcourt Brace, 1978).
5 Gordon Bowker, *Through the Dark Labyrinth* (London: Sinclair-Stevenson, 1977).
6 Letter 379 from Vincent to Theo, *The Complete Letters of Vincent van Gogh* (Greenwich: New York Graphic Society, 1959).
7 I. F. Walther and R. Metzger, *Vincent van Gogh* (Köln: Taschen, 1997), pp. 9–10.

8 Cited in *Times Literary Supplement* (May 30, 1980).
9 S. G. Shoham, *Sex as Bait: Eve, Casanova and Don Juan* (St. Lucia: University of Queensland Press, 1983).
10 S. G. Shoham and G. Rahav, *The Mark of Cain* (St. Lucia: University of Queensland Press, 1982).
11 A. Camus, *The Fall* (New York: Vintage Books, 1956), pp. 7–8.

Chapter seven Genius and Madness

1 A. Artaud, *Van Gogh: Le Suicidé de la Société* (Paris: Gallimard, 1974), pp. 14–64.
2 T. S. Szasz, "The Myth of Mental Illness", *American Psychologist* 15 (1960): 113–18.
3 Lubin, *Stranger on the Earth* (St. Albans: Paladin, 1956).
4 *The Complete letters of Vincent Van Gogh*, 2nd edn (New York Graphics Society, 1959).
5 *Ibid.*
6 S. G. Shoham, *Sex as Bait: Casanova and Don Juan* (St Lucia: University of Queensland Press, 1983).
7 S. Freud, *Mourning and Melancholia* (London: Hogarth Press, 1924).
8 S. G. Shoham, Lilly and Yitzhak Stein, "The Differential Pressures towards Schizophrenia and Delinquency" in Friday and Stewart (eds), *Youth, Crime and Juvenile Justice* (New York: Harper and Row, 1977).
9 B. Hursten, D'Esopo, "The Obligation to Remain Sick" in T. J. Scwell (ed.), *Mental Illness and Social Processes* (New York: Harper and Row, 1967).
10 T. J. Scheff, *Being Mentally Ill* (Chicago: Aldine, 1966).
11 T. J. Scheff, *Mental Illness and Social Processes* (New York: Harper and Row, 1967).
12 Artaud, *Van Gogh*, pp. 13–14.
13 A. Beer, *Du Demon de Van* Gogh (Paris: ADIA, 1974).
14 *Ibid.*
15 M. Addad, "Delinquency among Psychiatric Patients", *Crime and Social Deviance* 6 (1978): 129–34.
16 F. Minkowski, "Le Temps Vecu", *Etudes Phenomenonogiques et Psychologie Pathologique*, Neuchätel (1968).
17 Artaud, *Van Gogh*, pp. 14–64.
18 Letter from Vincent to Theo, *Complete Letters.*
19 M. Addad and M. Benevech, "Nouvelle Approche du Processus de Stigmatization en Criminology" (French, English and Spanish), *Revue Internationale de Police Criminelle* 356, pp. 66–72.
20 C. Harrison and P. Wood (eds), *Art in Theory 1900–1990* (Oxford: Basil Blackwell), p. 479.
21 Letter 582 from Vincent to Theo, *Complete Letters.*
22 *Ibid.*

Chapter eight St. Vincent – Absolute Authenticity

1 L. F. Walther and R. Metzger, *Vincent Van Gogh* (Köln: Taschen, 1997), p. 522.
2 Letter 509 from Vincent to Theo, *The Complete Letters of Vincent Van Gogh* (Greenwich: New York Graphic Society, 1959).
3 *Arles*, October 1888, Pasadena (Cal.) Norton Simon Museum of Art.
4 *Saint Remy*, Late August 1889, USA, Private Collection, Sotheby's Auction, February 25, 1970.
5 *Starry Night*, Saint Remy, June 1889, Lost, formerly in the Künsthalle, Bremen.
6 *Wheat Field with Crows. Auvers-sur-Oise*, July 1890, Amsterdam, Rijksmuseum, Vincent van Gogh, Vincent van Gogh Foundation.
7 *Auvers-sur-Oise*, late June 1890, Bern, Collection of H. R. Hahnlorer.
8 *Auvers-sur-Oise*, June 1890, whereabouts unknown.
9 *The Raising of Lazarus*, May 1890, Amsterdam, Rijksmuseum.
10 Letter 276 from Vincent to Theo, *Complete Letters.*
11 Letter 309 from Vincent to Theo, *ibid.*
12 *Orchards in Blossom*, Arles, April 1888, Amsterdam, Rijkmuseum.
13 Instance of this premise may be observed in *Orchard Blossom*, Arles, April 1888, Switzerland, Private Collection, and in *Almond Tree*, Arles, April 1888, Amsterdam, Rijksmuseum.
14 *Landscape under a Stormy Sky*, Arles, May 1888, Vaduz, Lichtenstein, Foundation Socindec.
15 *Starry Night over the Rhone,* Arles, September 1888, Paris, Musée d'Orsay.
16 *The Sower*; Outskirts of Arles in the background, Arles, September 1888, Los Angeles, The Armand Hammer Museum of Art.
17 *Two White Butterflies*, Arles, Spring 1889, Amsterdam, Rijksmuseum.
18 Letter 474 from Vincent to Theo, *Complete Letters.*
19 *Cypresses with two Female Figures*, Saint-Remy, June 1889, Otterlo, Rijdsmuseum Kröller-Müller.
20 *Starry Night:* Saint Remy, June 1889, New York, The Museum of Modern Art.
21 *Tree Trunks with Ivy*, Saint Remy, Summer 1889, Otterlo Rijksmusem, Kröller-Müller.
22 The biographical details are taken from *The World of Van Gogh, 1853–1890* (New York: Time Life Books, 1973). Page numbers in paranthesis in the text are from the text.
23 Letter 193 from Vincent to Theo, *Complete Letters.*
24 Letter 379 from Vincent to Theo, *ibid.*
25 Letter 312 from Vincent to Theo, *ibid.*
26 Walther and Metzer, *Vincent Van Gogh*, p. 228.
27 *Ibid.*, p. 8.
28 *The Good Samaritan*, Saint Remy, May 1890, Otterlo Rijksmuseum, Kröller-Müller.
29 Letter 195 from Vincent to Theo, *Complete Letters.*

30 M. Buber, *Daniel* (Jerusalem: The Bialik Institute, 1930), in Hebrew.
31 S. G. Shoham, *Sex as Bait* (St. Lucia: University of Queensland Press, 1983), p. 180.
32 *Auvers-sur-Oise*, June 1890, Paris, Musée d'Orsay and Christies Auction, New York, May 15, 1990.
33 *Saint Remy*, April–May 1890, Otterlo Rijksmuseum Kröller-Müller.
34 *Saint Remy*, May 1890, Amsterdam, Rijksmuseum.
35 Letter 339a from Vincent to Theo, *Complete Letters*.
36 Walter and Metzger, *Vincent Van Gogh*, pp. 442–60.
37 Walter and Metzger, *Vincent Van Gogh*, pp. 54–5.
38 *Ibid.*, p. 565.
39 A. H. Maslow, "Peak Experiences as Acute Experiences", *American Journal of Psyhoanalysis* 21, 1961.
40 F. Nietzsche cited in Walter and Metzer, *Vincent Van Gogh*, p. 54.
41 *Arles*, April 1889, Winterthur Collection, Oscar Reinhart.
42 April 1889, Japan, private collection.
43 *Starry Night*, Saint Remy, June 1889, New York, The Museum of Modern Art.
44 *Auvers-sur-Oise* 1890, Amsterdam, Rijksmuseum.

Chapter nine Antonin Artaud – Outside of Time

1 *Revue Oblique Consacrée à Antonin Artaud* (eds), R. Borderie and I. Pauvert, (Paris: Roger Borderie, 1976), p. 191. Page numbers in paranthesis in the text are from this book.
2 A. Artaud, "Le Suicidé de la Société", *Oeuvres Completes*, vol. 13 (Paris: Gallimard, 1982).
3 *Revue Oblique*, p. 13.
4 Artaud, "Le Suicidé de la Société", pp. 50–1.
5 Franco and Stefano Borsi, *Paolo Uccello* (New York: A. N. Abrams, 1992), p. 9.
6 Artaud, *Oeuvres Completes*, vol. 13, p. 13.
7 F. and S. Borsi, *Paolo Uccello*, p. 13.
8 *Revue Oblique*, p. 31.
9 Artaud, *Oeuvres Completes*, vol. 7.
10 F. and S. Borsi, *Paolo Uccello*, pp. 185–7.
11 *Revue Oblique*, p. 39.

Giora Shoham's Published Works and His Theory of Personality

There follows synopses, in chronological order, of all my published works that together form the Theory of Personality:

The stigma theory of crime and deviation (*The Mark of Cain* [1970]) regards the labelling and tagging processes as constitutive factors identifying an individual as criminal both in the eyes of others and in his own eyes. Derogatory labels are tagged on to an individual by relevant others and are internalized by that person as a part of his or her self-image. The social control agencies are thus responsible, by means of various branding mechanisms, for the distinction between the deviant and the conformist, irrespective of the structural or substantive nature of an individual's behavior.

Ultimately, a criminal, a deviant, or an antisocial person is one who is branded as such by a group or by individuals who have the power to do so. The branding of a person as deviant, queer, troublemaker, rigid, maladjusted, etc. is inherent in the normative authority of the power elite in a group. With crime there are some legal barriers to the branding machinery of society, but these do not operate in the stigmatizing of a person as deviant and maladjusted. The term "adjustment" itself is associated with the use of power and pressure to enforce conformity.

This pioneering work draws broadly from mythology, anthropology, sociology and literature, and concludes that in spite of criticism against the labelling frame of reference, some of which is justified, it still stands largely vindicated.

Society and the Absurd (1974) uses the concept of the Absurd – a concept that has previously been almost exclusively part of the discourse of existentialist philosophers and creative writers. In so far as it denotes the disintegration of man's ability to interact meaningfully with his fellow-man and with the world, the Absurd provides a relevant framework within which to explore a number of dominant social themes – social deviance, alienation, madness. The text draws on ancient and modern philosophy, and literature, as well as on historical, anthropological and ethnological research. Among the many thinkers whose writings contribute to the proposed synthesis are Camus, Durkheim, Freud, Heidegger, Kierkegaard, Koestler, Levy-Bruhl, Henry Miller, Nietzsche, Plotinus, Rosenzweig, Sartre, Spinoza, and Van Gogh. The book takes the true measure of, and deals effectively with, the human condition.

The Myth of Tantalus (1979) endeavors to formulate a new Personality Theory based on vectors that have not been fully utilized before in the behavioral and social sciences. Established theoretical frames of reference are not neglected or overlooked, but are incorporated, compared and contrasted with the new theoretical structure.

Existentialistic and ontological premises which have been largely dealt with by philosophers and novelists are here integrated into the theoretical structure. Some aspects of mysticism, meditation, and religious experiences as psycho-sociological phenomena are also dealt with. The empirical anchors are taken from varied sources ranging from the topical issues of Arab–Jewish relationships to the divergent personalities of the founders of the Hassidic movement.

Finally the Isaac Syndrome (adults tending to sacrifice their young), is contrasted with the Oedipal and other developmental conflicts within the family matrix.

An outline of the Personality Theory is given below:

The two opposing vectors that underpin the Theory are those of "participation" and "separation." Participation indicates the identification of Ego with a person (persons), an object, or a symbolic construct outside himself, and his striving to lose his separate identity by fusion with this other object or symbol. Separation is the opposite vector. However, as the vectors are multidimensional, the psychological pressures are much more likely to take place on the different planes of a space that represents the human personality than along a unidimensional continuum.

A specific human quality of special interest is man's subjective feeling of *separateness* – where Ego is perceived as an ontological entity. Other animals do not possess this ontological feeling of individuality. This *sui generis* quality of *Homo sapiens,* the ability to sense his separateness, has been subject to diametrically opposite value judgements. Schachtel regards the "activity affect" leading to the elaborate interaction of Ego with the objects around him as an ever-recurring pleasure. This interaction is not feasible if Ego is not ontologically separate. The stance adopted in Shoham's Personality Theory is to tread on the elegiac path formed by Freud, Heidegger and Eliade, where the coagulating of Ego's distinct identity is through painful encounters with obstacles, impediments, and conflicts. Unifications are temporary, and the desire for a blissful remerger of the individual and his entourage is a perennial longing expressed in religion, art, and philosophy but never fully attained in reality. The use of these opposing vectors of unification/fusion and separation/isolation as the main axes of the Theory is in conjunction with *three* major developmental phases. *First*, the process of birth: this abrupt propulsion from cushioned self-sufficiency into the strife and struggles of life outside the womb is a major crisis, which is recorded by the newborn's psyche and is in addition to any physical pressures that the process of birth itself might have on the cranium and the resultant impressionistic effects on the various layers of the brain. The Theory does not accept the "birth trauma" theories which stress the variability of birth-related physical violence as a clue to personality pathologies. The basic premise of the Theory relates to the separating effects of birth, which are universal. These effects initiate the opposite vector of participation, which is a directional driving force harnessing a diverse assortment of psychic energy toward union with given objects or symbolics. The fetus, at birth, is physiologically and psychologically capable of recording these colossal crises incidental to birth and is traumatized by them into a lifelong quest for congruity and unification.

The *second* process of separation is the crystallization of an individual ego by the molding of the "ego boundary." The infant shrieks and kicks his way into the world, but he still feels himself part and parcel of his environment. However, this pantheistic bliss is gradually destroyed by the bumps and grinds he suffers from the harsh realities of hunger, thirst, discomfort, and physical violence from hard objects in his surroundings, and a mother who is mostly loving but sometimes nagging, apathetic, hysterical, or overprotective. All this cajoles and pushes the infant into coagulating a separate identity (the *third* stage): to leave the common fold of unity with his environment and crystallize an "I." This individual self knows, then, that he is not part of and with everything but stands *vis-à-vis* his surroundings and opposite everybody. This realization of oneself through being forced to leave the security of engulfing togetherness is registered by the sprouting psyche as a fall from grace. Why we are pushed out is the great imponderable, the existence of which we take as given. *The Myth of Tantalus* explains the meaning and purpose of this *Geworfenheit*, and the opposing life-long vector to overcome it.

The process of separation continues in full force as a corollary of socialization, until one reaches, in Erickson's jargon, one's "ego identity," which is the post-adolescent's adjustment to the mandates of the normative system of society. The making of the "responsible person," the "stable human being," is achieved through constant indoctrination on the part of the various socialization agencies – family, school, church, and so on. These convey to the individual the harsh realities of life and urge him to "grow up," with the help of rigorous initiation rites. What it amounts to is that the child spreads out his arms to embrace with naive eagerness every person, every object and beast. He thereby exposes his soft body and tender psyche to physical injures and mental blows. These make him shrink with fright and pain. In due course, the scar tissue of experience and learning covers the sores and wounds. The child becomes less vulnerable but also less sensitive, and he is more reluctant to expose himself with a loving embrace to his environment. This is the lore of the rape of innocence by life. The end product is the separation of the alienated man, who is basically lonely. The sneer of the "tough guy" who walks and needs nobody is the folklore counterpart to the Protestant ethic and to the spirit of capitalism: "in this rat race everyone for himself." The strain to overcome the separating and dividing pressures never leaves the human individual. The striving to partake in a pantheistic whole is ever-present and it takes many forms; if one avenue toward its realization becomes blocked, it surges out from another channel.

Salvation through the Gutters (1979) is a comprehensive interdisciplinary work on the philosophy and theology of crime. Ideas and concepts from psychoanalysis, theology, comparative religion, literature, developmental psychology, and the Kabbala are woven together to present an interpretation of deviance in terms of behavioral and biopsychological developmental processes. Mysticism, meditation, and religious experience explained in psychosocial terms.

Sex as Bait: Eve, Casanova, and Don Juan (1983) is an interdisciplinary treatment of sex and love which draws on biology, mythology, psychoanalysis, and philosophy as well as on the Personality Theory, to construct a model of affective relationships between human beings. A mother-based sexual development theory is presented and related to the formation of a sexual typology continuum. This continuum, which ranges from the starkly carnal Casanova to the romantically agonized Don Juan, is illustrated by dramatic and literary sources. The separant Sisyphean Casanova tries to overcome the rift between himself and the object by the continuous conquest of female bodies; the participant archetype Don Juan longs to partake in and be possessed by the ultimate woman, by being in love with love and having love affairs in Tantalic succession.

A new theoretical framework for the maternal proscription of incest (based on mytho-empiricism) is put forward, which is related to the main role of woman in the formation of the nuclear family and of human culture. *Sex As Bait* presents the development of sexual identity, both male and female, based on a new approach to the oral development of the psyche. The sacred and profane aspects of love are presented as a phase of human development.

The Violence of Silence: The Impossibility of Dialogue (1983) considers the alienation of man from his fellow men and his estrangement from his environment in terms of the Theory of Personality. The analysis of man's alienation draws on the behavioral sciences as well as on theology, mythology, and existentialist philosophy. Illustrations are also provided from interpretations of the works of Sartre, Camus, Becket, Genet, and Sade. The book ends by providing a possible outlet from the impasse of alienation through rebellion, revelation, and creativity.

Rebellion, Creativity & Revelation (1985) takes as its stance the fact that alienation is neither a discovery of sociologists nor the invention of imaginative literature. Insights can be gleaned from sociology, from criminology, from literature, from psychology, theology, mysticism, Marxism, anthropology, art,

Printed and bound by CPI Group (UK) Ltd, Croydon, CR0 4YY

13/09/2026

14961101-0002